VANILLA

VANILLA

THE CULTURAL HISTORY OF THE WORLD'S
MOST POPULAR FLAVOR AND FRAGRANCE

PATRICIA RAIN

Produced by the Philip Lief Group, Inc.

JEREMY P. TARCHER/PENGUIN

a member of

Penguin Group (USA) Inc.

New York

JEREMY P. TARCHER/PENGUIN
Published by the Penguin Group • Penguin Group (USA) Inc., 375 Hudson Street, New York, New York 10014, USA •
Penguin Group (Canada), 10 Alcorn Avenue, Toronto, Ontario, Canada M4V 3B2 (a division of Pearson Penguin Canada
Inc.) • Penguin Books Ltd, 80 Strand, London WC2R 0RL, England • Penguin Ireland, 25 St Stephen's Green, Dublin 2,
Ireland (a division of Penguin Books Ltd) • Penguin Group (Australia), 250 Camberwell Road, Camberwell, Victoria 3124,
Australia (a division of Pearson Australia Group Pty Ltd) • Penguin Books India Pvt Ltd, 11 Community Centre,
Panchsheel Park, New Delhi—110 017, India • Penguin Group (NZ), Cnr Airborne and Rosedale Roads, Albany,
Auckland, New Zealand (a division of Pearson New Zealand Ltd) • Penguin Books (South Africa) (Pty) Ltd, 24 Sturdee
Avenue, Rosebank, Johannesburg 2196, South Africa.
Penguin Books Ltd, Registered Offices: 80 Strand, London WC2R 0RL, England

A list of illustration credits appears on page 372.

Library of Congress Cataloging-in-Publication Data

Rain, Patricia, date.
Vanilla: the cultural history of the world's most popular flavor and fragrance/Patricia Rain—1st ed.
p.   cm.
Includes bibliographical references.
ISBN 1-58542-363-7
1. Vanilla—History.   2. Vanilla—Utilization—History.   3. Cookery (Vanilla)   I. Title.
SB307.V2R25   2004   2004051641
633.8'2—dc22

Printed in the United States of America
1 3 5 7 9 10 8 6 4 2

This book is printed on acid-free paper. ∞

Book design by Stephanie Huntwork

Neither the author nor the publisher is engaged in rendering professional advice or services to the individual reader. The
ideas, procedures, and suggestions in this book are not intended as a substitute for consulting a physician. All matters
regarding health require medical supervision. Neither the author nor the publisher shall be liable or responsible for any loss,
injury, or damage allegedly arising from any information or suggestion in this book. The opinions expressed in this book
represent the personal views of the author and not of the publisher.

The recipes contained in this book are to be followed exactly as written. The publisher is not responsible for your specific
health or allergy needs that may require medical supervision. The publisher is not responsible for any adverse reactions to
the recipes contained in this book.

Most Tarcher/Penguin books are available at special quantity discounts for bulk purchase for sales promotions, premiums,
fund-raising, and educational needs. Special books or book excerpts also can be created to fit specific needs. For details,
write Penguin Group (USA) Inc. Special Markets, 375 Hudson Street, New York, NY 10014.

*This book is dedicated to my daughter, Serena; my
son-in-law, Brad; and my grandson, Theo. You
held me in the light through the difficult days
and gave me the gift of new life in Theo.
I am forever grateful for your love.*

· ACKNOWLEDGMENTS ·

Assembling and writing this book has been a truly collaborative effort. As no one has ever created a chronological history of vanilla from its origins in prehistory through its dispersal throughout the tropics, nor a history of the people who have grown it, I have reached out for assistance from our global community. Many of the growers whom I have met in person or via the Internet have been very generous with information even though, in most cases, English is not their native language. While I speak fluent Spanish, I have depended on translators in several countries, and even charades. It's amazing what you can do when words won't serve!

First, my heartfelt appreciation to Judy Capodanno and Terri Hennessy for their assistance as editors. (Fortunately, their English is impeccable.) They were also very supportive when I was diagnosed with cancer. Also included in the first tier of thanks are my two extraordinary assistants: the Contessa, Gina Tassone; and the Princess, Anita Howson. They took over managing most of the business while I concentrated on the book. Their dedication and assistance have been invaluable.

My thanks to the county research librarians in California as well as at the Library of Congress and the Smithsonian Institution, in Washington, D.C. Books I never thought I would find appeared, as if by magic, in the skillful hands of the librarians. Thanks also to David Karp, the Fruit Detective, for the use of his books and documents on vanilla. And thanks to Tim Ecott, a BBC journalist, who has just published a book on his travels in search of vanilla, for collaborating with me on difficult-to-find information about vanilla's history.

Thank you, Ken Cameron, of the New York Botanical Garden, Tom Miranda and Beth Page, of the Smithsonian Institution, Pesach Lubinsky (who is currently researching and documenting the species of wild vanilla throughout Mexico and Central and South Americas), and Michel Grisoni (formerly stationed in Tahiti and now in Réunion) for your botanical insights.

Growers, processors, and traders from around the world, you have been awesome in sharing information about your countries' history and cultures, as well as your personal experiences with vanilla! Special thanks go to: Heriberto Larios Rivera, Rocío Aguilero Madero, Victor Vallejo and Gloria Caserín, Joaquín Morales, the Gaya family, Cesar Arellano, Yolanda Arzani, the family of Don Fernando Patiño, Abel Alejandro, and the many people of Totonacapan whom I have interviewed over the years in Mexico; Madame Jeanne Chan, Marc Jones, Manu Martin, Alain Abel, Michel Bissal, Yannick Wong, and Dorothy Levy in Tahiti; François Bernard, Patrick Barthélémy, Thomas Fricke, and Sam Filiaci, growers and processors on Bali; Effendi Sutadisastra of Java; and the farmers and translators in Lombok, Indonesia; Maisen Windu, Nelson Wambeli, Mickey Puritau, Pete McGlynn and Harris, Michael Matmillo, and William and Jacinta Yanel, of Papua New Guinea; Vizzy George (who also was my attorney regarding a website piracy case), Jai Chaitanya, Rajesh Rajaram, Remi Chandran, and Abhilash Padival in India; Asiimwe Anania of Rwanda and Uganda; Bharat Pandya, Zakarya Abdirahaman and Richard Kutesa of Uganda; and Roger Rakotomalala, originally of Madagascar. A special thank-you to Hank Kaestner and Juan San Mames for their assistance when I wrote *The Vanilla Cookbook,* and for continuing to be two great supporters of my work in vanilla. And thank you, Rosamarí San Mames, for translating the document on the pueblo of Jicaltepec from French for me.

A big thank-you to all of the individuals in the vanilla industry, who shared their stories and family histories; I've attempted to include all of you in the book. And thank you to the support staff at the vanilla companies who made certain I received the information I requested.

And finally, my gratitude to *everyone* around the world who prayed for me—and continues to pray for me—after my cancer diagnosis. This was the greatest gift I could have received, and the inspiration to keep working to bring you, and the world, the story of our beloved vanilla.

—*Patricia Rain, Vanilla Queen, April 2004*

· CONTENTS ·

Unique Among Orchids

The sensuous aroma of a stalk of vanilla flowers; the heady perfume of a field of vanilla beans ripening in the sun. A basket filled with freshly harvested beans, brown and redolent in the lingering warmth of a tropical afternoon. A batch of freshly baked cookies, filling the kitchen with the warm scent of comfort and home.

If the above conjures olfactory memories of pleasures imagined or real, you are already under the intoxicating spell of one of the world's most powerful and beloved aromas. The saga of vanilla and its romantic journey from its original home in the deep tropics of the Americas, and into the collective consciousness of millions of people worldwide, has been filled with myth and legend, supposition and conjecture, fantasy and reality. And, if you question the premise that there is much more to vanilla than the fragrance that tweaks the nose, or tempts the palate, consider this: only the last of the descriptions in the first paragraph is accurate.

We are so absorbed in our lives that we rarely give thought to the small pleasures that make up our daily routine. A steaming morning cup of coffee or tea, the chocolate almond crunch bar we can't resist, the vanilla-bean ice cream that melts dreamily into the apple pie. Satisfying, affordable, soothing . . . and taken for granted.

If, by chance, we decide to explore further, we often find that our presumptions are a bit skewed. Naive vanilla romantics search for vanilla bean trees and bouquets of vanilla flowers, wonder if vanilla stalks can be grown for home use in the backyard, inquire as to where to purchase vanilla flowers to grind up for perfume, and even want to know how to juice vanilla fruits to make extract. While the questions are valid, they demonstrate how little we know about the products we love. In order to fully appreciate the legacy of vanilla, cast aside the trappings of daily life for a moment and suspend any mantle of sophistication to fully appreciate the unique and often surprising story of vanilla from its American origins, its circuitous path from Mexico in the early 1500s, its arrival in the United States, nearly three hundred years later, and its ongoing journey from the tropics to our tables in the twenty-first century.

VANILLA IS A MEMBER of the orchid family, one of the oldest families of plants in the world, a family that probably evolved more than 90 million years ago. Orchids are the largest family of flowering plants in the world, with over 25,000 species in the wild and more than 100,000 hybrids created in laboratories and hothouses. They are extremely diverse in appearance and range in size from the miniscule Venezuelan *Platystele ornata* that can only be seen under a microscope, to the 20-foot-tall *Renanthera storei* and the humongous *Grammatophyllum speciosum*, which grows as large as

Botanical print of vanilla from
the early nineteenth century

40 feet in circumference and weighs half a ton. (Remarkably, this gigantic orchid can be found most often growing as an *epiphyte*—a plant that lives on trees—high above the Borneo rain-forest floor!)

According to Dr. Ken Cameron, of the New York Botanical Gardens, and a specialist focused on the vanilla subfamily of orchids at the gardens, orchids originally emerged from the order Asparagales, a diverse group of plants that includes asparagus, amaryllises, daffodils, irises, onions, agaves, and yucca. Species in the vanilla subfamily exhibit a lot of primitive aspects, yet at the same time there are many very advanced and unusual features that make them unique among orchids.

Tracing the evolutionary history of orchids has, until recently, been obscured because, unlike the pollen of most plants which is nearly indestructible, the pollen of orchids is so delicate that no fossil records have remained to provide reliable clues to the date of the flowers' emergence. By using DNA to build evolutionary trees of the world's plants, it appears that orchids were the first and oldest of the Asparagales lineage, and that they branched off from this group about 90 million years ago.

Scientists have also found that orchids first lived on the ground, and that later they evolved to live on other plants as thousands of orchid species now do, a characteristic that may have helped them evolve into so many species. Although *lithophyte* orchids live on rock surfaces, *sacrophytes* live in humus and decomposing vegetation, and *terrestrials* live on the ground and root in soil or sand, the majority of orchids are epiphytes. There are also some orchids, such as vanilla, that belong in two categories. The vanilla plant produces long vines and depends on other plants for support, so, technically speaking, it's an epiphyte. But vanilla also produces roots that trail along the top of the forest floor, barely slipping beneath the soil, making the plant also a terrestrial. Contrary to popular belief, *none* of the many members of the orchid family is a parasite.

Another identifying characteristic of the Asparagales order is that its seeds are encased in a distinctive black, crusty coat. Orchids, in general, have very thin seeds, but there are exceptions— most notably, vanilla. The millions of black seeds in vanilla pods are very similar to the same crusty black-coated seeds as those thrown off by the feathery fronds of the mature asparagus! Nearly all orchids have three petals and three *sepals*, or modified leaves, but, beyond that, the variations are startlingly diverse. Orchids vary from brightly colored and showy blooms to small, unremarkable flowers, some individually on a stem, others producing large clusters of flowers. Some bloom only once a year, and some twice, while others bloom continuously.

As orchid seeds contain no endosperm, they obtain their nutrients in a curious and Machiavellian fashion. Microscopic fungi invade the orchid seed and infect the immature embryo within. When the seed germinates, it consumes the fungi that brought it to life. In the case of the vanilla orchids, if they are pollinated naturally in the wild, their seeds are fertile and can reproduce. If they are pollinated artificially by humans, they are sterile. As a result, propagating vanilla from seeds is nearly impossible unless it is done in a plant laboratory. On the other hand, because vanilla is a vine that also produces terrestrial roots, in the wild it can loop down from the tutor that sustains it, attach itself to the ground, and grow back up again. If part of the plant dies, the balance remains alive.

There are at least 150 species of vanilla indigenous to tropical regions worldwide. Despite the fact that varieties of the vanilla orchid can be found in such diverse places as Africa and Asia, the only vanilla species that have proved to be edible and useful originally came from the Americas. Further, there are only two members of the American vanilla family that have been used commercially—*Vanilla planifolia* (also known as *Vanilla fragrans*) and *Vanilla pompona Schiede*. (A third edible species, *Vanilla tahitensis*, is believed to have originated by crossing *planifolia* and *pompona* stock in a plant laboratory in Manila in the 1700s.) What makes these numbers especially surprising is that vanilla produces the *only* edible fruit in the entire orchid family.

Orchids typically do not self-pollinate because their male *(anther)* and female *(stigma)* sex organs are separated by the *rostellum* (a small flap of plant tissue), a quirk of nature that has led to very complex, and often deceptive and conniving, methods of attracting help from insect pollinators. In order to survive, orchids must be gaudy or bold enough to catch the attention of birds, bees, wasps, ants, and other small insects; have a heady, pheromonelike aroma; or produce a nectar or sticky fluid that provides sustenance or momentarily traps the insect visitors—this occurs at the same time that pollen is released on them as they struggle to break free. However, as producing nectar and fluids requires the plant to expend a lot of energy, some orchids have evolved to appear sexually attractive to the insects that will pollinate them, and produce only the tiniest amount of nectar, while others use deception and simply look as though they would offer a reward of pollen or nectar.

The vanilla orchids are no exception. The waxy flowers are a pale yellowish green, about 4 inches (10 cm) in diameter. While *Vanilla planifolia* itself is not seductively showy, other vanilla varieties are quite erotic, some with a "tongue" that extends from the long lip of the flower. Insects are intrigued by the tufts of flexible hairs on the tongue, or inside the cavernous lip of the orchids, so they climb onto them. These hairs move the insects inward to the pollen deep inside the flower. The insects have trouble getting out again without breaking the rostellum—thus pollinating the plant. In short, without their awareness, they make love to the orchids.

Vanilla orchids bloom very early in the morning, begin to wilt by mid-morning, and die by mid-afternoon *unless* they are pollinated. In the Americas, no one knows for sure about the natural pollinators of the vanilla. Pollination was possibly performed by the now rare Euglossine bees as well as the very small and nearly extinct melipona bees, which historically have been credited as the primary pollinators. Euglossines are the more likely candidates because they are the most common pollinators of orchids, they travel great distances, and their bodies are a good match architecturally with the vanilla flower. It is also possible that the orchid was pollinated by some long-billed hummingbirds that enjoyed the few drops of delicate nectar secreted from inside the flower and onto the orchid's lip, though this would be a difficult task as the tubular blossom has such a deep throat. The flowers also have an aroma that, to human noses, is faint if noticeable at all. Despite these two lures, the fact that the flower lives so briefly makes natural pollination a fairly random event, performed only by early-morning foraging insects and birds.

When vanilla cuttings were taken around the world, the plants thrived and flowered, but there are only a few documented instances where they actually produced a seedpod. It wasn't until the mid-1800s, at which time orchids were the passion of wealthy Europeans, that hand pollination was discovered and refined. Since then, wherever vanilla is grown, hand pollination of the orchids is necessary, even in their country of origin. Left to their own devices, even in Mexico, only a few flowers would be pollinated on each plant—a tiny percentage of the quantity needed for a world lusting after their delicate flavor.

Vanilla orchids produce inflorescences on *racemes*—small stemlike growths where the vanilla flowers form—which are attached to the vine and grow upward toward the light. Usually one flower blooms at a time on each raceme, though occasionally two or three might blossom the same day. The blooming period ranges from six weeks to two months, but there is a twenty-day period during which time the majority of activity occurs. Workers check each plant daily during this period, in order to pollinate the flowers before they fall. On a traditional forest plantation, workers can pollinate between four hundred and one thousand flowers a day. In the modern shade-cloth or intensive plantations, workers can pollinate as many as three thousand flowers. In every area vanilla is grown, this is known as "the marriage" of vanilla and is often performed by the women and children as their hands are small and deft, aiding them to reach into the throat of the flower to the pollen. Pollination accounts for about one-third of the laborious attention required by each vanilla plant.

In the countries where vanilla has been introduced, there are few—if any—predators. In Mexico, however, the chachalaca has a sharp eye and keen taste for the little flowers. A member of the crow family with an unsettling call that sounds remarkably similar to something heard in a fight in a chicken coop, the chachalaca will joyfully polish off the day's crop of orchids. It is the job of the boys in the family to pitch or shoot rocks and whatever other projectiles are available to keep the birds at abeyance. The occasional crack of a rifle during the pollinating season is not unusual, and the family usually has chachalaca and chili for lunch.

Once the plant has been pollinated, the ovary at the base of the orchid begins to swell. Within six weeks, the fruit, which closely resembles a huge green bean or a miniature banana, grows to its full length. However, it must remain on the vine for anywhere from six to nine months, depending on the region where it grows, before the fruits will be ready to harvest. Curiously, the cell walls of the vanilla fruits are among the strangest of all life; they are more like a matrix than a cell. Further, despite extensive studies by plant scientists over the past two hundred years, no one has been able to define precisely how vanillin—the most obvious chemical in vanilla, which contains about 25 percent of the flower's fragrance—is produced in the plant. In fact, no one has ever defined exactly how many organic compounds make up vanilla's

Green vanilla beans slowly maturing

flavor and fragrance profile, though it is estimated that there are somewhere between 250 and 500 distinct compounds that create its complex essence.

As harvest time approaches, the beans are checked daily, and, as they are harvested just before they are completely ripe, they have *no aroma and no flavor*. It is only after a several-stage curing-and-drying process that lasts between six and nine months that vanilla fully develops the characteristics that define its flavor and fragrance!

During the curing-and-drying period, the vanilla beans will be "killed" or "cooked" in ovens or near-boiling water, wrapped in cloths and stored in boxes for hours to days, massaged, manipulated, laid in the sun to dry each morning, and brought in to rest each evening. During this period the beans will lose as much as

80 percent of their original weight, turning into dark brown, oily, flexible, luxurious pods, with a powerful and enticing fragrance. Enticing, at least to all but insects who, surprisingly, are generally repelled by the aroma! Finally, when the beans are deemed ready, they will rest on wooden shelves for up to three months while they are "conditioned." Only then are they ready to be packed into tin or cardboard boxes, weighed, and shipped to more temperate climates where they will be used whole or processed into extracts.

While the progression from pollination to processed bean takes roughly one and one-half years, there is also the initial process of planting the vanilla cuttings. If the land to be used is forested, there is no need to plant tutor trees. However, the majority of commercial plantations require initial clearing, then the planting of tutor trees or the addition of posts, cement forms, or other methods of holding the vines. If the cuttings are at least 39 inches (1 meter) in length and if there is adequate humus, rainfall, and warmth, the vines might bloom within fourteen to eighteen months; more often it takes up to three years before the first blooms appear on the vines. Add this to the pollinating, growing, curing, and drying processes, and you can understand why vanilla is the most labor-intensive agricultural product in the world. And, as it only thrives within 25 degrees either side of the equator, and only then, where there is adequate rainfall and protection from the harsh tropical sun, this is why it is almost exclusively grown in countries where there is enough agricultural space to accommodate it and enough available cheap labor to produce it. This is why the aromatic brown pods and amber-colored liquid that create everyone's favorite flavor and fragrance are so expensive.

For the love of vanilla as a flavoring and as a perfume, and for its qualities as an aphrodisiac, medicinal herb, and healing aromatic, vanilla has been sought after and fought over ever since its discovery perhaps a millennium ago in the rain forests of the Americas. Its romantic journey throughout the last five hundred years is no less amazing than its evolution from among the oldest of flowering plants so many millions of years ago.

· 1 ·

XANAT, QUETZALCOATL, AND THE GODS' LEGACY

The story of vanilla begins in Mesoamerica, the ancient realm of the earliest Mexicans and Central Americans, an area that extended from what is now Mexico to northern Nicaragua, in the time before the Spaniards came to the Americas and conquered the indigenous people in 1519.

Vanilla grew wild in the humid lowland tropical forests in southern and eastern Mexico, Central America, and northern South America. In Mexico, from the area of central Veracruz on the Gulf Coast, vanilla's territory extended southeastward to the eastern slopes of the Andes, around through South America to the Guianas and northeast Brazil, and down the Atlantic coast of Brazil. On the western coast of Mexico, vanilla was found from Colima to Ecuador. It was also native to many islands in the West Indies. While it sounds as if vanilla grew nearly everywhere in the Americas, in fact it only hugged the coastlines and the forests that extended to the lower hills leading to the mountains.

THE DISCOVERY OF VANILLA

The tribes living in the northern regions of vanilla's natural range were the first to incorporate vanilla into their lives, perhaps as early as 2,000 to 2,500 years before the Spanish Conquest of Mexico in 1520. From Central Mexico to Costa Rica, there was a passion for pungent, aromatic fragrances. Vanilla had sacred and religious connotations as did corn and cacao. These were gifts bestowed upon them by the gods and were treated with reverence. Corn provided nourishment, cacao was a ceremonial drink, and vanilla was a fragrant incense. Vanilla beans were ground and mixed with *copal* (a dried resin from the Copalli tree with a pleasing pinelike odor) to perfume their temples. The native peoples were very knowledgeable about the medicinal use of herbs and may well have ground the vanilla bean for lung and stomach disorders as well as used the liquid from green beans as a poultice for drawing out insect venom and infections from wounds. Their medicinal skills far surpassed those of the Europeans at the time of their arrival in Mexico in the sixteenth century. And whereas the vanilla taken to Spain in the early 1500s was valued as a commodity, for the tribal peoples of the Americas vanilla was reverently considered a sacramental herb.

During Mexico's pre-classic period, beginning roughly around 1500 B.C., extensive trade routes developed throughout Mesoamerica, and the bartering of goods between groups living in the various different climates and altitudes brought about cultural exchanges including the sharing of important discoveries and spiritual beliefs. This is likely the time when vanilla was first used and traded among coastal tribes.

As the hunting-and-gathering nomadic lifestyle was slowly replaced by a more agrarian and settled existence, the population expanded, and adequate food production became increasingly important. Greater focus was placed on the nature gods such as Tlaloc and Xipe Totec, as it was believed that they controlled the rain, the sun, the winds, and the harvests. Pleasing the gods meant abundant food supplies.

It was during this time period that the Olmecs, the "mother culture" of Mexico, emerged. They lived in the humid forests and open savannas along the Gulf Coast of southern Veracruz and Tabasco and were known for their massive sculptures carved from basalt, their fine artistic abilities, and their skill in commerce. The Olmecs also made huge contributions to the development of what came to be the backbone of the Mesoamerican diet—maize.

Maize (corn) wasn't particularly important to the Mesoamericans until the Olmecs developed a technique that inadvertently changed the nutritional value for the better and, subsequently, literally fueled the growth and development of all of Mexico. Instead of boiling dried maize kernels until they were soft, or pounding them into powder, they cooked corn with white lime or wood ashes, then left it overnight in the cooking liquid. The transparent hull (pericarp) of the treated kernels now slipped off easily, making it much easier to grind the corn into a smooth dough (known as *nixtamali* in Nahuatl, the mother language of Mexico, or *masa* in Spanish). This simple shift in preparation changed corn from a low-protein grain into a high-protein food, creating Mexico's staff of life.

The Olmecs were quite possibly also the first to domesticate cacao (from which chocolate comes), another food of great importance in Mesoamerican culture and, subsequently, the rest of the world. And, with the domestication of cacao, the use of vanilla as a flavor followed at some point in this early history.

THE GOLDEN AGE OF MESOAMERICA

Centuries after the Olmecs dwindled away, the classical period or "golden age" of Mesoamerica began, an era which lasted for roughly a thousand years. The classic period heralded relatively peaceful times, when sophisticated urban city-states developed, replete with a strong religious structure, extraordinary architecture, artwork, math, science, astronomy, and hieroglyphic writing. The leaders of this era were the Maya, who lived in the tropical lowlands of northern Guatemala in the Peten Jungle and on the edges of the earlier Olmec territory. The Maya were brilliant artists, architects, and scientists spawning a renaissance in Mexican culture. They also made major culinary advances, including perfecting the cultivation of cacao and creating the drink, *chocolatl,* made famous much later by the Aztecs at the time of the Spanish Conquest of Mexico in the sixteenth century. And it was during the time of the Maya that vanilla was probably introduced as one of the flavorings for *chocolatl.*

SNAPAP QELA—ATOLE DULCE DE VAINILLA

The *atole* is a nutritious ancient Mesoamerican drink that has remained important in the modern Mexican diet. *Atoles* are made from white, yellow, or blue corn; may be sweet or savory; and are served hot or cold depending on the time of day or the meal. If at all possible, try to get *masa* from *caca-huazintle*, a special type of corn—it is well worth it.

1 cup fresh corn *masa* (ground corn flour)
9 cups water
2 vanilla beans
¼ cup honey

Mix *masa* with 2 cups of water until well blended. Place in a large ceramic jar (or saucepan), add remaining water and vanilla beans, set over open fire (or moderate heat on stove), and cook until the *atole* begins to boil.

Move to cooler section of fire (or lower heat), and allow mixture to simmer, making certain that it does not become lumpy. Remove from heat, add honey, and allow *atole* to cool. Serve cooled with spicy foods.

However, vanilla wasn't always used in this adored beverage. There were at least twelve different *chocolatl* versions, depending on the event and what was at hand, not unlike our flavor choices for coffee, milk shakes, and Italian sodas. While the Totonacs, an important group of people who emerged a little later in Mesoamerican history, were possibly the first to domesticate vanilla, their predecessors certainly enjoyed the fruits wild from the forest.

The collapse of the Guatemalan Mayan empire around A.D. 900 was triggered by overpopulation and the depletion of local resources. New cities were created farther to the north in what is now Mexico. The most important of the Mexican cities during the

The Pyramid of the Niches from the ruins of El Tajín, Veracruz, Mexico.
El Tajín is the bridge between the very early Mesoamerican and later cultures,
such as the Aztecs. The ruins show evidence of Olmec, Maya,
Huaxtec, and Totonac influences.

classical period was the enormous urban city-state of Teotihuacán. It was located about 25 miles (40 km) north of what is now Mexico City, and may have had more than 100,000 inhabitants. Also known for its fine art and cultural, economic, and political capabilities, the city's principal god was Quetzalcoatl ("Kay-zal-CO-at"), the great plumed serpent, who appears and reappears throughout Mesoamerican history. Teotihuacán was founded around 200 B.C., rose into prominence, then inexplicably fell into decline by A.D. 650 Soon it was overrun by the Tolteca-Chichimeca, a nomadic warring group from the north later known as the Toltecs, who were far less civilized than the southern tribes. Many of the inhabitants of Teotihuacán migrated east and south, searching for less populated and besieged lands.

The Totonacs, whom we will meet many times throughout vanilla's romantic history, most likely came to the Gulf Coast from Teotihuacán. Known as an artistic, peaceful people, they traveled east from the altiplano of Hidalgo and down into the tropics to the "Land of the Good and Resplendent Moon." The region of the Totonacs, known also as Totonacapan (the place of the Totonacs), covered a very large area during Mesoamerican times, and it is likely that the Totonacs also came from the altiplano of Puebla, extending their region of influence into the southern reaches of Veracruz.

The Totonac city-state of El Tajín gained prominence after the fall of Teotihuacán. Although we refer to El Tajín as "Totonac," its architecture and hieroglyphics contain Olmec, Maya, and Huaxtec influences as well, making El Tajín, in modern times, one of the important sites from Mesoamerica, and the bridge from the earlier cultures to those that came into power in the last years before the arrival of the Spanish.

According to Totonac legend and popular belief, the Totonacs were the first people to identify and domesticate vanilla. Available written history challenges this belief. The Totonacs who came from the Central Valley of Mexico probably knew nothing of vanilla until they came to the Gulf Coast. While the Olmecs may have been the first people who risked the possibility of poisoning in order to see if vanilla tasted as good as it smelled, we will never know for sure. What is known for certain is that vanilla has been central to the lives of the Totonacs for at least hundreds of years, and it has become so enmeshed with their history and lore that it belongs to them culturally.

The Maya called it *ziizbic*, the Zoques-Populucas called it *tich moya*, the Totonacs called it *xanat*, and, much later, the Aztec called it *tlilxochitl*. Interestingly, *xanat* (also spelled "xanath" and pronounced "CHA-nat") is the generic term for "flower" in Totonac. Despite vanilla's elevated stature within their culture, many nouns are generic in Mesoamerican languages. Vanilla is also sometimes called *caxixanath* ("catch-e-CHA-nat"), which means "hidden flower," as its orchid is neither showy nor prominent in the forest, and only lasts for a day.

Vanilla, in early times, was harvested from the forest when it was fully ripe and split open, filling the air with its distinctive fragrance. Instead of having one hundred to two hundred beans as is typical with hand-pollinated plants, there were eight or nine beans, pollinated at random by the forest insects. With vanilla boasting such a seductive aroma, it is certainly understandable that the coastal and low mountain forest dwellers would be drawn to the seedpods and experiment with ways to fragrance their lives with its alluring perfume. If cacao was the food of the gods, vanilla was definitely the nectar that accompanied it!

THE LEGEND OF VANILLA

Here is a Totonac legend about Mesoamerican times. The period of origin of the legend is uncertain.

In early times, the Land of the Good and Resplendent Moon was the kingdom of Totonacapan, ruled by the Totonacas. The palm-studded sands, verdant valleys, and shimmering hills and sierra in what is now known as Veracruz were overseen from several locations. One was Papantla, place of the *papan* birds. Another was El Tajín, the thunderbolt, an ancient city built in honor of the deity, Hurakan/Tlaloc, god of the storms. It was here in this dense, tropical rain forest that vanilla was first cultivated and cured. It was here that the fragrance from the vanilla was so exquisite that Papantla later became known as The City That Perfumed the World.

Xanat, the mysterious and elusive vanilla orchid, in "her" short-lived moment of glory

There was a time, however, before the reign of Tenitzli III, when there was no vanilla. In this city famous for its artists and sculptors, Tenitzli and his wife were blessed with a daughter so incredibly beautiful that they couldn't bear the thought of giving her away in marriage to a mere mortal. They dedicated her life as a pious offering to the cult of Tonacayohua, the goddess of crops and subsistence, a powerful goddess who affected their very lives and survival. Their daughter, Princess Tzacopontziza (Morning Star), devoted her time at the temple, bringing offerings of foods and flowers to the goddess.

It was during her trips from the forest, carrying flowers for the temple, that the young prince Zkatan-Oxga (Young Deer) first caught sight of Morning Star and immediately fell under her spell. He knew that even allowing his eyes to remain upon her for a moment, gazing at her innocent beauty, could bring him death by beheading, but he was obsessed to have her as his wife and companion. The love in his heart for Morning Star outweighed the dangers of being captured and killed. Each morning, before Morning Star went into the forest in search of flowers and doves as offerings for the goddess, Young Deer would hide in the undergrowth and await the arrival of the beautiful princess.

One morning, when the low, dense clouds clung to the hills, following the rain, Young Deer was so overcome with desire that he decided to capture Morning Star and flee with her to the sierra. As she passed close by, he leaped from the bushes, made his intentions known, then, taking her by the arm, ran with her, deep into the forest. Although Morning Star was startled by Young Deer's abrupt arrival and ardent passion, she, too, came under the spell of their star-crossed destiny and willingly followed.

Just as they reached the first mountains, a terrifying monster emerged from a cave, spewing fire, and forced the young lovers to retreat to the road. As they did, the priests of Tonacayohua appeared and blocked their path. Before Young Deer could utter a word, the priests struck him down and beheaded him. Swiftly, Morning Star met with the same terrible fate. Their hearts were cut from their bodies, still beating, taken to the temple, and placed on the stone altar as an offering to the goddess. Their bodies were then thrown into a deep ravine.

Not long after, on the exact site of their murders, the grasses where their blood had spilled began to dry and shrivel away as if their death was an omen of change. A few months later, a bush sprang forth so quickly and prodigiously that within a few days it had grown several feet high and was covered with thick foliage. Shortly after, an emerald green vine sprouted from the earth, its tendrils intertwining with the trunk and branches of the bush in a manner at once delicate and strong, much like an embrace. The tendrils were fragile and elegant, the leaves full and sensual. Everyone watched in amazement as, one morning, delicate yellow-green orchids appeared all over the vine like a young woman in love in repose, dreaming of her lover. As the orchids died, slender green pods developed, and over time they released a perfume more splendid than the finest incense offered to the goddess.

It was then that priests and devotees of Tonacayohua realized that the blood of Young Deer and Morning Star had been transformed into the strong bush and delicate orchid. The orchid and vine were designated as a sacred gift to the goddess and from this time on have been a divine offering from the Totonacas to their deity and to the world.

And so, this is how it came to pass that the blood of a young princess created the birth of *xanat*, or vanilla, the "nectar of the gods."

Post-Classic Mexico

After the fall of Teotihuacan and the great cities of the Maya, a major shift of power and lifestyle occurred. The military held more power than the priests. Wars of conquest were common, and the winners demanded tributes of goods and slaves from their captives. Human sacrifice increased, a necessary evil in order to appease both the nature gods and the gods of war. The northern warrior Toltecs came into the Central Valley of Mexico. Their leader, Topiltzin Quetzalcoatl, was an educated priest in the religious cult of Quetzalcoatl, the serpent god mentioned earlier. In 968, Topiltzin Quetzalcoatl founded the city of Tula. The Toltecs prospered and created the most important Mesoamericn city-state for the next two hundred years. Topiltzin Quetzalcoatl was known as a brilliant leader, but he was eventually deceived by his enemies and forced into exile. He promised to return; then he and his followers traveled south, crossing the Gulf of Mexico and into the Yucatan in 987.

QUETZALCOATL AND THE PROPHECY OF THE BLUE-EYED GODS

Quetzalcoatl, the great Mesoamerican plumed serpent, who at times appears with massive wings, figures prominently in the history and conquest of Mexico as well as in many myths and legends. In the legend of Quetzalcoatl, we are told that upon finding an obsidian mirror, and seeing himself for the first time, he was surprised and distraught to learn that he had the face not of a god but of a man! In his depression, he spent the night drinking pulque (a fermented alcoholic drink). Once intoxicated, he had an incestuous relationship with his sister. After awakening the next morning, hung over and ashamed, Quetzalcoatl was banished for his misdeeds. He left Mexico on a boat of serpents, telling the people that he would return from the East in "one reed year" (a date based on a sophisticated calendar where years were counted by combining a number and an object).

It's interesting to note that the human priest Topiltzin Quetzalcoatl also promised to return on a preset date before he was banished from Tula and headed south toward the Gulf of Mexico several hundred years before the Conquest.

Bernal Díaz says in his book, *The Discovery and Conquest of Mexico 1517–1521*:

> *It is a fact, as we now know, that their Indian ancestors had foretold that men with beards would come from the direction of the sunrise and would rule over them. Whatever the reason may have been, many Indians sent by the Great Moctezuma were watching for us at the river I have mentioned, with long poles, and on every pole a banner of white cotton cloth, which they waved and called to us, as though making signals of peace to come to them.*

Perhaps it was simply coincidence that Cortés and his conquistadors appeared on the shores of Veracruz in a one reed year, but, for a society that was besieged by war and upheaval, it must have appeared that the prophecy of the great Quetzalcoatl's return was true.

As the prophecy indicated that the returning gods would rule the humans, it's also understandable that Moctezuma might be uneasy about having Cortés travel to the center of his empire. Actually, Moctezuma didn't believe that Cortés and his soldiers were gods, a fact that he discussed with Cortés once he arrived in Tenochtitlán. Instead, he feared that these strange, blue-eyed men with beards had arrived as conquerors, fulfilling the prophecy in a far more sinister fashion.

Voladores *"flying" from a ceremonial pole in Papantla, Veracruz, Mexico*

In southern Mexico the new Maya civilization developed in the Yucatan. The postclassic Maya was also besieged by warfare and military control, and Mesoamerica was wracked with instability. The Totonac city of El Tajín was abandoned between 1180 and 1220, and not long after, only a few miles away, the Totonac city of Papantla was settled. From this inauspicious beginning, it would be difficult to imagine that Papantla would one day gain prominence as the center of the international vanilla industry and be known as "the City That Perfumed the World."

THE DANCE AND LEGEND
OF THE *VOLADORES*

The early history of the ceremonial flight of the *Voladores* is shrouded in the mists of antiquity. Information about the original ritual was partially lost when the invading conquerors from Spain destroyed so many of the documents and codices of the indigenous cultures. Fortunately, enough survived through legend and oral history, and in materials written by early visitors to New Spain, that anthropologists and historians have been able to document at least part of the story of this ancient religious practice and how it has evolved through time.

The Voladores were vanilla growers who were known as "those who fly," and were men who comprised an elite segment of the Totonac society. Not all growers were Voladores, but for those who "flew," vanilla cultivation and prayers to the Old Man of the Monte were interwoven with the dances and flight in honor of the spirits who provided the sun and rain.

A Totonac myth tells of a time when there was a great drought, and food and water grew scarce throughout the land. Five young men decided that they must send a message to Xipe Totec, the god of fertility, so that the rains would return and nurture the soil, and their crops would again flourish. So they went into the forest and searched for the tallest, straightest tree they could find.

When they came upon the perfect tree, they stayed with it overnight, fasting and praying for the tree's spirit to help them in their quest. The next day, they blessed the tree, then felled it and carried it back to their village, never allowing it to touch the ground. Only when they decided upon the perfect location for their ritual did they set the tree down.

The men stripped the tree of its leaves and branches, dug a hole to stand it upright, then blessed the site with ritual offerings. Then they adorned their bodies with tropical feathers so that they would appear like birds to Xipe Totec, in hope of attracting the god's attention to their important request. With vines wrapped around their waists, they secured themselves to the pole and made their plea through their flight and the haunting sounds of a flute and drum. The *caporal* or lead Volador, played a primitive flute and small drum with seeds attached to cords so that he could play both instruments simultaneously.

In Mesoamerican times, the ritual of the Volador was performed from Central Mexico to as far south as Nicaragua. It was performed once every fifty-two years at the change of their century, and the brotherhood of the Voladores was passed from father to son.

At the time of the Conquest, the Catholic Church fought strongly against what it considered heathen practices, and indigenous worship and rituals were silenced or held in secret.

Later, the Church combined native beliefs with religious dogma, creating a synchronization of faith. The flight of the Volador was considered an interesting game by colonial New Spain, and special plazas were constructed where the Voladores performed regularly for a curious public. Over time, the ritual slowly died out, until finally the Totonac and a few Otomi were the only groups performing this ancient practice.

Today, the Totonac people perform the flight of the Voladores for several reasons. First, it keeps a part of their traditional culture alive, allowing them to share their heritage with other Totonacs as well as people from around the world. Second, it provides additional income for the Voladores and their families. Non-Totonacs are asked to make a donation after each flight is completed, as well as for additional traditional Volador dances, which are frequently performed on weekends and evenings in the town plazas or in front of cafés. And last, it provides a sense of group pride. Like other folkloric dances and music from around the world, it's a way to celebrate heritage and diversity.

Vanilla continues to have a sacred place in the lives of the Totonac in the same way as the flight of the Volador, and the two have remained integrally connected. The Voladores are a source of great pride to everyone in Totonacapan. In Papantla, the hub of the vanilla industry, there is even a large stone Volador that looks down on the city from one of the highest points in town. Created by world-class artist, Teodoro Cano—who is part Totonac—the Volador is a moving testimony to the Totonac ancestors who founded Papantla in the 1200s, as well as to those who continue to maintain the rich cultural legacy in this region of tropical Mexico.

THE RISE OF THE AZTEC EMPIRE

While the northern Totonacs had little, if any, contact with the Aztecs who were soon to take control of Mexico, the Totonacs of Cempoala suffered under their rule, and most likely they provided vanilla as a tribute to the Aztecs for their beloved *chocolatl*.

Known as the Mexica (or Mejica) among themselves, the Aztecs traveled south from Aztlan in the early 1100s in search of their promised land. When they arrived in the Central Valley of Mexico, the best real estate had already been claimed, so they hired out as mercenaries for feuding chieftains until 1345 when they were able to occupy an islet in Lake Texcoco. It was here they built Tenochtitlán, which, by the time of the Conquest 150 years later, had at least 250,000 inhabitants.

The Aztecs were the most feared warriors of the tribes that came from the north. They worshiped many gods, including Quetzalcoatl, the plumed servant; Tlaloc, the god of the rain; and Xipe Totec, the god of spring and agriculture. It was to Huitzilopochtli, the god of sun and war, that they offered human sacrifices, which they believed were necessary to prevent major catastrophes and natural disasters. Interestingly, while the Aztecs were warriors, their culture was orderly and organized. Alcohol consumption was strongly discouraged, and cacao flavored with chilies, vanilla, herbs, and other flavorings was the beverage of choice for the aristocracy.

The Valley of Mexico averages over 7,000 feet in altitude, with some areas more than 10,000 feet above sea level. Altitude alone would make it impossible to grow cacao and vanilla here, and it certainly didn't grow in the dry, desert land to the north. So how did the Aztec know about these divine flavors of the east and south that they so quickly incorporated into their lives?

There were very sophisticated trade routes throughout Mesoamerica, making foot travel relatively easy for the athletic messengers who brought news from the tropics to the highlands. Long-distance traders, known as the *pochteca*, traveled to the Valley of Mexico relaying news as well as treasures from the lowlands—amber, copal incense, tropical bird feathers, jaguar pelts, and cacao, vanilla, and other tropical foods. So valuable were these products that the *pochteca* often arrived at their destination at night to avoid robbery. They may well have been the first to introduce cacao and vanilla to the Aztecs.

The fairly readily available cacao was used as money, and great storehouses were filled with cacao beans in the Aztec Empire. Because vanilla was much harder to come by than cacao, its value transcended even money and was jealously sought after.

Vanilla actually preceded the arrival of Cortés in its journey to Spain. In 1502, Spanish soldiers from Cuba obtained some vanilla from coastal Indians and sent it to Spain along with indigo and cochineal dyes. As the Spaniards' contact with the coastal tribes was limited, and as they didn't speak the native languages, vanilla's use was unknown. They thought it was a perfume.

THE CONQUEST OF MEXICO

Hernán Cortés was a Spaniard who came to Cuba in its early years under the Spanish crown. He participated in a couple of exploratory missions along the Gulf Coast of Mexico; then, in 1518, he was commissioned by the governor of Cuba to lead an army of his own to conquer Mexico. However, he overthrew the governor's instructions to visit the Yucatan to the south, instead landing his entourage of ships, men, and supplies to the north near what is now the capital of Veracruz state. Leaving some of his troops at a base camp, Cortés and fewer than five hundred soldiers began the arduous trek through the steaming jungles and swollen rivers of the lowlands and struggled over high mountain passes, finally arriving at the altiplano of Central Mexico.

It took Cortés and his army months to ascend to Tenochtitlán. They suffered from tropical diseases and fevers, hunger, and battle injuries in skirmishes with bands and villages of wary native peoples. Along the way, Aztec warriors arrived, bringing messages and gifts from their leader, Moctezuma, and the Spaniards sent gifts of glass beads and other trinkets in return. Moctezuma tried mightily to discourage the Spaniards from exploring Mexico, but to no avail.

On their slow journey to the highlands, the Spanish encountered first the Totonacs and then the Tlaxclalans, both of whom were unwilling subjects of the Aztecs. They were happy to assist in the overthrow of Moctezuma as he had caused them a lot of grief with his demands of taxes and tributes and the capture and sacrifice of their people. They were also wary of the soldiers who matched so well the prophecy of returning gods from the East, and therefore didn't give enormous resistance to the invaders. Between the two tribes, they increased Cortés's army with thousands of men.

In addition to their horses and supplies, the Spaniards had dragged guns, cannons, armor, and even greyhounds on their journey into the interior of Mexico. They had neither food nor warm clothing, however, to protect them from the highland chill, and they quickly used what few medical supplies they had brought with them, so they depended greatly on the assistance of the Indians. The Indians had, of course, never seen anything like horses, large dogs, and cannons. This furthered their belief that the invaders were sorcerers or gods, and they treated the Spaniards with wary respect.

When Cortés and his army finally arrived in the Valley of Mexico, they encountered a masterpiece of floating gardens, sophisticated architecture, and refinement, so astonishing and beautiful that Bernal Díaz, a soldier in Cortés's conquering army, described in his book, *The Discovery and Conquest of Mexico,* the Spaniards' wonder at the site before them:

> . . . *[And] when we saw so many cities and villages built in the water and other great towns on dry land and that straight and level Causeway going towards Mexico, we were amazed and said that it was like the enchantments they tell of in the legend of Amadis, on account of the great towers and cues and buildings rising from the water, and all built of masonry. And some of our soldiers even asked whether the things that they saw were not a dream. . . .*
>
> *And then when we entered the city of Iztapalapa, the appearance of the palaces in which they lodged us! How spacious and well built they were, of beautiful stone work and cedar wood, and the wood of other sweet scented trees, with great rooms and courts, wonderful to behold, covered with awnings of cotton cloth.*

Moctezuma greeted the Spaniards with great generosity, courtesy, and hospitality, housing the soldiers and preparing great banquets for them. The meals were finished with cups of highly flavored *chocolatl* laced with vanilla and served in lacquered gourds (rather than the golden goblets that Díaz had professed in his book). *Chocolatl* was not served as a beverage to be drunk with meals, but as an after-dinner delicacy in the way that banquets in western societies may be finished off with brandy, cognac, and cigars. The Spaniards were advised that *chocolatl* provided great endurance and helped tremendously in their success with women. The Spaniards, ever interested in aphrodisiacs, accepted this information as fact, and assumed that because Moctezuma had a large harem, he kept them happy by drinking *chocolatl*. While the Spanish soldiers may have encountered vanilla growing in the tropical forests or used as incense in the native temples, it was never mentioned or acknowledged until they drank *chocolatl* at Moctezuma's palace.

CHOCOLATL FRIO A LA AZTECA

Courtesy of chef Agustín Gaytan

This recipe for *chocolatl* is a modern adaptation of the early Aztec drink. This particular recipe has a number of modern shortcuts but contains most of the ingredients that could be expected of *chocolatl* in its traditional setting. The corn acts as an emulsifier for the chocolate since freshly ground chocolate can separate.

¼ lb cocoa beans, dark-toasted
¼ cup dry corn, toasted and soaked overnight in 1 cup
    water
1 vanilla bean
2 cups water

¼ cup raw honey, or to taste

4 ice cubes

Ground chili powder may be added to taste.

Materials needed:

Metate and mano (flat stone grinder and roller that's
   similar to a mortar and pestle, but bigger)

Blender and strainer

Presentation goblets

TRADITIONAL PREPARATION:

In a dry skillet, toast the cocoa beans, stirring constantly until
dark brown and fragrant, about 20–25 minutes. They should
be dark brown on the outside and deep, dark brown inside.
Cool and peel.

In the same skillet, toast the corn until it is golden brown
and begins to pop; stir constantly. Soak corn overnight in 1 cup
of water.

Form three small chocolate tablets (about 1 oz each) and put
them aside to cool. Place a lit alcohol burner or sterno under
the metate. The stone must remain hot, so check the flame periodically, replacing burner as necessary. Grind the cocoa pods
between the mano (stone roller) and the hot flat surface of the
metate. Repeat process until chocolate is well ground and
smooth.

In a small saucepan, simmer the vanilla bean in 1 cup of the
water over medium-high heat for about 10 minutes. In the same

liquid, melt a chocolate tablet. Stir constantly until it's completely melted. Set aside.

In the blender, grind soaked corn with its liquid at high speed for a full minute to form a smooth, loose paste. Strain. Grind remaining unground corn with ½ cup water. Strain and discard the leftover mush.

In the blender jar, combine melted chocolate (remove the vanilla bean), corn mixture, honey, and 4 ice cubes. Blend at high speed until frothy.

Serve in fluted goblets.

FOR QUICKER PREPARATION:

• Grind cocoa beans in the blender with enough hot water to form a loose sauce.
• Toast cornmeal instead of corn on a dry skillet and soak overnight.
• Blend all ingredients together with icy cold water and use vanilla extract instead of the bean.

SERVES 4 to 5 (2½ CUPS)

Cortés was a master of psychological warfare and manipulated people and events to his advantage. Moctezuma matched Cortés in skill. He was educated, revered by his people, and keenly perceptive. He knew that he was up against a difficult situation, and he handled the Spaniards with great consideration. He listened respectfully to Cortés's tales of the great monarchy of Europe and the value of abandoning a multitude of gods for the one true, supreme ruler. He acknowledged that the royalty of the distant lands to the East would be welcome to visit and that the god that guided Cortés was most probably a worthy deity, *but* he wasn't interested in converting to a new religion and giving up beliefs that he felt had kept their culture together for centuries.

Over a period of several months, the situation between the two groups deteriorated, ultimately ending in Moctezuma's death, stoned by his own people in a standoff between Moctezuma, the Spaniards, and the inhabitants of Tenochtitlán. Cortés and his men were then aggressively chased from Tenochtitlán by the infuriated warriors. Over the next weeks they regrouped, then returned to Tenochtitlán to lay siege to the city. The Aztecs fought with great ferocity, but they were no match for the Spaniards and their superior weapons. In the end, they could not withstand the relentless assaults, and the massive city-state built by the fiercest warriors of all Mexico fell and was completely destroyed.

Ironically, the Spaniards sought gold and jewels and treasures to enhance their own wealth as well as that of the monarchy. In fact, the greatest long-term wealth gleaned from the newly conquered Americas proved to be corn, cacao, and vanilla.

· 2 ·

INTOXICATING EUROPE
AND NEW SPAIN

The sixteenth century was an exciting and vibrant time in Europe for the titled, the aristocrats, and the adventurers. The spice trade was in full swing, and exotic flavors and fragrances such as cinnamon, nutmeg, cloves, black pepper, and myrrh arrived from around the known world on ships flying under an array of European flags. Sugar, the remarkable sweetener that brightened everything it flavored, was in such demand that plantations were needed in tropical outposts to satisfy discerning noble palates. Money was offered to people brave enough to leave everything that was familiar and safe to set sail to far-off, barely explored colonies filled with wild beasts and "heathens." This was the Renaissance, a time of expansion and exploration, a time of discovery not only of distant lands but of foods that fairly exploded with flavor; tapestries and textiles made from sumptuous silks and velvets; art, music, and architecture that dazzled the mind; and revolutionary new concepts in science and medicine.

Given Cortés's success in Mexico, it would make sense for him to return to Spain at once to show off the splendors he encountered in the New World and to be praised and honored by the king, Carlos I, with whom he would share his bounty. Instead, Cortés decided to take a two-year expedition to Honduras that eventually cost him his health, the wrath of jealous colonial rulers, and the loss of his personal property back home. It wasn't until 1528 that he returned to Spain with a remarkable display of the best the New World had to offer, intent on impressing the king and clearing up his name and reputation.

According to one account, Cortés brought cacao and vanilla beans along with sweet potatoes, haricort beans, and turkeys upon his return. While he may well have brought all of these items with him, this was not the first time that some of these foods went to Europe. Turkeys first went to New Spain in 1523, maize went to the Philippines in 1522, and chilies were taken to India by the Portuguese in 1525. It is also probable that vanilla and cacao would have traveled along with Cortés, at least as curiosities to titillate the senses, since certainly no one in Europe had any idea these flavors existed.

According to Michael Coe, Ph.D., an esteemed anthropologist and Mesoamerican specialist, Cortés does not mention in his journals that he brought plant products with him in 1528. He did write about a rather startling and eclectic variety of gifts from Mexico to impress the king: "These included one of Motecuhzoma's sons, 'many gentlemen and nobles of Mexico,' eight tumblers, ballplayers with their miraculously bouncing rubber balls (something never previously seen in Europe), and several albinos, dwarfs, and monsters (whatever these might have been)." Additionally, Cortés brought along a zoo, including jaguars, opossums, and an armadillo. Whether Cortés was impressed enough with chocolate and vanilla to include them in his traveling sideshow, we will never know for certain. What we do know is that once these two flavors caught on, they would launch a five-hundred-year craze that today continues to grow in popularity.

Chocolatl, as drunk by the Aztecs and other Native Americans, was such a strange-tasting brew that the Spaniards who tried it at the time of the Conquest were completely unimpressed until they doctored it with their own ingredients and made it more palatable. Indeed, a bitter drink containing fiery hot chilies, red clay, and ground corn, served with inches of foam on the top, would be an acquired taste—even with the counterbalance of fragrant vanilla—especially when you consider that the Spanish soldiers' preferred diet was meat, bread, and wine. Descriptive comments about the native drink ranged from "It [*chocolatl*] seemed more a drink for pigs, than a drink for humanity," to "It disgusts those who are not used to it, for it has a foam on top, or a scumlike bubbling." A recurring theme after the complaints was a grudging acceptance of *chocolatl* as it provided stamina and endurance, was comforting, and had medicinal importance. And, according to the Aztecs, it made a man *a man!*

In fact, it was thanks to the colonists of New Spain that chocolate became fit as a drink for European tastes. New Spain, under the leadership of its mother country, was to become self-sufficient by producing precious metals, supplying raw goods unavailable in Spain, and providing a market for Spanish manufacturers. Although New Spain had very limited gold, it was the highest producer of silver in the world. Vanilla, cacao, sugar, cattle hides, and red cochineal dye were the other important and profitable exports. Overseas transport was on Spanish sailing ships that traveled back and forth to Veracruz and Acapulco. This was the heyday of piracy in the Caribbean, and buccaneers and filibusters made their living attacking merchant ships. Travel was risky, especially if the ships carried valuable cargo. So the ships sailed in convoys once a year, and high prices and shortages of goods from home made life difficult for the colonists, who sometimes negotiated for desirable goods from the pirates themselves.

In 1532, Carlos I of Spain was crowned Charles V of the Holy Roman Empire by the pope. The church and state were one under his rule, and Franciscan, Dominican, and other religious orders were sent to New Spain to convert the native peoples, build churches and cathedrals, and attend to the religious needs of the colonizers. The priests and nuns were educated and cultured people from monied families. They served as teachers, operated the hospitals, and documented life in the colony. It was also partly due to them that vanilla and chocolate became more popular, first in the New World, then back home in Spain.

VANILLA IN NEW SPAIN

There are several accounts of vanilla in New Spain during the 1500s. An Aztec herbal book compiled and written in 1552 with the help of priests, and finally published in 1940, is the earliest known document that specifically mentions vanilla. The book tells us that the Aztec ground flowers with other aromatics and wore them around the neck as a medicinal charm or amulet. It's very likely that amulets such as these were first created by the Gulf Coast tribes who gathered the vanilla. At the other end of the spectrum, vanilla was made into an ointment as a treatment for syphilis. As we know that vanilla flowers last only one day, the flowers may have been dried, then brought by the *pochteca* traders to the Valley of Mexico, though there are anecdotal comments about Moctezuma's growing vanilla in his extensive botanical gardens. The book also contains the first known illustration of the vanilla plant.

The Aztecs were talented herbalists as were most of the Mesoamerican peoples. Whether they independently identified vanilla's curative powers or learned of them from the *pochteca* traders, the rare and valued vanilla was important as a medicine as well as an aphrodisiac in their culture.

In 1529, Franciscan Fray Bernardino de Sahagún came from Spain with the assignment of converting Aztecs to Christianity. The enlightened friar first learned Nahuatl, the Aztec "mother language," then taught young indigenous men to write their history in Nahuatl, using Spanish spelling. For the next three decades they collectively recorded all aspects of Aztec culture. The twelve-volume history, written in both Nahuatl and Spanish, went to Spain, but it was considered heretical by the Catholic Church, and much of the body of work wasn't published until 1829. However, the Aztec materials ultimately ended up in the Laurentian Library in Florence, Italy, where they became known among scholars as the Florentine Codex.

Fray Bernardino de Sahagún mentioned the widespread use of hot chocolate among the colonizers. He said, "It is perfumed, fragrant, precious, good, and a medicine. It is toasted and mixed with cacao. I add vanilla to cacao and drink it like vanilla." (These were his words; what he meant by "drinking it like vanilla" is uncertain.)

THE "ADDICTED" LADIES OF NEW SPAIN

Cacao and vanilla could both be purchased in the marketplace, but only the wealthiest people and the clergy in New Spain could afford their use. Whereas the men at the time of the Conquest had the opportunity to try the Aztec drink, the women in New Spain appeared to have quickly adapted it to their taste and incorporated it as a regular beverage, becoming "chocoholics" early on.

Bernal Díaz wrote about a huge banquet staged in the Great Plaza (now the Zocolo) of Mexico City, which was built on top of the ruins of the Aztec capital, Tenochtitlán. The event was to celebrate the peace treaty signed by archenemies Charles V of the Holy Roman Empire and Francis I of France. The affair was extravagant to the extreme, including fountains overflowing with wine. The women were not allowed to attend, so instead they gazed on the men from the windows and corridors of buildings surrounding the plaza. They were served sweetmeats and other costly tidbits along with glasses of wine. But they also received goblets of chocolate with vanilla to keep them calm and content, a beverage they far preferred to the alcoholic European standby.

One of the first changes the women made to the Old World beverage was to serve chocolate hot rather than cold or at room temperature as it was drunk in Mesoamerica. Delicate, sweet cane sugar was substituted for the stronger wild honey. Cinnamon, anise seed, and black pepper were substituted for the less appealing chili pepper and *Xochinacaꝫtli* (the sacred ear flower of the Aztecs), making vanilla the only consistent native flavoring to fragrance the ladies' favorite beverage. The final flourish was a refinement of a technique used by the Aztecs—the creation of a tablet or a ground powder to which sugar and water could be added, turning it into a "fast food" for any occasion.

The Creole ladies of Chiapas considered chocolate their own, and drank it several times a day. It was only a matter of time before they had their maids bring steaming *jícaras* (small clay bowls) of chocolate to them in church in order to endure the tedium of long masses and oratories. This enraged the clergy, whose services were interrupted by the maids' arrival with the chocolate. The clergy also believed that the women were addicted to the beverage and that it was perhaps immoral to imbibe chocolate and vanilla in such enormous quantities. The ensuing debate included the bishop announcing in strong terms that the ladies must give up their passion; they refused. The bishop then had an order placed on the door of the cathedral, excommunicating all who dared indulge in the cathedral during the services. The women responded by skipping mass at the cathedral, instead attending services at convents . . . with their chocolate brought by their maids. The cathedral was, by now, deserted, so the bishop announced that anyone not attending services at the cathedral was excommunicated. The bishop then fell ill from poison, served to him in a *jícara* of hot chocolate! He died eight days later after asking God to pardon his killers.

Who can blame these women for their indulgence? They may as well have been on another planet, so far from home and family, and all that was familiar and secure. Their husbands were often on journeys of exploration or commerce, so they were left alone at home with few privileges and entertainments. Between the theobromine and alkaloids that make chocolate a comforting stimulant and the soothing properties of vanilla, it's no wonder these ladies sought solace in a drink that nourished them, calmed their nerves, and gave them a slight buzz!

VANILLA AS MEDICINE

According to Fray Bernardino, chocolate, mixed with vanilla and two other aromatic herbs, was a cough remedy and a cure for spitting up blood. Based on Sahagún's comments, researchers until now have wondered whether vanilla was used to treat lung diseases such as tuberculosis, which plagued the native peoples since prehistoric times. Recent medical discoveries have found that another dreaded disease that caused severe lung distress may also have been what Fray Bernardino referred to in his notes.

In 1545, the worst drought in five hundred years struck North America, at times extending as far north as the boreal forests and from the Pacific to the Atlantic coasts. The drought severely affected every aspect of life on the northern continent. Recent scientific discoveries indicate that the epidemics known as *cocoliztli* (Nahuatl for "pests"), which first broke out in 1545, were probably hemorrhagic fevers triggered by an indigenous virus carried by rodents. This was similar to the Hanta virus that emerged in the late twentieth century in the drought-stricken southwestern United States. While the smallpox epidemic of 1520 killed between five and eight million native peoples, the *cocoliztli* virus felled an additional *seven to seventeen million people* between 1545 and 1576, making it one of the deadliest plagues in history! The epidemic only struck those in the dry highlands of Mexico and not on the tropical coasts, adding to the likelihood of its being a disease spread by rodents and not by humans.

The plague re-erupted during the time of the arrival of Dr. Francisco Hernández who came to New Spain in the mid-1570s. He treated patients with the disease and documented it in his writings. He may well have used vanilla as an attempted cure for the dreaded disease, though the likelihood of saving people from this scourge was very slim.

Dr. Hernández was sent to New Spain by King Philip II in 1570 to study the colony's natural history and the medical usefulness of the herbs and other native treatments, and to do an anthropological history of the country. He spent seven years in the Valley of Mexico, learned Nahuatl, studied indigenous medicine, and wrote his observations in Latin, creating *The Natural History of New Spain* (Rerum Medicarum Novae Hispaniae Thesaurus) a six-volume collection describing more than three thousand plants. The books were accompanied by ten folio volumes of illustrative paintings by Mexican artists.

In his writings, Hernández referred to vanilla by its Nahuatl name, *tlilxochitl*, which means black pod for the vanilla bean. However, he erroneously translated it to mean black flower, which led to centuries of confusion over the increasingly popular bean. He also classified vanilla as *araco aromática* Hernández wrote of the medicinal properties of vanilla that he learned from the native physicians: "A decoction of vanilla beans steeped in water causes the urine to flow admirably; mixed with *mecaxochitl*, vanilla beans cause abortion; they warm and strengthen the stomach; diminish flatulence; cook the humours and attenuate them; give strength and vigor to the mind; heal female troubles; and are said to be good against cold poisons and the bites of venomous animals."

In itself, vanilla sounds like a miracle cure, but Dr. Francisco Hernández also talks about three flavorings that excite "the venereal appetite," the Viagra of the sixteenth century. Vanilla, cacao, and *mecaxochitl* (a plant related to black pepper and known now as *acuyo*) were the top three contenders that would do the trick. In fact, centuries later, vanilla's reputation as an aphrodisiac was scientifically proved.

THE THEORY OF HUMORS

The keen interest by the European royalty regarding vanilla and other herbs as medicine has to do with popular medical beliefs that circulated throughout Europe for nearly one thousand years. Started by the classical Greeks, and known as the "humoral theory of disease and nutrition," this was a medical system that survived until the first half of the nineteenth century.

Hippocrates (ca. 460–ca. 377 B.C.) believed that the body contains four humors—blood, phlegm, yellow bile, and black bile. A balanced proportion of these results in health, while disease is brought on by an imbalance. Galen, a Greek physician born around A.D. 130, expanded on this concept that humors, diseases, and the drugs to cure these diseases could be hot or cold, and moist or dry. His theory was that a "hot" fever needed a "cold" medicine. And since foods were an important part of maintaining health, they were all classified according to this theory. In addition to the humors beliefs, there was also astrology, the use of plants that in some way resembled the illness, and talismans that were methods employed by doctors of the time.

Dr. Hernández classified the foods and herbs of New Spain according to the humors theory as "hot." This meant that someone with a fever should not be treated with vanilla but with something "cold." On the contrary, the Aztec belief was that if patients were "hot" with a fever, they should be treated with "hot" medicines to induce sweating to speed up healing.

The Europeans were as obsessed with health and diet as we are in our culture today, though their concern was not based upon calories and fat, but on what would make them joyful, melancholy, strong, weak, or sexually powerful. There was constant discussion about what to eat and drink, and the new foods arriving from the colonies were not exempt from this debate. By the 1600s, the humors process became so detailed that even the times of the day, the seasons, and the four cardinal points were divided up into hot or cold. Further, foods were given a degree of heat or cold. In 1658, Dr. Guillaume Pison published his beliefs in Amsterdam, indicating that vanilla "is hot in the third degree."

Dr. Juan de Cardenas of Mexico wrote in 1591 that while chocolate by its nature was "cold," the New World spices that were added to it are all "hot," so that the end result is likely to be neutral. He said that "hot" people drink it with *atole* (a corn drink) and sugar to make them "cooler" or drink it with honey and hot water. We can only imagine how confusing it was to plan meals in advance.

INTOXICATING EUROPE

Back home in Europe the demand for chocolate and vanilla was growing. After the Conquest, the demand for cacao pods and vanilla beans diminished in Mexico as the Aztecs no longer drank their beloved beverage in the accustomed quantity. It was only when chocolate was transformed by the colonial women in New Spain that the demand again increased. In 1585, the first official shipment of cacao came from Veracruz to Seville. It was then manufactured in Spain and mixed with the flavors the ladies of New Spain found so delectable.

CHOCOLATE MANUFACTURE IN SPAIN IN THE LATE 1600s

T his recipe was recorded by an Englishman, E. Veryard, and published in his tract, *Choice Remarks,* which documented his visit to Spain in the latter half of the seventeenth century, when he observed chocolate being manufactured.

"The *Spaniards* being the only People in *Europe* that have the Reputation of making Chocolate to perfection, I made it my business to learn the manner, which is as follows. Take twenty pounds of *Cacao-Nuts,* and dividing them into four or five parcels, dry each apart in an Iron-pan pierced full of holes, over a gentle Fire without the least flame, stirring them continually and without the least intermission. The coming off of the Husks is no argument of their being sufficiently dried, but you are to continue it 'till the Kernals slip between your Fingers, and being lightly pressed crumble into pieces, but not so as to turn into Dust. The Cacao being thus prepared, put it into a Box or other Vessel, stopping it up close, and stirring it every two Hours, and twice or thrice during the Night-time, for otherwise it's apt to take fire. The next Day work it gently on the Stone with a Roller, that the Husks may come off, which are to be separated by winnowing, and such as remain afterwards must be carefully pickt out, and the Dust separated by a Searce [sieve]; when it is thoroughly cleansed, grind it on the Stone with a little Fire under it in a Chafendich [chafing dish] 'till it be wrought into a Mass. Weight the whole, and add to it as much Sugar finely powder'd as will make up twenty-five Pound, with four Ounces of Cinamon, working them all together very well with your hands, 'till they are mixt and united. Then you must grind it as before, but with greater force and longer, 'till it be well incorporated and look as if it were all *Cacao*. Next you are to add twenty-five *Bainillas* [vanilla pods] (more or less according to every one's palate) finely powder'd, proceeding to mix and grind it again as you did before with the Sugar. After this some put in a Drachm of Musk powder'd in a Mortar with a little dry Sugar, and to work it over again. Others add a small quantity of *Acciote*, which is a sort of red Earth brought from the West Indies, and serves to give it a Colour; but neither of these two latter ingredients are necessary. Lastly, you may form it into Cakes, Bricks, or Rolls, according to your fancy. The Rolls are made by dividing a Sheet of brown Paper into four parts, and laying as much of the Mass on each as you think sufficient (which you may regulate by weight) shaking and rolling it from side to side 'till it be formed. You may make the Cakes by putting about ten or twelve parcels on a sheet of the same Paper, and beating it against the Table to make it run abroad. For making the Bricks, the Paper must be forced into that shape, and the Chocolate put in. It must remain in the Papers 'till it be cold and dry."

While cacao was domesticated and grown in quantity, vanilla was still gathered wild and grew in limited quantities. Fortunately, explorers discovered that vanilla actually could be found in several areas of southern Mexico as well as in Guatemala and even over on the Pacific coast in Michoacán. The native people gathered it in the forest, dried it, and sold it to the merchants. The merchants then transported it to the ports where it would travel back to Spain. The Spanish grew increasingly wealthy as they controlled the world's vanilla and chocolate supply . . . at least until the seventeenth century.

It was during the late 1500s that vanilla's name changed from the Nahuatl *tlilxochitl* to *vainilla*, which meant "little scabbard" due to its similarity in appearance to the covering for swords. The bean itself was called *vaina*, which comes from the Latin "vagina." (The Totonacs attributed the characteristics of women to vanilla as well, perhaps because of its sensuous and erotic properties.) This change of name was first credited to Alonso de Molina who, in 1571, wrote *Vocabulario en lengua castellana y mexicana*, a well-known dictionary at the time. His translation for the word *tlilxochitl* was "ciertas vaynicas de olores," referring to the beans as "various fragrant scabbards." Vanilla was well on its way to becoming an international star, being the only important food from the New World that left its traditional name behind; its Spanish name was then adapted to the languages where it traveled throughout the seventeenth and eighteenth centuries.

Reflecting for a moment, as we learn about vanilla's travels throughout Europe in the 1600s, it's interesting to have a perspective on what was available, what was popular, and what was yet to be introduced. In 1582, coffee was mentioned for the first time in England. This bitter drink was not an instant hit. Tea from China was unknown. Sugar was a divine luxury—even spread over roasting meats—but available only to royalty and the wealthiest classes. Until the prohibitively expensive chocolate was cut with quantities of sugar, and until the price of sugar dropped significantly enough to make it affordable, the middle classes only heard about the delights of a cup of chocolate or the wonders of vanilla. As for the peasant classes that made up the vast majority of the population, King Henry IV of France said to a friend that he wished his peasants could have a chicken in every pot on Sundays. The reality was that peasants lived on bread and gruel. So all that was splendid and provocative in the food realm was sampled by only a very few.

Until the beginning of the seventeenth century, vanilla in Europe was only considered a flavoring for chocolate, but this would soon change as vanilla's popularity among the elite quickly spread from Spain to France, Italy, and England. In 1602, the apothecary and pastry

Stylized print of a vanilla vine

chef to Queen Elizabeth I, Hugo (aka Hugh) Morgan, suggested to Her Majesty that she might enjoy having vanilla as a flavoring on its own. Elizabeth was passionate about sweets—so much so, that fairly early in life her teeth rotted and she suffered dearly (though not enough to cure her of her obsession). As sugar was the penultimate sweetener of the day, she spread it on everything. Adding vanilla brought a new depth and dimension of flavor to her love of sweets, and she indulged herself with vanilla-flavored sweetmeats for the remainder of her life.

Morgan passed on some vanilla beans to Charles de l'Ecluse (aka Carolus Clusius) in 1605. Clusius, a brilliant botanist known, among other things, for his work with Dutch tulips, found the beans a curious oddity, dissected them, and classified them as *Lobus oblongus aromaticus,* though he neither knew their country of origin nor how they were used. Vanilla beans were not always properly cured and dried, and apparently the ones that were sent to Clusius were mildewed or decomposing as he commented that they smelled like benzoin, enough so to provoke headaches.

A few years later, Anne of Austria brought Spanish chocolate from her native Spain to her fourteen-year-old husband, Louis XIII of France, to be served at their wedding feast. Although the marriage was a disaster, the chocolate laced with vanilla was an instant hit, and word of the delectable drink spread like wildfire.

Chocolate was, of course, a big hit in Italy, where it was again transformed to Tuscan tastes. Francesco Redi, scientist and physician of Cosimo III de' Medici of the court of Tuscany, invented a wildly popular Jasmine Chocolate beverage. He noted, "The fresh peel of citrons and lemons, and the *very genteel* odor of jasmine, which, together with cinnamon, amber, musk, and vanilla, has a prodigious effect upon such as delight themselves in taking chocolate." So carefully did he guard his recipe that it wasn't until after his death in 1697 that the naturalist Antonio Vallisnieri got possession of the secret recipe of the Jasmine Chocolate. Curiously, the recipe doesn't mention citrons or lemons.

THE RENOWNED JASMINE CHOCOLATE OF THE GRAND DUKE OF TUSCANY

fresh jasmine flowers
10 lbs toasted cacao beans, cleaned and coarsely crushed
8 lbs white sugar, well dried

3 oz "perfect" vanilla beans
4–6 oz "perfect" cinnamon
2 scruples (⅟₁₂ oz.) ambergris

IN A BOX or similar utensil, alternate layers of jasmine with layers of the crushed cacao, and let sit for 24 hours. Then mix these up, and add more alternating layers of flowers and cacao, followed by the same treatment. This must be done ten to twelve times, so as to permeate the cacao with the odor of the jasmine. Next, take the remaining ingredients and add them to the mixed cacao and jasmine and grind them together on a slightly warmed metate (granite grinding stone); if the metate is too hot, the fragrance might be lost.

By 1635, chocolate houses came into vogue in Germany, France, and the Iberian Peninsula, and by 1669 the drink was so entrenched in London, the Cocoa Tree club opened on St. James Street, serving steaming cups of hot chocolate, beer, and some foods. The chocolate houses were gathering places for the men, a place where no respectable woman would set foot. Gambling was enjoyed and politics were discussed.

At the same time that chocolate enjoyed great popularity, tea and coffee were becoming better known. All three beverages were soon accepted, causing a couple of noteworthy and interconnected events. Up to this time, Spain controlled the supply of vanilla and cacao beans. In 1621, the Dutch chartered the Dutch West India Company. They set up massive sugar plantations that brought the price of sugar down enough to make it more affordable as well as available in Europe. The introduction of coffee and tea, along with the sweetened chocolate, created a surge in demand for sugar. As sugar production was very labor intensive, this triggered a rise in the need for slaves, and the world slave trade surged. Slaves were captured and purchased not just from Africa but also from other countries along the trade route, including Madagascar, where warring tribes sold their enemies to the European slavers. Ironically, while Madagascar was largely an unknown country at this time, within two hundred years it would become the greatest producer of vanilla in the world.

THE JEWS IN
THE VANILLA TRADE

A little-known chapter in the history of vanilla belongs to the Sephardic Jews of Spain and Portugal. When the Dutch created the Dutch West India Company, they needed colonizers and offered money to those who would come to the Caribbean. Many of the Jews who had fled to Amsterdam in the previous century signed up to travel to the new colonies. Word spread quickly, and Jews from the Azores and Italy joined them. They established flourishing sugar plantations near Recife in northern Brazil, only to be forced to leave along with the Dutch twenty years later as the Portuguese gained control of Brazil. They moved on to Barbados, Cayenne (now the Republic of Guiana), and Pomeroon (now French Guyana), where other Jews came from Europe in 1661 and, later, from Curacao. Over time, they set up very successful sugar mills and also became active in growing cacao.

While in Brazil, David and Rafael Mercado invented the process and machinery for refining sugar. Leaving Brazil, the brothers went to Barbados where they set up a sugar-refining mill. It went so well that others were soon engaged in the business in several of the Caribbean islands. Their success incurred the jealousy of some of the settlers, and in Barbados and Jamaica they lost many of their rights as citizens and, over time, were not permitted to have indentured servants or slaves. As the production of sugar requires large numbers of workers, the merchant/millers needed a less labor-intensive business. They chose cacao and vanilla. They quickly secured a monopoly in the vanilla trade, sending the much-desired flavor to their merchant friends and families in Europe.

BUTTERSCOTCH FINGERS

This recipe is a carryover from the Jewish sugar mill days in the Caribbean. Note that vanilla is also in the recipe.

¼ lb butter
2¼ cups light brown sugar
2 eggs
2 cups sifted flour
2 teaspoons baking powder
pinch salt
1 teaspoon pure vanilla extract
1 cup toasted, chopped nuts
confectioners' sugar

PREHEAT THE OVEN to 375°F. In a large bowl, cream the butter and brown sugar until light and fluffy. Add the eggs, one at a time, beating after each addition. In a small bowl, combine the flour, baking powder, and salt. Gradually add the flour mixture to the butter mixture. Mix well. Add the vanilla and chopped nuts.

TURN THE MIXTURE into a greased 9-x-11-inch baking dish and bake in the oven for about 25 minutes. Do not overbake. The finished product should be slightly moist and chewy. While dessert is still warm, cut into squares or bars. Sprinkle with sifted confectioners' sugar.

(Recipe adapted from *Jewish Cookery from Boston to Baghdad* by Malvina W. Liebman)

The early Jewish settlers of Pomeroon learned the local languages and lived peacefully with the Native Americans. The Indians gathered and processed cacao and vanilla, using secrets they kept from most of the European settlers. However, they showed the Jews their processing techniques, and the Jews improved and modernized the industry. The Pomeroon Jews then exported the vanilla and cacao to the Sephardic Jews living in Amsterdam, Hamburg, Bayonne, and Bordeaux, where they set up cocoa processing plants and perfected chocolate manufacturing in solid bars and rounds for use in hot chocolate and sweetmeats. Some became master chocolatiers. Indeed, Bayonne is known as the birthplace of *la patisserie française* (French pastry), in large part owing to the Portuguese Sephardic Jews from the Americas sending their relatives the coveted sugar, cacao, and vanilla.

An example of the Jews' importance in the vanilla trade is demonstrated in the following exchange between the purchasing agent Abraham Beekman and the Dutch West India Company. In March of 1684, Beekman wrote:

> *The Jew Salomon de la Roche having died some 8 or 9 months ago, the trade in vanilla has come to an end, since no one here knows how to prepare it so as to develop the proper aroma and keep it from spoiling. I have not heard of any this whole year. Little is found here. Most of it is to be found in Pomeroon, whither this Jew frequently traveled, and he used sometimes to make me a present of little. In navigating along the river, too, I have sometimes seen some on the trees and picked with my own hands, and it was prepared by the Jew, although I was never before acquainted with the virtues and value of this fruit. . . . The Jew has without my knowledge secretly sent a deal home. I shall do my best to obtain for the Company, in Pomeroon or elsewhere, as much as shall be feasible but I am afraid it will spoil, since I do not know how to prepare it. I shall take care that no private business be carried in it.*

Beekman is reproofed by the company on August 21 of that same year:

> *. . . [As] to the vanilla trade, which we recommend you carry on for the Company, where upon you answer us saying that this trade has come to an end through the death, 8 months ago of Jew Salomon de la Roche . . . a meager and poor excuse.*

The Jews were proud of their skill with vanilla, and they kept the extraction process secret. In Martinique a Catholic priest tried, without success, to spy on a Jew who, having come from the Guianas, knew how to prepare extract. Then, in 1689, the French plundered Pomeroon, and Abraham Beekman was dismissed in

1690. All that is now left of the Jews in the vanilla trade in Pomeroon is a recipe for Pomeroon Mousse Pie.

POMEROON MOUSSE PIE

For the crust:
1 cup sifted flour
grated rind of 1 orange
2 tablespoons ground almonds
¼ cup oil
2 tablespoons orange juice

For the filling:
6 oz good-quality semisweet or bittersweet chocolate
1 egg
2 egg yolks
2 teaspoons pure vanilla extract
2 egg whites
1¼ cups whipped heavy cream
shaved bitter chocolate

MAKE THE CRUST: Preheat the oven to 400°F. In a bowl combine the flour, orange rind, and ground almonds. In a small bowl combine the oil and orange juice and beat until frothy. Add the orange juice mixture to the flour mixture. Blend well. Form the dough into a ball and roll it out on well-floured wax paper, large enough to fit a 9-inch pie pan. Transfer the dough to the pie pan. Flute the edges of the crust and prick all over with a fork. Bake for 10 minutes or until lightly browned. Cool on a wire rack.

MELT THE CHOCOLATE in a double boiler over simmering water. Remove from heat and beat in, one at a time, the egg and the two egg yolks, then add vanilla. Beat the whites until stiff but not dry. Whip 1 cup of the cream and fold into the chocolate mixture. Fold in the egg whites. Spoon into the baked pie shell. Chill.

SWEETEN AND WHIP the remaining cream and use as a garnish on top of the pie along with bitter chocolate shavings.

(Recipe from *Jewish Cookery from Boston to Baghdad* by Malvina W. Liebman.)

By the late seventeenth century, the French, more than any other inhabitants in Europe, became passionate about vanilla. The gluttonous Louis XIV, the "sun king," reveled in his cups of chocolate laced with vanilla. After his death in 1715, Philip II of Bourbon served as the regent to the five-year-old heir to the throne, Louis XV. Although the sun king had made much of gastronomy, it was through Philip II that French cuisine flowered. Nobility and aristocrats alike attempted to outdo one another by securing the best and the brightest chefs who invented entrées, sauces, garnishes, and desserts named for their masters.

At the same time, vanilla use declined in Spain and England. The Spanish favored cinnamon over vanilla as a flavoring in their chocolate. By the end of the seventeenth century, so many Spaniards had moved to their colonies that their population at home dwindled, and they were soon to be considered a third-rate power. As a result, most of the vanilla that came through Spain was exported to France and Italy.

In 1708, the United East India Company commissioned with England to bring tea in bulk to the English. By 1711, tea edged out breakfast beer for a morning eye-opener. Although coffeehouses remained the most important place for socializing and discussing politics, tea continued to grow as the beverage of choice. Vanilla was used mainly as a flavoring for those who still enjoyed a luxurious cup of chocolate, and perhaps as a condiment for sweetmeats in the homes of the very wealthy.

France, however, continued to refine the use of vanilla in cuisine. It graced the delicious new ice creams and sorbets enjoyed by the aristocracy in the 1700s, and by 1750 vanilla-flavored ice cream was sold year-round in Paris. Pastries fragranced with vanilla were also an everyday indulgence among the wealthy.

The French also expanded the use of vanilla into the perfume industry. By the late 1700s, perfumes were commonplace, and what would be more delightful than to use vanilla to soften the strong nuances of Oriental spices and highlight the sweetness of delicate herbs and flowers?

Perfumes were originally created to mask strong body odors at a time when bathing and washing clothing were not everyday affairs. The malodorous streets were often rank enough to cause even the heartiest souls to swoon, and protection was needed against the vapors and fevers that abounded in public places. By the late 1750s, perfumes and pomanders were quite popular among the nobility. Often made from fine porcelains, with tiny holes in their lids to release the fragrances, pomander jars contained a mixture of exotic spices, citrus, and crushed, dried flowers. Handkerchiefs were perfumed with fragrances to refresh the nose. Even French tobacco and snuff were fragranced with the compelling aroma of vanilla.

VANILLA COMES TO THE AMERICAN COLONIES

The British American colonies were isolated enough from much of the excitement of European fads as to be completely unaware of vanilla. Chocolate probably arrived in the colonies near the end of the seventeenth century. It's altogether possible that the famous diarist and gourmand Samuel Pepys introduced it as he was the first to suggest that chocolate be made with milk. It's also possible that chocolate may have first come to the colonies from Jamaica. Physician James Baker bankrolled the Irish-American chocolate maker John Hannon in 1764, beginning the first chocolate company in the colonies. But there is no mention of vanilla until none other than bon vivant Thomas Jefferson returned from France.

As one of the greatest epicures and connoisseurs of his era, Thomas Jefferson deserves more than a fleeting mention for his far-reaching effect on America's collective palate. Passionate about the art of good living and fine food and wine, he introduced a wealth of well-detailed and documented information on everything from the growing, to the preparation, to the dining of a vast array of gastronomic delights unknown or underutilized in a young United States of America.

In 1784, Jefferson set sail for France as minister plenipotentiary to the court of Louis the XVI, leaving behind familiar Virginia fare such as ham, fried chicken, boiled greens, and batter breads. He quickly became enamored of French cuisine, and for the four years he spent in France, he devoted himself to the documentation of the meals he enjoyed, copying everything in his own hand. This was often in a blend of French and English. In fact, Jefferson's love of French food was so great that his archrival, Patrick Henry, once denounced him in a political speech as a man who had become so thoroughly "Frenchified" that he "abjured his native victuals."

When Jefferson returned from France in 1789, his protégé and confidential secretary, William Short, who remained in Paris as chargé d'affaires, was called upon frequently to provide a particular recipe or ingredient. Vanilla's intoxicating flavor had won over Jefferson during his French tour of duty, and shortly after his return to the United States, he sent his aide to the marketplace to buy vanilla pods. The aide returned, announcing that no one had ever heard of such a thing as vanilla. Jefferson then wrote to William Short, imploring him to send fifty vanilla pods wrapped in the middle of newspapers. With the flourish of a pen and the help of a friend, he saw that vanilla had traveled nearly full circle back to the Americas.

THOMAS JEFFERSON AND THE PHILADELPHIA ICE CREAM PHENOMENON

The icy, smooth elixir that soothes dry throats and cools fevered brows was quite the rage in the American capital during the late seventeenth century. Not for everyone, however, as only the rich and famous had access to blocks of ice stored in caves and underground pits and, later, in icehouses, during the hot and humid Philadelphia summers. Nor was sugar, a pricey tropical commodity, found on the shelf in every family pantry. Although it would be quite a while before ice cream was a pleasure for the masses, our founding fathers and their friends refreshed themselves with ices, sorbets, and freshly churned ice creams at state functions and private gatherings.

EMANUEL SÉGUR, a Frenchman, is believed to have introduced ice cream to Philadelphia. It was after the Revolution, and our young country still maintained strong ties with Europe and an eye for its latest culinary trends. French confectioners, often with credentials, were in demand. Ice cream became such a hit with the elite that George Washington bought Martha an ice-cream machine in 1784, Abigail Adams produced it in her home, and Thomas Jefferson, a great fan of French cuisine, experimented extensively with ice-cream making.

ALTHOUGH THEY WERE flavors of the Americas, chocolate was a luxury largely reserved for drinking, and vanilla was unknown in the United States at this time. Refreshing and available at least part of the year, lemons provided *the* flavor of choice.

ALL THIS CHANGED with Thomas Jefferson's request for vanilla pods from France. The irony of his request is the fact that the vanilla pods destined for Jefferson's pleasure traveled from Mexico or the Caribbean to France and then back to the United States, on sailing ships *during the middle of the French Revolution!* Was vanilla an expensive commodity? You bet!

PHILADELPHIA has prided itself since the early days on having ice cream made only with "pure" ingredients: milk, cream, sugar, and flavorings—what is now known as "Philadelphia ice cream." Jefferson's recipe called for eggs, a product that Philadelphia purists considered an "additive." His recipe was based on creating a French custard base, then freezing it. This velvety-rich ice cream later was called French custard ice cream or French vanilla ice cream, and was possibly the origin of the term "French vanilla."

Philadelphia-style ice cream, not French custard ice cream, became the standard of what American ice cream should be, but Jefferson's introduction of vanilla as a flavoring for the frozen treat was an instant success: lemon moved into second place, and vanilla reigned supreme. Small dark flecks of vanilla bean were a staple of true Philadelphia ice cream. This trend has since spread throughout the United States, and speckled vanilla-bean ice cream can be found in ice-cream parlors and grocery stores everywhere.

Jefferson kept meticulous accounts of all his purchases and expenditures. He also implored of his overseas guests to bring him delicacies that were not yet available in America. In 1792, he paid $4 to a Mr. Theophile Cassinove, the representative of several Dutch banking firms, for 100 vanilla beans (about 1 pound weight). It would be interesting to know the path that Jefferson's vanilla had traveled. Did it originate in New Spain, the West Indies, or South America? Had it traveled to Spain, France, or Holland? By the end of the eighteenth century, vanilla could have come from several sources and traveled to several possible destinations before arriving in the United States. Yet despite its growing international reputation, vanilla discovered its journeys had just begun. Within the next two hundred years, vanilla would be planted, grown, and used worldwide.

Jefferson created a book of his recipes, which included entries, or "receipts," as they were then known, from his French chef; family friend, Mary Randolph; Mary's daughter, Virginia Randolph Trist; and Mary's sister, Ellen Randolph Coolidge. First, here is Jefferson's method of preparing ice cream, in the original wording:

THOMAS JEFFERSON'S VANILLA ICE CREAM

2 bottles of good cream
6 yolks of eggs
½ lb. sugar

Mix the yolks and sugar.

Put the cream on a fire in a casserole, first putting in a stick of vanilla.

When near boiling take it off and pour it gently into the mixture of eggs and sugar.

Stir it well.

Put it on the fire again, stirring it thoroughly with a spoon to prevent its sticking to the casserole.

When near boiling, take it off and strain it through a towel. Put it in the sorbetiere [ice pail].

Then set it in ice an hour before it is to be served. Put into the ice a handful of salt.

Put ice all around the sorbetiere—i.e., a layer of ice a layer of salt for 3 layers.

Put salt on the coverlid of the sorbetiere and cover the whole with ice.

Leave it still half a quarter of an hour.

Then turn the S. in the ice 10 min.

Open it to loosen with a spatula the ice from the inner sides of the S.

Open it from time to time to detach the ice from the sides.

When well taken (prise) stir it well with the spatula, put it in moulds, jostling it well down on the knee then put the mould into the same bucket of ice.

Leave it there to the moment of serving it.

To withdraw it, immerse the mould in warm water, tossing it well until it will come out and turn it onto a plate.

WHILE THE MOLDED ice creams were fine for regular dinners, on state occasions it was quite popular to create a more elaborate dessert similar to the later popular "Baked Alaska." One White House visitor reported that at a presidential dinner, the ice cream was brought to the table as small balls, encased in warm pastry—a feat that caused great astonishment.

CHOCOLATE CREAM

by Mrs. Mary Randolph

Scrape ¼ pound chocolate very fine. Add 3 tablespoonfuls of water and stir over a low flame until melted. Add 4 cups of scalded milk. Beat the yolks of 6 eggs until light, add 6 tablespoonfuls of sugar and a pinch of salt. Pour into first mixture and stir until it thickens. Add 1 teaspoonful of vanilla. Strain into a glass dish.

PHILADELPHIA PUDDING

by Mrs. Virginia Randolph Trist

Wash 1 cupful of rice well and stir it into 3 pints of milk. Sweeten to taste, add pinch of salt, and flavor with nutmeg, vanilla, or cinnamon. When all is mixed, set over a very low flame for five or six hours. It must not be stirred or put over too hot a fire.

3

TROPICAL MIGRATIONS

As vanilla's popularity grew, so, too, did the demand for it, especially as it became the darling of the European cognoscenti. By the late seventeenth century, it was clear that more vanilla was needed to fill the demand for its use in beverages, pastry making, medicine, and aphrodisiacs. The complication lay in understanding how vanilla grew and reproduced and where it could be grown. Because demand so far outpaced supply, the prices for vanilla were extraordinarily high, though for royalty and the upper class, price was of far less concern than having a ready supply of the luxuries that made life more "bearable."

THE BIRTH OF AN INDUSTRY

As the coastal forests of Central America, Panama, and even Venezuela and Cuba were scoured for wild vanilla that could be turned into plantations and exploited, the vanilla "industry" was on its way. What began as scouting parties and exploratory adventures developed into a lucrative business for the Spanish and, later, others who had access to vanilla.

William Dampier, a British pioneer in scientific exploration, observed vanilla growing in the Bay of Campeche in Southern Mexico in 1676 and in 1681 in Bocas del Toro, Costa Rica. In his *A New Voyage Round the World*, he wrote:

> *We found a small Indian village, and in it a great quantity of Vinello's drying in the sun. The Vinello is a little Cod (pod) full of black seeds; it is 4 or 5 inches long, about the bigness of the stem of a Tobacco leaf, and when dried much resembling it; so that our Privateers at first have often thrown them away when they took any, wondering why the Spaniards should lay up Tobacco stems. This Cod grows on a small Vine, which climbs about and supports itself by the neighboring trees; it first bears a yellow Flower from whence the Cod afterwards proceeds. It is first green, but when ripe it turns yellow; then the Indians (whose manufacture it is, and who sell it cheap to the Spaniards) gather it and lay it in the sun, which makes it soft; then it changes to a Chestnut colour. Then they frequently press it between their fingers, which makes it flat. If the Indians do anything to them besides, I know not, but I have seen the Spaniards sleek them with Oyl.*

Later, when Dampier went to Costa Rica, he attempted (unsuccessfully) to dry the beans himself. He asked the Spaniards how this was done, and they didn't know, so he concluded that the native peoples had secret methods. He noted:

> *Could we have learnt the art of it, several of us would have gone to Bocca-toro* [sic] *yearly, at the dry season and cured them, had*

freighted our vessel. We there might have had Turtle enough for food and store of Vinello's. . . . [T]hey are commonly sold for 3 pence a Cod among the Spaniards in the West Indies, and are sold by the Druggist, for they are much used among Chocolate to perfume it. Some will use them among Tobacco, for it gives it a delicate scent. I never heard of any Vinello's but here in this Country about Caibooca and at Bocca-toro.

At three pence a pod, had Dampier learned how to dry the beans, and organized the trade, he would have had a very lucrative business. Farther south, as the Jews had developed an independent vanilla trade, by the middle of the 1600s, vanilla was available from a variety of locations though certainly not in abundance. Even wild vanilla varieties that did not have the same aromatic properties as the beloved *Vanilla planifolia* were gathered and sent to Europe where vanilla was vanilla and they wanted as much of it as they could get.

Sometime in the early to mid-1600s, vanilla plantations were established in an organized fashion in the area of Teutila, Oaxaca, Tabasco, and northern Guatemala. These plantations were the primary sources for vanilla in New Spain. In 1765, Fray Francisco de Ajofrín, in his travels to Oaxaca, passed through the province of Teutila where he observed the vanilla industry. Within a one-hundred-year period, the plantations flourished, and vanilla was an excellent source of income for the area, a crop of great commercial importance that kept the villages well funded. Fray Francisco's writings describe how vanilla was planted, harvested, and cured. He mentions that when the beans are harvested in December and January, "they have no aroma until they are cured by the force of the sun, which is strong. After a few days in the sun they begin to change from green to dark and the aroma or balsam from the oils

Vanilla vine growing wild up a tree trunk. Wild vines often grow to the top of the forest canopy, but they don't produce many flowers as they expend their energy in producing the vines.

is so aromatic that you cannot suffer, but the fragrance can make you feel light-headed." According to Fray Francisco, the vanilla was packed in bundles of fifty beans and tied with a fine thread from the Ojonote tree, then boxed for the trip to Spain and other European provinces and Africa. (Where he got the idea they went to Africa is anyone's guess.)

A document from the Mexican Archivo General de la Nación indicates that the vanilla business was well established in Papantla as early as 1743, but that the pods were still gathered in the wild. It tells us that the Totonacs gathered vanilla pods growing on plants in the hills and then sold them to a group of buyers in town. The buyers, in turn, cured them. "This is the way it was always done," the record states, implying that the beans had been gathered this way for at least several decades. The Totonacs received up to 2 pesos per purchase and were far better off than most indigenous people in Mexico who struggled to survive under the brutal Spanish *encomienda* system.

For those who cured, dried, and sold the vanilla (known as the *beneficiadores*), the vanilla business was quite profitable. The *alcalde mayor* (bureaucratic chief) attempted to corner the local vanilla market for his own benefit. He issued a decree, prohibiting the harvest of the vanilla before December 8, at which time he would purchase the entire supply himself. Whether he was able to get away with this is not recorded, but his interest illustrates the hold the fragrant crop already had on the area's economy.

For the Totonacs of the central Veracruz coast, vanilla plantations were established a bit later. This is probably due, at least in part, to the fact that this area of Mexico was isolated enough so it wasn't as greatly affected by the Aztecs in the central highlands of Mexico, or by the subsequent Conquest and Spanish rule as were the native peoples to the south and east. The Totonacs here were not subjugated and forced to provide tributes of vanilla in Mesoamerican times, and the Spaniards did not seek vanilla from this region in the early colonial years.

J. A. Villaseñor y Sánchez's two-volume account about life in the provinces of New Spain from 1746 to 1748 concurs that the Spanish traders were buying vanilla that was still gathered in the hills around Papantla. Agapito Fontecilla, who also documented life in the canton of Papantla, wrote *A Brief Treatise Over the Cultivation and Processing of Vanilla*, in which he states that he had seen documents in the Papantla archives that indicated that vanilla plantations had existed in this area as early as 1760. This is the first mention we have of vanilla being planted rather than gathered from the forest in the Papantla region.

Other documents from the Mexican Archivo General de la Nación give us a more concrete glimpse into the early days of the industry. One, from Teutila in 1738, tells of a complaint that was made over two boxes of vanilla coming from Oaxaca that had been kept illegally in the port of Veracruz instead of traveling with the fleet to Spain. The vanilla was valued at 45 pesos per thousand pods and double that in Spain. Considering that the vines depended on insect pollination, that's a lot of vanilla. The bigger question is why such a valuable commodity would have been kept in port. One wonders if the plan was to hoard the vanilla, thereby forcing the prices even higher. Whatever the reason, vanilla from Teutila was held in such high esteem that it was considered the standard for excellence in Spain up until the early 1800s when the industry there had nearly disappeared.

A HOT COMMODITY

The Totonacs of Colipa (near Misantla) began planting vanilla in the hills surrounding their village in the early 1760s. This was an area that had, up until then, been dedicated to growing tobacco and chili peppers as cash crops, so vanilla cultivation was still a new business at the time the Totonacs filed a formal report in 1767. The Totonacs complained that thieves were stealing their beans and they were losing a large part of their harvest.

The Totonacs were caught in a difficult position. There was a government regulation already in place that stated the first day that vanilla could legally be picked. The regulation was created to ensure that the vanilla would be ripe before picking so that it would meet the high standards set for exported vanilla. As vanilla beans were certainly easy to steal, the only hope the growers had was to sleep by their vanilla plants, machetes by their sides, as harvest season approached, then keep the beans under guard until they were sold.

Sadly, the problems that plagued the Totonacs of Colipa still exist today. As soon as vanilla became a commercial commodity, farmers around the world have struggled with theft, assault, and even homicide over their precious holding. Modern times are no different. Harvest dates are set and enforced worldwide, but des-

peration—and greed—often override the law, and vanilla is sometimes picked so green it is nearly useless.

KILLING THE BEANS

Alexander von Humboldt, the renowned German naturalist, zool-
ogist, sociologist, and explorer, staged an expedition from 1799 to
1804 with his good friend A.J.A. Bonpland, whereby they traveled
through Central and South Americas, Mexico, Cuba, and the
United States. The materials Humboldt gathered during his expedition were published in the *Voyage de Humboldt et Bonpland,* often
referred to as *The American Journey,* in which he provides some of
the most specific information in print about the Mexican vanilla industry in the early nineteenth century. He carefully documented
the agricultural practices that he observed along the way, including
the working vanilla plantations and the trade in the Orinoco basin
in South America. In 1803 and 1804 he traveled along coastal Mexico, getting a firsthand view of the Mexican vanilla industry.

Humboldt describes the varieties of wild vanilla growing
throughout Central and South Americas and the Caribbean and
compares the quality of the different vanilla species. He was very
fond of the Misantla Valley, claiming that it is a "delicious valley
where there isn't the same plague of mosquitoes and other insects
that abound in the port of Nautla." His accounts provide details
about the cultivated plantations in the Misantla Valley, including
the fact that each plant could produce as many as forty beans per
season—a lot when you consider that with plants growing wild in
the forest only six to eight beans were gathered from each.

The Indians harvested the beans and sold them fresh to the
Creole Mexicans and mestizos (people of mixed Indian-European

blood), whom Humboldt referred to as "people of reason." They cured and dried the beans, using a technique called *beneficio de poscoyol* (or *poscoyon*), where the beans are wrapped in wool blankets and then dried in a native oven "over" low heat to stop the fermentation of the beans. This technique, known as "killing the beans," is the first time that this practice is mentioned in print. Given that *poscoyol* is a Totonac word, the Indians may have used a similar technique for curing beans when they were unable to get the green beans to the curing houses quickly enough, or it may simply refer to the type of oven that was used.

Humboldt also mentions that although there was some vanilla coming from the canton of Papantla 62 miles (nearly 100 km) away, the quantities were limited and the beans were poorly dried, though very aromatic. The farmers of Misantla were certain, however, that the Indians of Papantla and Nautla, who supposedly still gathered beans from the forest, were stealing beans from their more organized plantations.

According to Humboldt, the annual production from Misantla was about 700,000 beans, Teutila in Oaxaca was only producing about 110,000 beans, and the Papantla district yielded about 100,000 beans yearly. Assuming Humboldt is referring to dried beans, this amounts to about 3½ tons of dried vanilla annually, a respectable amount of vanilla considering it was being naturally pollinated rather than artificially, or hand-pollinated.

THE ELUSIVE ORCHID

Back in Europe, although vanilla was "the flavor of the moment," no one knew that the plant was an orchid. In fact, scientists were hard at work simply trying to understand how plants reproduced.

In 1694, Rudolph Jacob Camerarius, a professor and botanist, proved that plants had sexes, a revolutionary breakthrough in horticulture. He identified their reproductive parts and also demonstrated the role of pollen in plant reproduction. But the secrets of vanilla were still not understood. A few years later, Charles Plumier described the genus *Vanilla* in *Nova plantarum americanarum genera* and wrote about three species from the West Indies, but somehow managed to neglect *Vanilla planifolia*, the "mother" of commercial vanilla. It wasn't until 1799 that O. Schwartz definitively established the genus *Vanilla* with two species, *V. aromatica* and *V. claviculata*. But scientists had yet to learn the secrets of orchid propagation, and until this code was broken, the commercial production of vanilla in countries other than the Americas would not be possible.

Around 1740, the fancy of the upper class and nobility turned to botany, and plants were transported on sailing ships from around the world to Europe's royal greenhouses. This was actually just the beginning of a plant frenzy that grew to amazing proportions in the 1800s. Orchid fever overtook the wealthy hobbyists, and they financed expeditions into the farthest reaches of tropical jungles and forests in search of the next best orchid, ideally one not yet discovered. Rather than risking their own lives and limbs, they would find a young man thirsting for adventure; if the young man was lost forever or eaten by the locals, well, that was just part of the adventure.

Fortunately, gathering vanilla wasn't nearly so risky, and sometime before 1759 vanilla plants were sent to the greenhouse at the Jardin du Roi in Paris, with the plan of propagating them and sending them to French colonies. As the horticulturists couldn't get the plants to flower, the project fizzled. Nevertheless, simply having vanilla vines in the royal gardens was a prestigious oddity, though, as there are no records of what became of these vines, it is likely that they eventually died out.

The Spanish established a tropical laboratory in the Philippines sometime in the late 1700s. It was here that *Vanilla pompona Schiede* (also known as "Vanillon" or "Guadeloupe vanilla," as plants of this species were either indigenous to—or brought from—Mexico to the West Indies early on) and *Vanilla planifolia* were first crossed, creating the plant stock that later evolved into *Vanilla tahitensis*. Cuttings traveled to and from the laboratory for at least another fifty years, but no information about the Manila laboratory appears to have survived.

In 1793, a Monsieur Millier imported vanilla from Martinique, Guadeloupe, and Guyana, bringing the cuttings to Paris. The Marquis of Blanford also introduced vanilla plants from the West Indies in the late 1700s or early 1800s, and sometime before 1807 one of these plants actually flowered in Paddington Gardens (London), in the collection of the Right Honorable Charles Greville. Even more remarkably, the orchids produced fruits! A frenzy of excitement ensued, including the inviting of Francis Bauer, a famous illustrator of the period, to create botanical prints of the plant with its fruit. This is the first record of vanilla's actually being produced in Europe, though after the fact, since no one has any idea of how it happened. Cuttings were sent to botanical gardens in Paris and Antwerp with great hopes of finding a way to produce the treasured beans, but . . . it never happened again.

Nevertheless, in 1819 two cuttings from the plants Greville sent to a Dr. Somme at the Botanic Garden of Antwerp made the journey to Buitenzorg (now the gardens of Bogor) in Java. The one plant that survived the voyage flowered in 1825, but none of the flowers produced beans. The botanist Carl Ludwig Blume mistak-

The racemes, where vanilla flowers will form. Usually only one flower blooms at a time on each raceme, but occasionally there will be two that appear simultaneously.

enly described the plant as *Vanilla viridifloria*, though it had already been classified as *planifolia* stock by Henry Andrews in 1808.

In 1819 a Commandant Philebert brought *Vanilla pompona* (or possibly *Vanilla mexico mill*) cuttings from Cayenne to Réunion, the island in the West Indies. Referred to as the "great vanilla" and called *Vanilla guianensis* (or *surinamensis*), some of this vanilla was taken to Manila in 1819, and then brought back again in 1820 (why it was brought back is unknown). Then in 1822 *Vanilla planifolia* arrived in Réunion, some of it as cuttings from the same infamous plant that flowered and fruited in Paddington Gardens. Although it was essentially a decorative plant until the 1840s, when producing plantations were finally established, it later provided the stock that created Bourbon vanilla.

THE CURSE OF MOCTEZUMA

While the other two very popular tropical plants, cacao and coffee, thrived and reproduced in their new tropical environments, vanilla didn't, and scientists and hobbyists alike were frustrated. What was the problem? The climate was right, the soil was right, and the vines flourished. So why wouldn't vanilla produce fruit? Rumors spread that perhaps vanilla was somehow jinxed; perhaps it was just as the Indians of Mexico had said: "You can plant it, and you can grow it, but you won't get it to fruit." Was it the "curse of Moctezuma" coming back to haunt the descendants of the men who destroyed the great Aztec empire and plundered the country? No one had a reasonable explanation for the perplexing riddle of reproducing vanilla.

Then, as so frequently happens, the time for solving the mystery of vanilla propagation was at hand, and within eleven years, three people independently of one another made the discovery that would dramatically change the vanilla industry.

In 1830, a gardener known only as Neumann is credited with pollinating vanilla orchids in the glass houses at the Musée de Paris. This information is anecdotal, and little appears to have been written about Neumann, so whether it is true or not is uncertain. However, in 1836, Charles Morren, a professor of natural science at the University of Liege in Belgium, who had recently been nominated to the directorship of the Liege Botanical Garden, dissected a vanilla orchid in his quest to better understand the plant. In the process of cutting the labellum, the lip separating the rostellum and the stigma, with a scalpel, he discovered how the male and female segments of the orchid were separated and how the pollen needed to be manually transmitted if the plant was not in its native habitat.

This was an especially clever epiphany as Morren was an academic, not a horticulturist. By this time, scientists and orchid fanciers had figured out that many orchids needed to be hand-pollinated; the problem was in actually obtaining a vanilla orchid to see if this was true for vanilla as well. As the flowers rarely bloomed in European greenhouses and as they only lived for a day, the window of opportunity to observe the flowers was very narrow.

Morren then traced the ancestry of the plant he had studied back to the one that had originally flowered in the collection of the Right Honorable Charles Greville. In 1838, Morren's paper "On the Production of Vanilla in Europe" was read before the British Association at Newcastle and published the following year. As important as Morren's discovery was, in and of itself it did not create a major change in vanilla production.

That occurred three years later when a twelve-year-old boy named Edmond Albius uncovered the secret that launched the vanilla industry throughout the Indian Ocean, Indonesia, and Tahiti, and greatly expanded its production in Mexico.

Not much is known of Albius. He was the child of a sister's maid, on the plantation of Ferréol Bellier-Beaumont, an amateur botanist residing in Réunion. Monsieur Bellier took an interest in Edmond and taught the young boy about orchids and pollination. One day, Edmond was examining vanilla orchids in bloom, and he applied a similar technique of pollination to the one he used for Monsieur Bellier-Beaumont's orchids. With a splinter of bamboo, he lifted the thin, flaplike rostellum that divides the male anther and female stigma organs and pressed the pollen against the stigmatic surface. This simple process was accomplished in a matter of a few seconds. Within a couple of days a vanilla bean began to form, proof of the success of the pollination.

It would be gratifying to say that Albius made a fortune for himself and brought great honor to his patron, but unfortunately it didn't work out that way. There is no indication that Monsieur Bellier-Beaumont benefited directly or indirectly from his protégé's discovery, and Albius never saw a penny for his brilliant endeavor. He was freed from slavery in 1848, married, and died in 1888 in a pauper's residence. The only acknowledgment in honor of Edmond is a crude plaster-cast monument that was erected in the Réunion capital city of Saint-Denis in 1981, but his accomplishment is documented in books and papers—a simple technique that changed the industry forever.

HEADING FOR THE TROPICS

Albius's discovery came not a minute too soon. The quantity of vanilla coming from all areas of Mexico declined dramatically in the years after 1810 when political upheaval in the country over the autocratic and inadequate Spanish colonial rule triggered an eleven-year struggle for Mexico's independence.

At the same time, vanilla's importance in Europe continued to soar, creating an ever-increasing need to grow it in other tropical colonial holdings. The flavoring was becoming a staple in upper-class families and entrenched in European culture. In 1845, Lord Sidney Smith bestowed the following compliment upon his very eligible single daughter, one Lady Holland: "Ah, you flavor everything: you are the vanilla of society."

The time also witnessed a growing interest in food as more than sustenance. There was a proliferation of cookbooks and recipes in the early to middle 1800s. In 1825 Jean Anthelme Brillat-Savarin published *The Physiology of Taste*. He wrote a treatise about chocolate and included a favorable comment about vanilla as well:

We have come to think of chocolate *as the mixture which results from roasting together the cacao bean with sugar and cinnamon: such is the classic definition. Sugar is an integral part of it; for with cacao alone we can only make a cocoa paste and not chocolate. And when we add the delicious perfume of vanilla to this mixture of sugar, cacao, and cinnamon we achieve the* ne plus ultra *of perfection to which such a concoction may be carried.*

In 1846 Alexis Soyer published *The Gastronomic Regenerator* with recipes for two thousand dishes that ranged from elaborate banquet entrées like roast peacock to simpler daily roasts and hashes. His initial printing of two thousand copies sold out in two

In 1849 Soyer wrote *The Modern Housewife*, or *Menagere*, a book written for the emerging middle-class families of Europe. He instructs the readers on how to make "Sugar of Vanilla," as follows:

Chop a stick of well frosted vanilla very small, and put it into a mortar with half a pound of lump sugar, pound the whole well together in a mortar, sift through a hair sieve and put in a bottle or jar, corking up tight, and using where required.

months, and four editions were printed in less than a year—a re-markable number of books for the time.

Vanilla was in great demand and innovative plans had to be devised to get it. The logical place for vanilla plantations were the islands of the Indian Ocean, an area that had played an essential role in the control of the spice trade routes. Réunion, the very same island where Edmond Albius made his discovery, had been the staging area in the wars between the French and British for control of the shipping routes to India.

Réunion, along with Mauritius and Rodrigues, are part of the Mascarene island chain. Réunion is much like Hawaii as it sits on a hot spot on the earth's crust, a volcanic island with rich tropical soil. Although the Arab and Malay travelers visited it, it was uninhabited when the Portuguese navigator Pedro de Mascarenhas came upon it in 1512. In 1642, the French took it for themselves as their main base for the French East India Company, and the king of France, Louis XIII, named the island *Ile de Bourbon*. The English wrested control of the island in 1810 during the Napoleonic wars and renamed it *La Réunion*. Although the island was given back to the French five years later, its original Portuguese name Réunion remained, though two hundred years later the Mascarene Islands are still often referred to as the Bourbon Islands.

Coffee was the first cash crop planted in Réunion, and African slaves from Madagascar and East Africa were brought in to work in the fields, as there were no native peoples there to put to work. The coffee plantations were destroyed by cyclones in the early nineteenth century; when the British took control of the island, sugar became its primary crop. In 1850, sugar plantations began to fail; with cheap labor and an ideal climate, vanilla plantations were quite successful and quickly became the island's primary income producer, and plantations were established not long after in nearby

Mauritius. In 1848 Réunion exported 110 pounds (50 kg) of cured and dried vanilla; within ten years they produced 6,600 pounds (3,000 kg), and at its apex, Réunion had a record of 200 tons of vanilla in 1895. Although very little vanilla now grows in Réunion, the name *Bourbon* is synonymous with Indian Ocean vanilla.

Now that vanilla could effectively be grown in any suitable tropical climate, cuttings and plants traveled around the world like migrating birds. Around 1840, vanilla was first introduced to Madagascar. Fifteen years later, it was again brought to Madagascar and was taken to the Seychelles two years later. In 1846, vanilla was introduced as a cash crop by Johannes Elias Teysmann, director of the Botanic Gardens at Buitenzorg (Bogor) on the island of Java. Admiral Ferdinand Alphonse Hamelin introduced the first vanilla plants from Manila to Tahiti in 1846, and the industry took hold in 1880. A Monsieur Le Compte brought vanilla from Manila to Gabon in 1848, and then in 1874, a Monsieur Klaime took vanilla from Gabon to the Musée de Paris. And in 1875, vanilla cuttings traveled from Martinique to Réunion, then Madagascar, and on to the Comoro Islands where vanilla became an important cash crop. By 1886, world vanilla production was greater in the Mascarene Islands and Java than in Mexico! The monopoly of the Americas was forever broken, the curse of Moctezuma dissolved, and vanilla would soon become a household necessity for the cookies, cakes, and ice creams that became synonymous with the comforts of home.

INDEED, vanilla plantations had become big business. S. J. Galbraith wrote a bulletin in 1898 published by the U.S. Department of Agriculture, Division of Botany, that provides us with a glimpse into the life of a vanilla plantation in the Seychelles. The bulletin was published in part because Puerto Rico and Hawaii had recently been annexed to the United States, and there was considerable interest in growing vanilla on these two tropical islands close to home. As France controlled the Indian Ocean islands as well as Tahiti, Indian Ocean vanilla for the U.S. market was mainly purchased through France. Most of the American vanilla came from Mexico at this time, with small additional amounts from the West Indies. If Hawaii and Puerto Rico could supplement the Mexican vanilla supply, the United States could expand its market share and fill the need of its growing food-service industry. In the bulletin's introduction there is a listing of the monies made in tropical colonial countries at the time of publication as an incentive for potential growers: Réunion earned $560,563 from its vanilla crop in 1892, the small island of Tahiti earned $172,295 in 1897, and the Seychelles earned $246,600 the same year.

Galbraith begins by telling us that if vanilla is kept free from disease, it is a plant of extraordinary vitality. This was an important observation, as, at one point, plants were grown so closely together that workers could barely pass between them. This created an enormous per acre yield, but when disease broke out in a vanillery (and it often did), destruction was rapid and complete. Initially, trees were used in the Seychelles, but many planters, says Galbraith, "made use of hardwood posts & bars, the former being notched on top and the latter laid in the notches, resting thus from 4 to 5 feet from ground."

Probably from personal experience, he suggests planting each vine on a tree of its own in a place where land is cheap, nine feet between trees ("which can be topped"), and followed by a heavy mulching with leaf mold. Galbraith adds that while this is more expensive as the workers have more area to cover for pollination, and more mulch and fertilizers will be needed, the process provides increased security against sick plants and spreading disease.

Galbraith says, "There used to be a story current here, no doubt with some grain of truth in it, to the effect that in a very wet season the only vanilla planter who had any crop was one whose pigs had got adrift in his plantation and spent the night in grubbing up vanilla roots. This method of producing flowers is not recommended, but it is quite possible that careful and systematic root pruning might be carried on with advantage in wet years, if one could tell beforehand when these were coming."

As was true in most vanilla plantations around the world, the pollination of flowers was done mainly by women and children. Galbraith says, "The operation is a very simple one, and an average Negro will acquire the knack after being shown a few examples. . . . An ordinary hand can fecundate a hundred or more flowers per hour. Early morning from 7 to 9 is the best time for fertilizing; but the work may be started with sunrise and carried well into the afternoon though about midday flowers begin to close some and work goes slower."

Galbraith employed a "triple dipping" method of hot water in his curing and drying process, a method developed in the Indian Ocean as vanilla production got under way. He says that the price for vanilla in June of 1897 was $6 per pound. The ordinary estate laborers were paid $3.40 per month, women earned $2.60 a month, and children were paid 7¢ per day, however long the day took. Those who tied the vanilla packets were paid 58¢ per 100 bundles of 50 pods each.

Unfortunately, there isn't much information on daily life at the Indian Ocean plantations, either about the growers and their families or the workers who labored to produce the vanilla. However, the Mexican vanilla industry, which by now was largely centered in the canton of Papantla, had great cultural significance as well as economic importance for the region as well as the country, so daily life was carefully documented in books, music, and poetry as well as in business accountings. The golden age of vanilla in Mexico was exciting and rich, and the subsequent struggle to save the industry against all odds was a remarkable odyssey to keep a spiritual heritage alive. While Mexico no longer controlled the international vanilla trade, it nevertheless continued to maintain its reputation for producing the world's finest vanilla.

4

THE CITY THAT
PERFUMED THE WORLD

PAPANTLA

In the center of the state of Veracruz, about 16 miles (26 km) inland from the Gulf Coast, the city of Papantla de Olarte (changed from Papantla in the 1930s) is tucked into the folds of hills and arroyos of the Montes de Papantla. Its whitewashed buildings and red tiled roofs sit atop a rise in the land a little more than 900 feet (265 meters) above sea level, leading from the torrid tropical coast up to the Sierra Madre Oriental, one of two great mountain cordilleras that divide Mexico into three distinct longitudinal sections. Founded in 1230 by the Totonacs, the city of Papantla is located close to the majestic ruins of what was later discovered to be the twin cities of El Tajín, dedicated to the rain gods Tlaloc and Huracan. The world-famous Voladores de Papantla hail from the canton of Papantla, many of them following in the footsteps of their ancestors as guardians of the forest and cultivators of its extraordinary vanilla. In Mexico, Papantla is synonymous with vanilla. Although it was not a commercial center of vanilla production until the mid-1700s, it nevertheless proudly carries the reputation as the birthplace and hub of the Mexican vanilla industry.

The canton of Papantla has a rich and complex history filled with wars, rebellions and revolutions, piracy, and intrigue; an abundance of valuable natural resources; the proud, indigenous Totonac culture that was, at one time, the wealthiest group of native people in Mexico; and the capacity to survive great obstacles and challenges. If we could open the window of time to get a glimpse of Papantla during the *bella época,* the period when vanilla was queen of Mexico, we would find a small but very prosperous city doing international business with big brokers in New York, South America, and Europe, and winning awards for its prized vanilla at the Universal Columbian Expositions in the United States as well as expositions in France.

In 1910, Papantla had over 6,000 residents, and more than 50,000 people throughout the canton. While Papantla was still one of the smallest of the state's urban centers—the capital city, Xalapa, had 80,000 people, and the port of Veracruz boasted a population of 100,000—it nevertheless was a major hub of activity.

In addition to its vanilla industry, the canton of Papantla was known for its tropical hardwoods, tobacco, cochineal dye, corn, beans, and chili, as well as huge cattle ranches producing beef and hides. The most lucrative and sought-after resource, however, was petroleum. The entire Gulf Coast region sat on great oil reserves, which were first explored in the 1860s, and by 1910 the oil fields were actively pumping and producing oil along the coast. The

The coat of arms for Papantla. It is divided into four equal parts to represent the four original colonial barrios of Papantla: Santa Cruz, Naranjo, San Juan, and Zapote. The first section is turquoise blue and contains hieroglyphics that symbolize the name and founding of the city. The second, of silver white, shows the ritual dance of the Voladores. *The third section is cream colored and contains three hieroglyphics that represent three hearts (Tutu Nacu), which stand for the name of the Totonacs. It also represents the three original cities of the Totonacs: Tajín, Paxil, and Cempoala. The fourth, in a deep burnt umber, represents the pyramid of El Tajín, the synthesis of the cultural richness of Totonacapan. The border denotes five symbols of Mesoamerican Totonac sculpture as well as the characteristic hospitality of the city:* Min Chic Huila *(Totonac) and* Estas en tu casa *(Spanish), which both translate as: "You Are in Your Home."*

At the top is the stylized headpiece worn by the men who perform the Mesoamerican Dance of the Hua-Huas. It represents the solar splendor and potency of Totonacapan. Finally, the coat of arms is bordered with vanilla vines, leaves, flowers, fruits, and the sacred vanilla plant cultivated and processed with excellence by the inhabitants of the region of Totonacapan. At the base is a ribbon with the colors of the flag, symbolizing the ascendance of the Mexican culture and the way it is tied to the beautiful vanilla that has traveled the world.

revenue from these valued resources made the region the wealthiest in the nation.

The Totonacs were the vanilla growers, originally gathering the beans wild in the forest and, by the 1700s, establishing plantations where vanilla was grown domestically. Planting took place in the early spring followed by pollination which began in late March and lasted until early May, with the major pollinating occurring from mid- to late April. After the late 1870s, when the discovery of artificial pollination finally arrived in Mexico, the women and children were the primary pollinators, though the men climbed the trees to pollinate the blossoms that trailed up into the forest canopy. But most of the wild vanilla was pollinated by insects and hummingbirds. The entire region was still heavily forested, though this was quickly changing as petroleum companies laid pipelines to Mexico City and other coastal locations.

Harvest coincided with the Christian winter holidays: *El Día de Guadalupe*, December 12; *La Noche Buena*, December 24; *Los Tres Reyes*, January 6; and *Candelaria*, February 2. The Totonacs traveled by horseback and on mules to bring the vanilla in from the ranchos and villages from throughout the canton to the town of Papantla and to Gutiérrez Zamora, located on the Tecolutla River. The proprietors of the *casas de beneficio* (the export houses where the vanilla was cured and dried, then sent to market) purchased the Totonacs' vanilla, then began the labor-intensive process of curing and drying the beans. More than six thousand workers were employed by the *casas de beneficio* during the vanilla season, which lasted nearly six months.

The names of the export houses reflected the diversity of the region and the international flavor of the community. Predominantly run by Spanish, Italian, and French families who had settled in the canton during the past fifty to seventy years, the houses included: Fontecilla, Tremari, Chena, Montini, Trueba, Curti, Gaya, Cueto, Cuagliotti, Arzani, Fiorentini, Yorio-Lammoglia, Marie, Zardoni, Tognola, Cajigal, Magrassi, Garmilla, Buil, Guerrero, Patiño, Zubieta, La Fuente, Pardo, Gutiérrez, Gomez, Winfield, Nava, Larios, Morgado, and Bautista.

The *casas de beneficio* were often extraordinary compared to the humble homes of the Totonacs; though some were relatively modest, many were two stories high and some covered a half city block or more. Typically constructed of masonry, with beams and trim of exquisite tropical hardwoods and tiled roofs, the casas were crafted by skilled tradesmen who directed local workers in their construction. Cedar, mahogany, and palo morado accents and detailing were lacquered or oiled to a fine sheen. At the street entry, heavy wooden doors stood tall and wide enough to accommodate large carriages and wagons. This entry led into the side of the property alongside the courtyard.

The front doors opened into a large room where business was conducted. The *beneficiadores* inspected the vanilla brought in from the ranchos by the Totonacs, who were dressed completely in white and always wore hats. The dry vanilla was stacked on wooden stretchers *(camillas)* that were, in turn, placed on floor-to-ceiling shelves known as *espigueros*. The aroma of the beans—rich and heady at the tail end of the curing and drying process—filled the rooms like an invisible seductress and drifted out into the streets to envelop passersby.

A private family parlor adjoined the business room. A doorway behind this room led into large, multi-use courtyards and patios. To one side of the courtyard, arched wooden doors opened to low-heat ovens where the vanilla beans were "killed" (to stop fermentation) before sun drying began.

The family's living quarters in some of the casas included a grand second story with rooms facing out on to the streets, the tall windows flanked by heavy wooden shutters to shut out the harsh tropical light and heat. Heirloom furniture arrived by schooner from Europe and the Orient—exquisitely carved chests, armoires, tables, and finely upholstered couches, chairs, and love seats. Rooms were also furnished with locally constructed furniture in the Spanish colonial style as well as rustic furniture made from hand-turned wood and chairs with rush seats. Huge mirrors, oil paintings of the countryside, portraits of family members, and religious tableaus adorned the walls.

Second-story floors opened on to covered balconies that overlooked courtyards bordered with tropical plants. During the peak of the harvest and drying season, the vanilla was spread out like lush dark carpets, filling courtyards and patios and lining the town's streets, forcing pedestrians and horses alike to detour. Even flat rooftops were spread with mats, then covered with vanilla beans. The beans were put into the sun early in the morning until the peak heat of the day. Too hot to touch with bare hands, the vanilla beans were carefully gathered and placed in large wooden boxes where they would spend the rest of the day and night sweating liquid and synthesizing the oils and resins that give vanilla its extraordinary fragrance and flavor. When the vanilla lay in the sun, the balsamlike aroma was so fragrant that travelers could smell the town long before they could see it, catching the first whiff of vanilla as far as $5\frac{1}{2}$ miles (9 km) outside of town. It was during this time that Papantla was aptly dubbed "the city that perfumed the world."

Vanilla was so valuable that robbery was a constant threat. Lawlessness throughout the hills and mountains was common. On the ranchos, men armed with machetes slept with their crops before harvest. The Totonacs could not trust the Europeans to safe-guard their money for them, and they considered paper money useless. They only accepted silver or gold in payment for their vanilla. In the words of Guadalupe Muñoz Lopez of Papantla about the trade in 1907, "During this time, the only money of value was the *Azteca de Oro* peso and the *peso plata* 0.720, which is how they paid the vanilla growers, who then returned to their ran-chos with their mules loaded with saddlebags filled with gold and silver."

Robbers ambushed Totonacs returning to their ranchos, mak-ing travel alone or in small numbers very dangerous. Señor Juan Simbrón Méndez of El Tajín said that in 1914, "They jumped us on the royal road to Tajín, the road called Caracatlocos. There they took our money, at times the same money that they paid us. To me, they burned my house there at km 14, and for that I quit the vanilla as much that has happened was too sad."

Pacotilleros ("shady traders") purchased the stolen vanilla, then sold it to intermediaries who then would resell it in Papantla. Small buyers crowded the trails in the late autumn, attempting to per-suade the farmers to sell to them. The price of vanilla went up considerably from October to January, as the vanilla had remained longer on the vines and therefore was more valuable. However, most Totonacs couldn't wait till January to sell their vanilla as they needed the money, and often they sold simply because having the vanilla on hand meant it could be stolen and they would be killed at the same time. Although there were laws to prevent early har-vest, many farmers did so nevertheless. They also didn't dare leave their fields just before harvest season as they knew their beans would be stolen.

As another Totonac farmer said sadly, "One plants, one pollinates, and someone else harvests. My son was killed on his way to the vanilla field; now, I prefer to keep the other sons than have money."

Because of the constant danger, the Totonacs secretly buried their money, often dying without disclosing the whereabouts of the family's fortunes. It is said that the hills and mountains to this day contain great stashes of hidden and forgotten money.

HOLIDAYS AND FESTIVALS in Papantla were magnificent. Although there were many celebrations throughout the year, Easter week, Corpus Christi (the Eucharist), and *Todos Santos* and *El Día de los Muertos* (All Saints' Day and the Day of the Dead) were always the most memorable. The devoutly religious Totonacs traveled from the ranchos and mountain villages throughout the canton, walking, or riding horses, and dressed in their finest clothing. The men and women were always in white, the men's hats decorated with tropical feathers, flowers, and vanilla beans; the women in skirts delicately embroidered with the tree of life in cross-stitch, overskirts, and head coverings in organza. Gold filigree jewelry adorned their throats, wrists, and ears; their black hair, oiled and glistening, was plaited with ribbons and flowers.

The center of town was laid out in typical Mexican colonial fashion. The church, Santa María de Papantla, served as a cornerstone for the development of the city, and was built in 1730 of great cedar beams and thick, whitewashed walls. At the base of the church was the central plaza where the town's events and fiestas were held.

The courtyard around the church was transformed for the holidays by Totonacs under the watchful eyes of the local clergy. At each of the four cardinal points in the courtyard, a simple lean-to of wood and palm was assembled with a back wall, thatch roof, and partial sides. Men and women wove intricate palm decorations to adorn the temporary altars that filled the small palapas. Across from the church, a towering sixty-foot pole would be hewn from a tree brought from the forest for the flight of the *Voladores,* a solemn tradition that would follow the church services and procession through town.

Stalls would be set up where Totonac women sold *tamales* and *pulacles,* and meat stews rich with chunks of pork and thickened with *masa. Aguas frescas,* beverages made from fresh fruits and juices, as well as the traditional *atoles,* flowed from large earthen jugs. *Aguardiente,* the powerful liquor made from sugarcane, would certainly be available. The pungent odor of frying onions, chili, and other spices would fill the air as the sauces for fiery *moles* (regional sauces) were prepared.

The Totonacs who traveled from the farther reaches of the canton would bring bedrolls and stay in the plaza for the duration of the fiesta. The town became a sea of white as the faithful Totonacs walked in the religious processions or gathered in the plaza.

Family and friends of the European and mestizo families in Papantla came for holidays and celebrations from as far away as Mexico City. The new railroad brought people to the coast from the highlands; then they traveled by boat up the Tecolutla River and finished their journey on horseback. A trip of this magnitude required a visit of a few weeks.

In the homes of wealthy Papantecos, preparations for the holidays required the help of several maids. Kitchens were set in the back of houses, often in a separate building and, in modest homes, in a covered section of the patio. The ladies of the house would oversee food preparation for the elegant midnight buffets in the wealthiest homes. Kitchens would be filled with the aroma of delicacies that would later grace long tables lit by candlelight. Families also prepared the foods of their homeland, and tamales were served in every home on special occasions. Maids would set out decanters of French and Spanish wines or homemade *rompope*, a rich, creamy drink made with cane alcohol and vanilla, for guests to sip throughout the evening gala. *Pasteles* and *natillas*, fragranced with vanilla, and steaming cups of Mexican coffee and cognac would be served into the early morning hours. Concerts and dances were part of the holiday celebrations, with waltzes and fox-trots, and even rousing Mexican *tapatias* and *ʒapateados*, enjoyed to the music of *mariachis* and *jorochas*.

NATILLA

This beloved Mexican dessert originated in Europe—probably Spain—but has been a part of Veracruz tradition for more than one hundred years. Each family has its own version of this comfort food. Some cooks use condensed and evaporated milk, some use panela or dark brown sugar, and some *natillas* are even baked in the oven. The one constant in the *natillas* from Papantla is that they always contain pure vanilla.

3 tablespoons cornstarch
2 cups milk
6 large egg yolks
¾ cup granulated sugar

THE CITY THAT PERFUMED THE WORLD

¼ cup dark rum, or ¼ cup additional milk
1 tablespoon vanilla extract
1 cup raisins

IN A MEDIUM BOWL, thoroughly whisk cornstarch into ½ cup of the milk. Let rest for 1 minute, then whisk again. Whisk in egg yolks.

IN A MEDIUM SAUCEPAN, combine remaining 1½ cups milk, sugar, rum, and vanilla extract and bring to a scald over medium heat. Whisking constantly, slowly drizzle the hot liquid into the egg mixture. Return the mixture to the saucepan and cook over medium heat, whisking constantly and scraping the bottom of the pan, until tiny bubbles boil up for 10 seconds.

STRAIN THE MIXTURE through a fine strainer into a bowl. Fold in the raisins. Divide the pudding among 6 dessert bowls. Let cool to room temperature, then cover and refrigerate until chilled.

SERVES 6

This idyllic picture of a city made famous for its fragrant gift to the world is only part of the story. Struggle, loss, and the determination to persevere were recurring themes for the native people and newcomers alike from Mesoamerican times to the present.

THE TOTONACS

The Totonacs, considered one of the most artistic of the Mesoamerican tribes, came to the Gulf Coast after the fall of the great city-state Teotihuacan, around A.D. 650 There are several theories about the origin of the name "Totonaco" (anglicized here as Totonac). One popular interpretation is that the name is derived from *Tutu Nacu* or "three hearts," the three centers of power of the ancient Totonac empire. The Totonacs of Papantla prefer the interpretation of anthropologist Melgarejo Vivanco that says the name alludes to the heart in the sense of tenderness and love. Therefore, Totonacapan is the place of the people of love and tenderness.

The origin of the name "Papantla" most likely came from Papan, Papantzin, or Papan Tecutli (Señor Papan), who led a group of descendants of the ancient people who had established the city-states of El Tajín and those whose predecessors had more recently arrived from Teotihuacan, to settle on the land that is now Papantla. As the name *papan* is the Nahuatl word for the large crow-like bird that still fills the region with its plaintive cries, Papantla (or Papantlan) is the place of the papan birds.

The Gulf Coast tropics provided an enviable wealth of natural resources and foods for the Totonacs, including game animals, fish, birds, herbs, roots, insects, an array of tropical vegetables, fruits and berries, edible flowers, and wild honey. When Fray Juan de Torquemada arrived in New Spain, he documented the diversity of foods from the tropics and noted that the climate permitted three harvests of corn each year. The dry highland regions of Mexico were not as blessed, and as the Aztecs from the north settled into Central Mexico and grew more powerful, they overran the Gulf Coast native populations. This was in part to obtain tributes of foods, cacao, vanilla, hardwoods, animal skins, feathers, cotton, and other desirable commodities.

For the Totonacs, water, air, earth, stones, plants, animals, and insects had souls and feelings and had their place in which to dwell in harmony with the divine guardian. This vision of the world dictated their customs, traditions, and beliefs, what they ate from the forest, and how they maintained harmony and balance with the world. Kiwikgolo was the god of the forest, and it was necessary to request his permission to enter the forest to hunt, fish, gather foods, or cut wood. His feminine companion (or persona), Kiwichat, was the ancient grandmother. It is she who taught the ways of medicine and of curing ills; she also taught her people what foods to eat and where to find them. Kiwichat represented life, fertility, and the land. The two personages of Kiwikgolo and Kiwichat were intertwined, and it is to them that the traditional Totonacs dedicated their lives.

THE SPANISH COLONIAL RULE

When the Spanish arrived, they appropriated large sections of land where they created enormous haciendas to raise cattle for internal use and for export to Spain. The Totonacs withdrew into the vast forests and maintained their lives as separately as possible.

The vast resources of the tropics came with a price for the new settlers: unrelenting heat, torrential rains, and regular outbreaks of cholera, fevers, malaria, and other virulent diseases. Every few years there were devastating storms, ruinous winter freezes, or another violent epidemic. Despite leading a life both difficult and very different from that at home, the Spanish persevered, establishing homes in the city of Papantla and on the headwaters of the Tecolutla River.

The Totonacs controlled vanilla production. By the mid-1700s, the domestic vanilla trade was thriving in the Misantla Valley south of Papantla, and locally the first domesticated vanilla stands were established. In the early days of vanilla cultivation, the Totonacs harvested the beans when they were brown and partially dried, and completed the drying process by placing the beans in the sun and then in the shade; in unusually wet years, they put the beans to dry over slow fires in their homes. This process was inexact and did not allow for the many organic components that make up the flavor and fragrance of vanilla to develop fully. Too much drying made the beans brittle; too wet, and they mildewed. Smoke from the home fires changed the flavor and fragrance. The Creoles and mulattoes took over the curing and drying process, buying the beans from the Totonacs; then, once the beans were processed, they sold them to the Spanish for the European market.

In the rural areas of the canton, the indigenous people had appointed chiefs who supposedly represented them, but the Spanish oversaw the government, through local *alcaldes,* or mayors, and through larger government bodies in the capital of each state. The government created a monopoly of the tobacco trade and taxed agricultural crops such as vanilla and sugarcane, and *aguardiente,* the alcoholic beverage. The taxes were biased in the favor of the Spanish crown. In 1767, the Totonacs rose up in protest and were quickly squelched, but in 1787 they rose up again, this time capturing several of the resident Spanish and not permitting them to escape. Word got to the capital in the port of Veracruz, and 200 soldiers came to quell the rebellion. But shortly thereafter, rebellions again flared throughout the region. The government forbade them to grow tobacco, a traditional crop; they made the smallest share of profit of everyone in the vanilla industry; and their communal lands were rapidly disappearing to aggressive landowners.

Known as the *gente de razón* (people of reason), the Europeans and Creoles considered it necessary to manage the affairs of the Indians. The last years of the colonization of Mexico (the early 1800s) were filled with constant racial and ethnic tensions, with Papantla's own Serafin de Olarte (whose surname was added to the official town name in 1935) leading local indigenous rebellions. Despite the constant skirmishes and struggles for autonomy between the Totonacs and the Europeans and Creoles, the demand for vanilla in Europe was enormous, and the industry continued to grow. As the center of the world's vanilla supply, Papantla thrived.

The War of Independence

Spain's troubles at home began to impinge on the colonies they established worldwide. Struggling with loss of power and the Napoleonic wars, Spain drastically increased taxes in its colonies. At the same time, the wars impeded the country's ability to import goods from overseas. The settlers and Indians alike were not interested in supporting wars in a foreign land, especially without a market for the goods they were being taxed for. This was just one of the reasons for discontent that sparked the War of Independence, but for growers and exporters it was significant.

The War of Independence began in Guanajuato but quickly spread throughout the country. The entire Gulf Coast region was at war, with many battles fought in the coastal ports. Papantla was attacked several times and overtaken by the Spanish in 1819. Serafin de Olarte was the indigenous hero who retook Papantla and burned the Spanish sector as well as held at abeyance the Spanish in the mountainous regions of the canton. After his death in battle, his son, Mariano, took his father's place and fought valiantly throughout the civil war and then continued leading indigenous rebellions after the war ended. Not only did the rebels defeat the Spanish, they were only armed with bows and arrows whereas the Spanish had guns.

The war seriously disrupted all regional commerce as the port of Tecolutla was destroyed. As overseas trade was impossible, the vanilla industry and other local businesses came to a halt.

INDIGENOUS STRUGGLES

After gaining its independence, Mexico was unstable and uncertain as a new nation. The government changed hands dozens of times. Corruption, extortion, and bribery on the part of the government authorities were common. Locally, the illegal appropriation of native lands where vanilla and food crops were grown, the frequent abuses toward the Totonacs by the local Spanish and Creoles who monopolized the processed vanilla market, and the religious prohibitions placed upon the Indians created intense local trouble. Where there had been Spanish law, now there was Mexican law.

The Totonacs, like most native groups, practiced slash and burn along with crop rotation. This was in harmony with the forest as enough time was allowed between the clearing of the land and the next planting, and crop rotation and rejuvenation of land were part of the process. Slash-and-burn techniques could be maintained as long as there was enough communal land to support the people who lived on it. However, the communal lands were rapidly disappearing or being destroyed by grazing cattle. The *acahual* trees that served as shade for the forest understory, the bushes on which the vanilla grew, and even the vanilla vines were eaten by the cattle, leaving the land exposed to the harsh tropical sun and invasive weeds. The shade-loving vanilla could not survive without the protective forest canopy, which caused resentment over the loss of a beloved crop.

By 1845, Papantla was a city struggling between the old ways and modern development. The main part of town was growing rapidly, with a variety of trades and services represented along with merchants and, of course, the vanilla industry. At least 900,000 vanilla beans a year were exported to Europe, and the industry was considered enormously successful. Then, the capricious weather dealt a major blow to the farmers with a fierce hurricane and massive flooding, which destroyed the plantations, obstructed the roads, and caused considerable loss of life. Before there was time for recovery, the Mexican-American War began.

THE WAR YEARS

The Gulf Coast was vulnerable because of the major ports that connected Mexico to the rest of the world. Four American warships arrived in the port of Tecolutla, and armed soldiers marched into Papantla. Over the next months the activity escalated, and Papantla was presented with a document declaring that it was now part of the United States of America. Within days, four hundred Mexican national guardsmen armed with guns and another three hundred foot soldiers bearing machetes rallied in Papantla, and all routes that led to the central highlands were closed by the locals, effectively blocking the invasion and causing the Americans to retreat. Nevertheless, the Americans, with superior manpower and resources, overwhelmed other areas of Mexico, and despite its heroic resistance, Mexico was forced to cede almost half its territory to the United States.

Between 1858 and 1868, Mexico endured another civil war as well as a war with France, leaving the economy in ruins and the entire infrastructure of the country in chaos. Throughout this period of countrywide warfare, Papantla also faced continued battles at home. The Totonacs stubbornly refused to relinquish their territory to the settlers. As the indigenous people were fortunate to have a variety of food crops and forest game and fish to maintain them and as vanilla provided them with cash, they were strong enough and had good reason to fight hard for their land.

IMMIGRANTS

At the same time, the pressures of a growing population faced the canton. Papantla was solicited by President Benito Juárez and other officials to open its lands to European farmers as a way to improve the economy. In the early 1830s, a French agricultural community developed along the coast in Jicaltepec. Enduring great hardship, and depending on the local Totonacs for survival, the immigrants eventually established sugarcane plantations and created businesses producing cane alcohol and, later, vanilla farming, curing, and selling.

In the late 1850s, five hundred Italian families arrived in Tecolutla, but the official in charge of the immigration abandoned the people, leaving them to die of hunger and disease. According to local oral history, one of the immigrants finally approached the local people and begged for assistance. The families were fed and given medicines. One day a local came upon an Italian cooking a vulture. When the Papanteco explained to the Italian that the locals never ate these scavenger birds, the Italian responded, "Anything that flies is good enough for the table!"

The Italians suffered greatly. The same official who had invited them to Mexico neglected to mention that they would be farming in a rural area, and many of the people who came were actually artists, writers, merchants, and others with no experience tilling the land. They settled in the village of Cabezas del Carmen, now known as Gutiérrez Zamora, near the port of Tecolutla. The heat and incessant clouds of insects made living near the port tortuous, and many of the families moved inland to Papantla. Others persevered, adapted to the climate, and eventually created successful businesses. They established vanilla houses in the canton and became both farmers and *beneficiadores* of vanilla and other crops, as well as merchants, teachers, and office workers.

Rompope came to Mexico with the Italians and quickly became a popular holiday beverage. This is the recipe used by the Arzani family of Gutiérrez Zamora.

ROMPOPE

Courtesy of Yolanda Arzani

1 14-oz can sweetened condensed milk
2 14-oz cans water
1 Mexican vanilla bean, sliced open
5 egg yolks
¼ cup grain alcohol (or vodka, rum, or brandy), or to taste

IN A SAUCEPAN, mix the milk with the water, using a wooden spoon, and heat over medium-high heat until mixture boils. Reduce heat and add the vanilla bean. Simmer for about 5 minutes, stirring occasionally. Let cool completely.

WHEN COOL, stir together the egg yolks and strain them into the milk mixture. Return the saucepan to low heat, stirring constantly with a wooden spoon, until the mixture begins to boil. (Some of the mixture will stick to the wooden spoon at this point, which is another indication that it is done.) Remove from heat and let cool.

WHEN IT IS COMPLETELY COOL, gradually add the alcohol, stirring constantly. Strain the mixture into clean bottles and refrigerate. *Rompope* can be kept in the refrigerator for about six months.

USE CHILLED or at room temperature as a beverage, or as a sauce for cake or ice cream.

THE PORFIRIO YEARS

After the French were driven out, the Veracruz government turned its attention in earnest to the privatization of the communal lands of the Totonacs. The Totonacs appealed to the state congress for the protection of their land, but their requests fell on deaf ears. When Porfirio Díaz became president of Mexico in 1877, he quickly reparceled much of the state of Veracruz to the advantage of the Europeans. As a native of Veracruz and the husband of an Italian, he had a vested interest in the outcome and supported European interests at home.

Díaz developed an impressive railroad system, providing the

*An early-twentieth-century advertisement for Mexican
vanilla used by McCormick & Company*

first major source of mass transportation throughout the country, which in turn stimulated industrialization. He encouraged American business interests—luxury crops such as vanilla, coffee, and cacao, as well as tropical hardwoods, were desirable for the wealthy, industrialized nation to the north. But the promise of oil, an industry that would soon cast a dark pallor over the Mexican vanilla industry, began to attract American investors. The two governments forged bonds for control of the Gulf region of Mexico. However, since the Mexican-American War, there was a major distrust of the powerful country to the north, enough so that Díaz was quoted as saying, "Poor Mexico, so far from God and so close to the United States." It could be said that it was an alliance of necessity by proximity, but not one of great friendship.

The city and canton of Papantla were growing rapidly. By the beginning of the 1870s, the population was between 15,000 and 21,000. Although the census was probably not completely reliable, people had emigrated from other areas during the wars, which probably accounted partially for the dramatic increase in the population. There were 84 merchants, 18 cigar makers, and 24 carpenters. Papantla, Santo Domingo, and Espinal each had schools, and Papantla even had a pharmacy. The plaza was laid out with uniform streets and the church was improved and a bell tower was added to it. Even telegraph service arrived. Unfortunately, despite areas of major progress, public health was still an area of grave concern. The first years of the 1870s were plagued with yellow fever and smallpox, killing many in the population.

Vanilla production continued to grow despite the uprisings, epidemics, and changes that came to the canton of Papantla. The Totonacs were still producing vanilla and the Creole families cured and dried it, making the Papantla vanilla industry the largest in Mexico and valued at 256,000 pesos, an exceptional amount of money for the time.

IMPROVEMENTS IN CURING AND DRYING

Sometime in the mid-1800s, a mestizo man named Juan Perez invented a method of oven-drying to stop the enzymatic process of green vanilla. This process, known as *poscoyon,* for the Totonac word *sweating,* used simple bread ovens. Perez found that by placing the beans in the mouth of the ovens at 140°F (60°C) for 30 to 36 hours, the heat effectively stopped the fermentation process in the beans and both hastened and regulated the drying process. This process required exact precision as some beans could easily burn if the ovens were stoked with too much wood while others remained green. A maid leaked the secret of Juan's ovens, and other *beneficiadores* quickly adapted this technique throughout the entire region. This imprecise method remained just that, until the Tapia family in Misantla and the Gaya-Capellini family in Gutiérrez Zamora introduced the calefactive oven, which brought about a more complete and uniform curing of the beans.

ARTIFICIAL POLLINATION

The French colony of Jicaltepec, near San Rafael, prospered over time, and the immigrants decided to grow vanilla. Sometime between 1874 and 1877, three men from the colony went to France and, much to their surprise, discovered healthy vanilla plants in the tropical greenhouses at the Musée de Paris. The plants had been artificially pollinated, a concept that, if it ever existed in early times in Mexico, had long since been forgotten. The men returned to Mexico and taught this remarkable technique to their country-men, charging $10 each for the information. The son of one of the men went to Papantla to expand on the project, and within a few days he collected $800! According to local history, when the To-tonacs saw the enormous crops produced through artificial polli-nation, they believed that the Europeans were stealing their beans. For the safety of everyone involved, the French then taught the Totonacs their secret technique.

In order to benefit from artificial pollination, an entirely differ-ent method of planting was necessary. A thousand vines were planted per 2½ acres (or hectares), which, when they started to produce, would remain active for six years. After that, the land was rested for ten years and new forests were sought—ideally, virgin soil that was still nutrient rich. This intensive planting system re-quired additional land, and the issue of communal versus private lands escalated.

Everyone benefited from the French import of artificial polli-nation, as in 1890 around 297 tons (270,000 kg) of vanilla were produced with a value of $600,000. In 1899, an account of vanilla production in Mexico stated:

> *The greatest part of the vanilla produced in this area is grown around Papantla, from where it is exported via Veracruz because it is easier to get to Veracruz by sea than to Papantla by land. I don't think that Papantla offers, as far as vanilla growing is concerned, better natural conditions than other soil in this region. Success in this area is owed to the colonists that settled there years ago: the pa-tient and industrious Frenchmen, profoundly hardworking, who arrived in poverty with their large families. Around two million pesos worth of vanilla was exported from Papantla to the United States.*

The success of vanilla in the colony of Jicaltepec was, sadly, short-lived. On September 8, 1888, the most destructive flood in the history of Jicaltepec and San Rafael occurred; the high water and currents destroyed everything—harvests, animals, houses. In a few hours, ten years of hard work disappeared.

Seven years later, on February 13, 1895, the temperature dropped to ten degrees below zero Celsius (14°F). The vanilla was nearly completely destroyed, and only a few of the plants were salvaged. The freeze was followed by a severe drought, and rats ate the weakened plants. This, combined with the ongoing problem with the theft of harvests, left the farmers in ruin. According to Jean-Christophe Demard, in his publication *Jicaltepec: Terre d'Argile, A Chronicle of a French Village in Mexico:* "They watched day and night under the cold rain and the north winds that swept the region during several days or even weeks. They were exposed to bad weather, as well as to attacks from thieves that would not hesitate to kill the guard to take the coveted fruit."

The growers organized to regulate the harvest and trade of green beans in an effort to get better harvest prices and to fight theft. To ensure safe passage, they even accompanied their vanilla to France. Despite their most valiant efforts, the French colonies in the Indian Ocean had grown enough to create serious competition, and the famous vanilla of the San Rafael region lost its hold in the world market.

Despite all that challenged the vanilla industry, the entire cycle of growing, pollinating, harvesting, curing, and drying the beans had been refined to such a degree that Papantla vanilla (which included Gutiérrez Zamora and other local towns) was hailed as the finest in the world. Pedro Tremari and Domingo Fuente of Papantla and Pascual Montessoro of Gutiérrez Zamora won medals for their vanilla in New York, and Antonio Chena won a gold medal in Paris. Vanilla sold for exorbitant prices in New York, with the *beneficiadores* making enormous sums of money. By the turn of the century, the cultivation of vanilla in Mexico cost $9 a pound in the United States, and produced nearly 1,400 pesos for each acre of land, or 4 million pesos a year!

While the Porfiriata—the thirty-three-year period that Porfirio Díaz ruled Mexico—saw a great transformation of the country and there was enormous progress in transportation, schools and education, and commerce, the costs of change were borne on the backs of Indian Mexico, both rural and urban. In 1896, a group of engineers arrived in Papantla with the task of redelineating and dividing the land. The Totonacs once again rebelled; the battles were bloody and fierce, and local jails were filled with those who were caught. A permanent military presence was established in the region in an attempt to keep the Indians under control; the survey proceeded as planned.

By the late 1800s, the Europeans and Totonacs populated the canton of Papantla in nearly equal numbers. Between 10,000 and 15,000 people from each group spoke either Spanish or Totonac. This number reflected the balance of power between the Europeans and the Totonacs—the Europeans were landowners who could conduct business throughout Mexico and Europe, whereas the majority of the Totonacs lived outside town, most did not speak fluent Spanish, and only a handful were literate.

Despite being the wealthiest of the indigenous peoples in Mexico, the Totonacs retained their traditional customs and lifestyle, preferring to remain apart rather than assimilate with the more modern culture of the Europeans. The Europeans adhered to this unspoken isolationism as well. Although there was some intermarriage, and there was regular interaction between the native Mexicans and those whose families came from outside the country, Mexican culture was strongly defined by class. Upper classes associated with others of their class—and typically married only those of the same Spanish, Italian, or French heritage—and families spoke with pride of having maintained "clean bloodlines" that they could trace back to their European homeland. This distinction diminished among the merchant and working classes among whom intermarriage was not uncommon. The wealthy families depended on the Totonacs and mestizos to help manage and maintain their

A fan from the early twentieth century promoted the virtues of Papantla vanilla, courtesy of an ad from McCormick & Company.

homes, care for their children, and work in their businesses, but the social gulf between them was enormous and perpetuated by a great invisible wall.

The depth of futility and despair the Totonacs must have felt is difficult to imagine. Their traditional communal lands were largely gone, their sacred vanilla reduced to a material commodity over which they had limited control, and they were marginalized as humans and considered simple. Only their deep spiritual and religious faith and their closely knit communal system sustained them.

Traditional Totonac Vanilla Farming

The Totonacs produced their own vanilla in a similar environment to the way it grows naturally in the forest. Their method and rituals were virtually unchanged until the 1970s. Today, the Totonac farmers continue to produce vanilla in a similar fashion, but most of the rituals surrounding the cycle are no longer practiced.

Before any work began, Kiwigilo, the "old man of the forest," was consulted and permission was asked to clear the land. When permission was asked, it was also requested that no venomous snakes come on to the vanilla plantation.

It was customary to make a promise to Kiwigilo at the time of planting to guarantee a good harvest. A ritual meal of *mole* with turkey was prepared and given to the land as an offering for fertility and to ensure that the vanilla thrived. Small tortillas were prepared in the numbers of two, four, five, eight, ten, and twelve to use as ritual foods for the gods. These were traditional numbers that were syncretized with Catholicism to represent the twelve apostles.

There were two altars in the traditional Totonac home. The main altar, the one most people saw upon entering the house, was the Catholic altar. It was—and still is—decorated with woven palm ornaments, pictures of saints, icons, flowers, and candles. In a prominent spot there would be offerings of food and drink.

The traditional Totonac altar was below the main altar and dedicated to Kiwigilo. It was usually hidden behind small, decorative, cut paper banners *(papel picado)*. Fabrics decorated with ritual designs covered the altar. Idols and figures made of stone or iron—legitimate archaeological pieces found by the Totonacs in the countryside during their work in the fields—sat on the altar. These idols were passed from fathers to sons over the generations. Offerings consisted of native plants and fruits, minerals, bones, animal skins, bird feathers, maize and seeds, earth, and water. Cigars made from locally grown tobacco were also placed on the altar. In the Catholic churches in the rural areas throughout Totonacapan, it is still common to see the patron saints of the town dressed in traditional Totonac dress with small offerings of water, *refino* (sugarcane alcohol), and maize kernels at the feet of the saints. Placed there at the beginning of the planting season, these help to guarantee a good harvest.

Next, the land was cut back and then burned to clear out the forest understory. *Acahual* trees were allowed to remain as they provided the necessary shade for the vanilla. Rapid-growing bushes that were easy to propagate were planted to serve as tutors for the vanilla; traditional bushes and small trees included *ramón*, *laurel*, *chaca*, *capulin*, *pata de vaca*, *balletilla (cachuapaxtle)*, *cojon de gato*, and *pichoco*. These bushes were chosen for their small leaves and year-round foliage so that the sun/shade balance would be maintained. Healthy vanilla vines *(esquejes)*, 2 to 3 meters in length, were cut from the forest and planted individually or in twos next to the tutors.

For the Totonacs, each of the many varieties of vanilla that grew in the region had religious significance. *Vanilla pompona*, called *la vainilla bastarda*, was considered the "queen of vanilla," and was always planted at a key point on the plantation. As *Vanilla pompona* is larger and hardier than *planifolia*, it was believed that it would protect the other plants, and that if bad spirits or harm to the family came through disease or curses, it would affect the *pompona* first and be absorbed, leaving the family safe. *Vanilla planifolia* was known as *Vainilla mestiza*. *Vainilla rayada,* also known as *Vainilla rayo* or *Vainilla de taro* (bamboo vanilla), has a striped leaf and a fragrance similar to *planifolia*. It was the vanilla that was always dedicated to the most important cult of fertility. There was also *vainilla de puerco* (pig vanilla), *vainilla de mono* (monkey vanilla), *vainilla oreja de burro* (donkey ear vanilla), *vainilla de monte alto* (vanilla of the tall forest), and others. Each had its own special story, most of which, unfortunately, have never been recorded and are probably lost forever.

Traditional plantations ranged in size from 25 to 75 acres (10 to 30 hectares). A compost of dead leaves and other forest matter was applied to the base of the plants in February, August, and December.

It took between three and four years for the first blooms to appear at the traditional plantation. March 18 was the *Fiesta de Fecundación,* the celebration of fertility. Flowering commenced at this time and continued into early May. During pollination there were dietary restrictions. Beef and fish were prohibited as were some other foods, in order not to compromise the setting of the flowers. The Totonacs also abstained from sex during the period dedicated to pollination.

Once artificial pollination was discovered, it was always called "the marriage of vanilla." Because pollination was done manually with a small stick, moving the pollen from the male anther and depositing it on the female stigma, it was similar to intercourse. Since it took between eight and nine months for the vanilla bean to develop, the entire cycle was not unlike that of human procreation. For this reason, the vanilla was perceived, in the Totonac vision of the world, as divinely tied to humankind.

Vanilla orchids have both male and female plants. The males

produce lots of flowers but the beans don't "set," or stay on the vine, and quickly drop off. As the plants essentially look the same, those that hadn't produced in four years were removed from the plantation, a practice that is continued today.

The stick used for pollination was—and still is—carefully prepared. Some farmers believed that the type of wood didn't matter, but others thought that the heart of the *chaca* was the only wood to use. The tip was whittled with a knife or machete until it had a thin, chisel-like point. Plants high up and out of reach were pollinated because they were less likely to be stolen. Ropes or ladders were used to reach the blossoms. The *Vanilla pompona* was sometimes used for pollination. The flower was cut and carried to the cultivated vine; the pollination process was the same except that it used two flowers rather than just one. The pods from this cross were larger and heavier, but not as desirable. A day or two after pollination, the flowers were checked to make sure the beans had set. If not, additional flowers were pollinated to ensure maximum production.

Once the vanilla was pollinated, there was little that needed to be done for the plants until the time of harvest. This allowed time for caring for the family *milpa* (cultivated crops), hunting, and other necessary tasks. It was also a time of concern, especially if the rains did not return on time. Papantla has always had very inconsistent rainfall, and consequently there has been great preoccupation with the rain cycles. As the soil is thin and much of the land sits on a great limestone shelf, the heavy rainfall is quickly absorbed into the land. If rain does not return by May, it can be disastrous for vanilla and food crops alike. Therefore, prayers and offerings were made for rain on a continual basis.

The beans were originally harvested when they were ripe and beginning to dry. Later, as techniques improved and standards were set, the beans were harvested when they were nearly ripe. The finest beans—those with the greatest amount of oil—were harvested in late January and early February. The majority of the vanilla was brought to the *casas de beneficio* and sold green. Depending on where the families lived, it was sometimes easier to keep the beans on the ranchos and dry them there. Also windfalls and vanilla that matured early were dried at home. These beans were not considered premium quality. However, some of the Totonacs became *beneficiadores* and purchased beans from their neighbors, then dried them, using the same methods as the Europeans and mestizos. This was especially common in the pueblos tucked into the sierra that were not easily accessible to Papantla, though a few of the *beneficiadores* in Papantla would travel to the ranchos to collect the vanilla.

In the first days of commercial vanilla production, vanilla beans were counted by the thousands. Later, they were sold green in lots of 100 pods. Then vanilla was sold by the pound in rolls of 3 to 5 pounds each; 100 green beans were considered about 5 pounds. Now vanilla is sold by the kilogram (2.2 lbs), both as green and as dried beans.

Papantla was known as Kachikin, or "the city." Trips to Kachikin were planned for the delivery of beans or for festivals and holy days, and were combined with picking up supplies unavailable outside town. Burros were the primary method of transporting goods. When the vanilla was finally ready for shipment from Papantla, it was loaded into tin boxes and then into larger cedar boxes. The boxes were carried by the mules either through the hills to Tecolutla where they were floated in flat-bottomed boats called *chalanes* or were taken by mule back into the mountains to the rail head at Tezuitlan, where the vanilla traveled to the port of Veracruz. The majority of the vanilla was headed to the United States, but until the early years of the twentieth century it also went to Europe.

The *beneficiadores* established five grades of Mexican vanilla, standards which are still used today:

- *Superior* consists of the finest black beans.
- *Buena* are usually as good as *superior* but perhaps a little shorter and not quite as oily.
- *Mediana* are average and usually used as extract beans.
- *Ordinaria entera* are extract grade whole beans.
- *Picadura* are the small pieces and splits.

A successful harvest and sale were always celebrated, usually with local fiestas. The successful transport of money back home was as important as the sale. Robbery, assault, and homicide have always been problems integrally tied in with producing vanilla, just as being "tied to the company store" has been a problem for small farmers everywhere. Many of the *beneficiadores* had stores and essentially kept the Totonacs in servitude. They wouldn't tell the Totonacs the going price for their vanilla, but instead would issue credits, which rarely covered the cost of supplies. These two problems were always in the forefront of the minds of the growers. However, as Spanish wasn't spoken fluently by most Totonacs, and even those who spoke Spanish were usually illiterate, the growers had no access to the current prices for vanilla, and so were forced to accept the pay or not sell at all. As vanilla often went through several hands until it reached the *beneficiadores* in Papantla, the price difference between what the farmer got and what the vanilla ultimately was sold for would be significantly different.

The families who either dried their own vanilla or who worked in the *casas de beneficio* used the vanilla oil that ran off during the first stages of curing and drying to rub on their skin or to add shine to their hair. The vanilla was also used as an air freshener and a perfume for clothing. Dried beans were tucked into hatbands along with flowers and feathers. And a vanilla-flavored *aguardiente* was always prepared for baptisms, weddings, and other significant family events.

Although originally the Totonacs didn't use vanilla in their cooking (it was typically only incorporated into alcoholic beverages), it has become more popular over the past thirty years. The following recipe is one way vanilla is used by the Totonacs today.

XATMAKLHUKIN NIPXI (CALABAZA EN TACHA)—SWEET BAKED PUMPKIN

1 medium pumpkin or other flavorful squash, left whole
2 teaspoons baking soda
2 quarts water
3 lumps *piloncillo*, or ½–¾ cup dark brown sugar
6 vanilla beans
¼ cup hot water

PREHEAT OVEN to 300°F. Pierce all over the skin of the pumpkin or squash. In a large bowl or pot, dissolve the baking soda in 2 quarts of water and submerge the pumpkin for 1 hour. Drain well.

IN A SMALL BOWL, dissolve the *piloncillo* (sugar) with the vanilla beans and ¼ cup hot water until the mixture forms a thick honey. If necessary, break the *piloncillo* into pieces to facilitate making the honey.

PLACE THE PUMPKIN into a tight-fitting baking dish; then pour the vanilla honey over the pumpkin, ladling it repeatedly to cover the pumpkin. Make small slits in the pumpkin and insert the vanilla bean pieces into the slits, if desired. Bake the pumpkin in the oven for about 2 hours or until the pumpkin is very soft.

CUT THE PUMPKIN open and remove the seeds. Serve in small bowls decorated with new vanilla bean pieces.

THE MEXICAN REVOLUTION

On November 20, 1910, the long-simmering discontent throughout the country finally erupted in revolution. Porfirio Díaz was forced to surrender his power, but the political fragmentation that followed came from the revolutionaries' inability to agree on what they had gained. Violence plagued the entire country for the next decade.

On September 15, 1914, the war came to the canton of Papantla. Although the majority of the battles were focused in Tuxpan, all commercial routes were closed, the indigenous people took to the mountains, and hunger and epidemics plagued the entire region. The oil companies, however, continued to produce without a glitch, thanks to an alliance with one faction of the government.

The year 1915 was particularly difficult for the canton of Papantla, which suffered the fallout of the Villistas, Carrancistas, and Peleacistas. The town was repeatedly sacked, and there were kidnappings and shootings. Some people took refuge in Tuxpan or Tampico and others went to the petroleum camps. The local economy came to a standstill. By 1916 the mountains were completely under siege. When peace finally came to the majority of Mexico in 1920, Papantla began the hard work of restoration. Vanilla and oil helped the economy recover here far more quickly than elsewhere in the country.

The Mexican Revolution completely changed the country, and of course made its impression on the native people. Here two Mexicans share their memories of the fateful time in Mexican history. Fernando Patiño lived in the city of Papantla, and Catalina Vasquez-Vega was a Totonac mountain woman.

FERNANDO PATIÑO
ON THE MEXICAN REVOLUTION
IN THE CITY OF PAPANTLA

I was a little boy at the time of the Revolution, but I remember a lot of what happened. The Revolution didn't come to Papantla right away, but there were groups like the Villistas and Carrancistas, and they were coming back and forth throughout the region. All the young men joined the war and went to the states of Puebla or Mexico. The Villistas came through town and blew up the government palace. The first Papanteco to die was the wife of a Frenchman who was in the courtyard working at the Casa de Tremari. There had been shooting going on all afternoon and a sniper killed her, but I don't know if he meant to shoot her or if it was intended for someone else. After that, they shut down the vanilla businesses as everyone was too afraid to work. The vines were pretty much let go. My father, who worked at the Casa de Juventino Guerrero, sold meat during the Revolution. Everyone knew each other in those days and my father would go to the ranchos to get the meat and then sell it in town.

The Revolution stopped briefly each time a new president came into office. Every time a big battle broke out, everyone who could would leave town and we'd head out to the ranchos to stay until it was safe again. After a while it was impossible to travel on the roads and there wasn't enough food to eat. It was a terrible time.

I was about eleven when my father and I went by horseback to Tuxpan where we had rich relatives who had a big cattle ranch. My father returned home and I stayed on at my uncle's house, but then the war took a turn for the worse and I was trapped there for three months. My uncle had to slaughter all the cattle because the soldiers wanted meat. They blew up the plaza and the streets were filled with blood. Each side would go to Tuxpan so finally the government was attacking locals because they didn't know whose side anyone was on. There was a boat offshore filled with silver and gold to keep the money safe.

The government closed the port and no one could leave town. At night was the worst; that's when most of the killing happened. It was a bad time, and it didn't get better for a long time after the Revolution officially ended. After the war the vanilla business started up again and a lot of the Totonacs got rich because they had stored it up out on the ranchos.

CATALINA VASQUEZ-VEGA ON THE REVOLUTION IN THE MOUNTAINS AROUND PAPANTLA

My parents were killed in the Revolution. I was five years old at the time, and I lived with my sisters and brothers in the mountains near Coxquihui. After that we were pretty much on our own. We were sometimes hidden in the thorn bushes for our safety as soldiers would come through the area and rape the girls and they'd kidnap the boys to take as soldiers. We gathered flowers and roots to stuff tamales and then sold them to whoever was coming through in order to keep ourselves alive. We were hungry all the time, and very scared. The fighting was fierce in the mountains and we didn't know if we would live. My parents were traditional growers, but I don't remember much about it because the Revolution came when I was so young. I married a local boy at fourteen so that I would have a home. He grew vanilla the old way until we came to Papantla during the terrible freeze of 1964, and I supported us by taking in washing for others and raising my family.

By 1920 the overseas market for vanilla dominated world production by an enormous margin. Eighty percent of the vanilla came from the Indian Ocean islands, with a much higher production per acre than seen in Mexico. Mexico produced only 15 percent of the world crop and was destined for the United States while the Indian Ocean market went primarily to Europe. Nevertheless, Papantla initially made a good comeback after the war, and the vanilla brought in a considerably higher price than other regions did due to the product's fine quality and reputation.

The new generation of *beneficiadores* established their operations with radically different ways of doing business. They opened branches in cities like Philadelphia and New York. They sent their orders directly to their branches for future sales, and they established quality control and an association to combat the use of artificial extracts. Production of vanilla in 1925 was 132 tons. Vanilla syndicates such as the *7 de Enero* syndicate were formed, and the Totonac and mestizo workers organized.

One of the concessions gained by the Totonacs as a result of the Revolution was the *ejido* system—communally shared lands for indigenous families. Many of the haciendas were broken up and land was given to the native peoples throughout Mexico, land that could not be taken away from them. While at first this system appeared ideal, after a few generations it became problematic, especially if there were several boys in the family, as there simply wasn't enough land to maintain the growing generations of family members.

Due to the Revolution and the drop in prices brought about by Indian Ocean production, the vanilla-growing regions in Misantla and San Rafael died out, and nearly all the Mexican vanilla was produced in the canton of Papantla. Until 1945 the industry was a major source of income for Papantla, employing much of the community, which assisted them during the Great Depression. Regardless, Papantla's days as the world's largest producer of vanilla were numbered. Petroleum exploration expanded, and during the 1920s and 1930s the beautiful forest was stripped by petroleum workers who laid oil lines to the interior of Mexico. Growing vanilla became increasingly difficult as the climate began to change without the forest canopy. By 1930, Madagascar vanilla plantations produced over 80 percent of the world's vanilla and monopolized the world's vanilla market. Nevertheless, for years to come, Papantla and Gutiérrez Zamora would retain their reputation for their fragrant and flavorful contribution to the world.

· 5 ·

THE FLAVOR
FOR EVERYONE

While the introduction of artificial pollination appeared to be a simple and relatively insignificant scientific breakthrough, its impact was remarkably dramatic. No longer a flavor and fragrance for just the elite and titled, vanilla was now available in enough quantity to make it affordable to nearly everyone, if only in a scoop of vanilla ice cream. Pharmacists found that vanilla effectively masked unpalatable medicines as well as provided a comforting aftertaste, and its use became commonplace in liquid medications and "medicinal elixirs." Druggists also prepared small bottles of extracts for the American homemaker who trusted her pharmacist to guarantee purity and quality, and to provide her with the best value for her money.

Plantations of a size unimaginable a century before were developed throughout the tropics, and vanilla was now imported to Europe and the United States from the Indian Ocean islands, Indonesia, and Tahiti, as well as Mexico, Central America, and the

Caribbean. While in most places the farmers and workers made far less than the middlemen and exporters, vanilla was nevertheless a valuable source of income and a cash crop that was more lucrative than cane sugar, which was, by now, grown throughout the tropics.

In fact, now that sugar was so affordable, its use in daily fare was commonplace. By the mid-1800s, candy factories were sprouting up throughout Europe and the United States. Cadbury, Lindt & Sprüngli, and Nestlé were big names in Europe, challenging France for the title of producing the world's finest chocolates. In the United States, Baker's chocolate was a leader in candy making, but there were many new companies coming into the marketplace, often with humble beginnings in the home kitchen. Henry Maillard's "Celebrated Vanilla Chocolates and Breakfast Cocoa" were "sold by grocers everywhere" in the 1870s, according to New York ads, and Maillard offered free lessons on how to make chocolate correctly at his "chocolate school." And caramel maker, Milton Hershey, created chocolate-covered caramels and his first bar chocolate in the late 1800s.

But it is the soft drink and ice-cream industries that will ultimately make the greatest use of vanilla. In 1886, Coca-Cola went on sale at Jacob's Pharmacy in Atlanta and was advertised as an "esteemed Brain tonic and Intellectual Beverage." Dr. Pepper was introduced the same year, announcing their product as "The King of Beverages, Free from Caffeine," and Pepsi-Cola came into the marketplace in 1898. Two of the inventors were pharmacists, and all three had mixed soft drinks for their in-store soda fountains. In addition to the soft drinks that were packaged, vanilla-flavored syrup was a favorite in the soda fountains and ice-cream "saloons."

Atlanta physician and chemist John S. Pemberton, a former Confederate officer, invented a variety of elixirs and patent medicines, including "Globe of Flower Cough Syrup," "Triplex Liver Pills," and his popular "French Wine of Coca." He sold the latter as a cure for nervous disorders, gastric disturbances, and impotency.

In November of 1885, Atlanta voted to become a "dry" city, so Pemberton decided to remove the wine. He created a flavored syrup, adding a fair dose of sugar, essential oils, vanilla, and fruit flavors to make it tastier. Frank M. Robinson, Pemberton's bookkeeper and business partner, suggested the name "Coca-Cola" for the extracts of the African kola nuts that were part of the syrup. Robinson felt that instead of "Coca Kola," using two "Cs" would look better for advertising purposes; he wrote the name out in flowing script, and the new product was marketed as a "brain and nerve tonic" in drugstores.

Robinson created an ad in the *Atlanta Daily Journal* shortly after the formula was finalized: "Coca-Cola, Delicious! Refreshing! Invigorating! The New and Popular Soda Fountain Drink, containing properties of the wonderful coca plant and the famous Kola nuts. For sale by Willis Venable and Nunnally & Rawson." By year's end, they had sold twenty-five gallons of Coca-Cola syrup at $1 a gallon.

Unfortunately, Pemberton was not a businessman. After a falling-out with Robinson, Asa Candler bought the business and Robinson went to work with Candler. Pemberton died in 1888, having no idea his invention would become the world's most popular soft drink.

Candler and Robinson were a fine team. Candler owned one of the largest drug businesses in Atlanta and had a good sense for business, and Robinson had a flair for graphics and advertising. The business took off, and by 1919 there were bottling plants in every major city in the United States. In 1916 the trademark bottle for which Coca-Cola has become known was designed as a way to make it distinctive from other similarly flavored soft drinks. Coca-Cola has continued its success and is still the leading industry soft drink worldwide.

ICE-CREAM MANIA

There was something about the cool, smooth, sweet creaminess of frozen desserts that triggered love at first bite for Americans—at least once they had the opportunity to try the delicious comfort food. Although ice cream came to the United States in the late 1700s, and the first ice-cream establishment opened in New York in 1796, the availability of ice cream as a treat for the average person didn't come about until the mid-1800s. In 1851, Jacob Fussell opened the first large-scale commercial ice-cream plant in Baltimore, Maryland. Considered the "father of American ice cream," Fussell helped to make ice cream all the rage.

Despite the popularity of the frozen dessert, until the late 1800s, flavoring ice cream with vanilla was still an expensive proposition. Once the trickle-down effect of artificially pollinating vanilla orchids made the beans and extracts more affordable, vanilla quickly became the favorite flavor of ice-cream eaters. And why not? The comfort and satisfaction of a delicate flavor that slides effortlessly down the throat while cooling and soothing the body at the same time is a hard act to beat.

As the American ice-cream industry was growing, so, too, was the popular soda fountain. Also known as "phosphate parlors," imitation mineral waters were first created in 1810, then flavored with syrups. The first ice-cream soda wasn't served in a public place until 1873 when a soda fountain ran out of cream. Vanilla ice cream was substituted, and we can easily imagine how well it was received: creamy vanilla ice-cream floating in charged water flavored with fruit syrup was a divine revelation for visitors of the parlors and fountains across the country, enough so, that the first fountain serving ice-cream sodas was soon averaging $600 a day! Interestingly, as ice cream was most often served as a Sunday treat (and often with the ice-cream parlor as a family destination point), it was the inspiration for the name "ice-cream sundae."

In 1904 the St. Louis Exposition and World's Fair had fifty ice-cream booths to refresh attendees making their way through the exhibits during the hot and humid summer months. While there is controversy over exactly who invented the ice-cream cone, the consensus is that it emerged at the fair, and may have been independently developed by several different vendors using warm waffle cookies and other baked, thin cookie dough. A pharmacist apprentice invented the banana split the same year (the original "split" contained *only* vanilla ice cream), and by 1909 U.S. ice-cream sales reached 30 million gallons a year. There were forty-nine ice-cream manufacturing plants in Philadelphia along with fifty-two ice-cream "saloons," and in New York there were more soda fountains than bars and saloons serving alcoholic beverages.

The Eskimo Pie came on to the scene as the "I Scream Bar" in 1919, and by 1921 it was selling at the rate of two million bars a day!

Hot on its heels was the "Good Humor" bar; by 1924, Americans ate 6.8 pounds of ice cream per capita per year, with vanilla as the leading flavor of choice.

In 1926, the first successful continuous process (or motorized) freezer was perfected, and packaged ice cream could now be purchased at the grocery store. The last piece of the puzzle for keeping ice cream cold and delicious fell into place in 1930 with the advent of dry ice, an invention intended specifically to keep ice cream cold (with the backup ability to create fog and smoke for theatrical performances and the movies). The American public could now have frozen dessert on a stick or in a cone anywhere, anytime. The demand for vanilla in the ice-cream industry exploded, and has only continued to grow, with 29 percent of all ice-cream lovers choosing vanilla as their favorite flavor, far ahead of chocolate, which, at 8.9 percent, weighs in as a distant second.

ICE CREAM AT THE TURN OF THE TWENTIETH CENTURY

In the late nineteenth century, Fannie Merritt Farmer was the director of the Boston Cooking School, a place for young women seeking a career, as well as for the housewife who had not learned to cook or who wished to further her skill in the kitchen. As a teen, Fannie had a paralytic stroke, which had forced her to drop out of high school, but she recovered enough to start cooking, and her family sent her to the Boston Cooking School where she was graduated in 1889. She wrote

The Boston Cooking-School Cook Book (later changed to *The Fannie Farmer Cookbook*) in 1896, imploring her readers to use precise measurements and carefully follow instructions. Her book has been revised and modernized dozens of times and remains in print today.

IN THE EARLY books there was a recipe for Vanilla Ice Cream I (Philadelphia), which called for: "1 quart thin cream, ¾ cup sugar, 1½ tablespoons vanilla, Few grains salt. Mix ingredients and freeze (found on page 558)."

The directions for freezing on page 558 included an ice shaver and tub *or* wooden mallet and canvas bag, a heavy cloth or newspaper to cover the freezer once the ice cream has been frozen, coarse rock salt, and ice or snow. She then provided detailed instructions on how to proceed; in later editions, a freezing method was included for modern readers who owned a mechanical refrigerator. There were a large number of variations on the theme, based on strawberries, raspberries, quince, praline, pistachios, black walnuts, prunes, and so on.

THERE WERE ALSO fancier desserts to be made, using vanilla ice cream as the base. Ice Cream Croquettes could be concocted as follows:

> *Shape ice cream in individual molds or with an ice cream scoop, roll in macaroon dust made by pounding and sifting dry macaroons, or rolling in Jordan almonds, blanched, shredded, and browned in the oven.*

This would make a nice dessert for a ladies' luncheon or a card party. If all the stops were pulled out for a dinner party, there was the very popular Peche Melba created by chef Auguste Escoffier in honor of Australian *grande cantrice* Dame Nellie Melba (Helen Porter Mitchell), who performed Richard Wagner's opera *Lohengrin* at Covent Garden in 1894.

Peche Melba is made by scooping fresh vanilla ice cream onto peeled and poached peach halves, then covering it with Sauce Cardinale, a puree of raspberries flavored with aged kirsch and topped with almond slivers. Occasionally either this recipe, or a variation thereof, still appears in food magazines and on menus in trendy restaurants.

CHOICES FOR THE MODERN HOMEMAKER

Other changes in American demographics occurred that also affected the use of vanilla. By the beginning of the twentieth century, one in four American families had live-in domestic help, but by 1920 the ratio of domestic service in the general public had dropped by half. Middle-class women entered the kitchen in ever greater numbers, and most needed to learn how to cook. Cookbooks and cooking schools proliferated, as did helpful advice in women's magazines. Advertising was big business, and women took the messages to heart.

In the late 1800s, the fledgling flavoring industry took off, with salesmen selling the company's elixirs door-to-door to urban homemakers. The more adventurous of the sales force traveled by

Early vanilla bottles from the Watkins Company

buckboard wagon into the rural eastern, midwestern, southern, and western states, offering everything from cleaning powders and patent medicines to cooking supplies. They sold their products to general stores and sometimes even ventured out to the ranches and farmhouses. Flavorings such as vanilla, peppermint, lemon, black walnut, and almond brought exotic possibilities to farms, ranches, and even homesteaders, with vanilla by far the favorite. Vanilla was advertised in magazines and newspapers, in free recipe booklets, on the back of paper dolls, on postcards, and in handouts at fairs and other public events. And, with the popularity of vanilla in ice cream, it was a logical step for it to show up as a home flavoring.

Names like Adams, Baldwin, Dittman's, Kell's, Lochhead,

McCormick, Mother Murphy's, Nielsen-Massey's, Sauer's, Virginia Dare, and Watkins have survived through the years, but dozens of pharmacists and small companies also had products for sale. In 1885, the *Detroit Commercial* listed vanilla wafer cookies, vanilla concentrates for vanilla soda, and vanilla made by the Seeley Manufacturing Company that came in panel bottles, taper panels, and round Rx bottles at $2 per dozen for the two-ounce size. The Joseph Burnett Company of Boston advertised their vanilla as "a fine flavor for ice cream, cake, custards, etc." The Francis H. Leggett Company in New York offered pharmacists Bourbon vanilla beans at $6 to $10.50 a pound and $11 to $17 a pound for Mexican beans in the "Medicine and Drugs" section of the Premier Enquirer catalog in 1909. Morrows Pure Vanilla Extract promoted its "Purity and Strength." Thomas and Taylor Spice Company of Chicago carried Gold Band Flavoring Extracts that were "Next to None."

There was Aromanilla; No-al Trademark; Thurber's Fine Flavorings and Extracts; Perston and Merrill Culinary Chemists; Royal; Foss; Wellman Foods; Royal Flavorings and Extracts; Kellogg's Extracts by Adams & Eaton; and scores of other companies through the years that provided the modern homemaker with flavorful options for the finest baked goods and cream desserts.

BRANDS THAT BECAME HOUSEHOLD NAMES

Some of the vanilla extract manufacturers whose businesses have endured through time began with products unrelated to the flavors they later produced. Twenty-five-year-old Willoughby McCormick began his business in the late 1800s in a cellar in Baltimore, Maryland, producing fruit flavorings as well as glue and pesticides (flea powders and soaps). His Uncle Sam's Nerve and Bone Liniment and Reliable Brand patent medicines were two other specialties. His growing business was completely destroyed in the great Baltimore fire of 1904, and he struggled over whether to rebuild or to start over in a new field. He wrote a letter to his mother, saying he felt responsible for his employees who depended on him for work so he decided to keep going, but instead of producing private label products for others, as he had to this point, he would now manufacture under his own name. In 1906 he bought a spice company from Philadelphia, then expanded into the tea industry (he had one of the first automated tea-bag machines in the world). He created the Bee Brand name, which he used to label most of his extracts and spices, chosen because bees symbolized industriousness, cleanliness, and teamwork, three traits that he fostered among his employees. The exact year he launched his vanilla lines— Bee Brand and Silver Medal—has been forgotten, but his vanillas have graced grocery shelves for decades. Silver Medal was finally dropped, and the Bee Brand was slowly phased over to the McCormick brand during a period of expansion in the 1940s; McCormick & Company is now the largest spice and extract producer in the world.

Twenty-eight-year-old entrepreneur Joseph R. Watkins founded the J. R. Watkins Medical Company in 1868 in Plainview, Minnesota, launching one of America's first natural-remedies direct-marketing companies. His product was Watkins Red Liniment, made from Asian camphor and red pepper extract—a product that is still sold today.

In 1895, Watkins entered the specialty-food market by introducing vanilla extract, black pepper, and cinnamon. Some of his products were used by the American soldiers in World War I. In 1928, he received Gold Medal honors at the Paris International

Watkins assembly line, 1930s

Exposition for his vanilla, black pepper, cinnamon, and other ground spices, and the spice and flavor component of his business flourished.

Nielsen-Massey Vanillas, the world's largest producer of just vanilla flavors and extracts, set up business in 1907 in Sterling, Illinois. Richard Massey was a businessman, and his partner, Dr. Otis Klein, was a chemist. Their product line? Fragrances for the cleaning industry! Known as Massey's, Inc., the two men were apparently not compatible, as Massey moved without Dr. Klein to Webster Avenue in Chicago in 1917, and the business switched to the manufacture of flavorings. Chatfield John Nielsen Sr. joined the company soon thereafter, vanilla became the focus, and business boomed.

Jacob Beck and a Mr. Doyle launched the Beck and Doyle soda fountain around 1910. Part of their operation included making phosphates, and syrups became their passion. Their vanilla syrup became popular for use in Coca-Cola fountain drinks. They then convinced the owner of a Beatrice Dairy down the street from them to use their vanilla extracts in ice cream, and soon their business focused exclusively on vanilla. When Dairy Queen soft ice cream opened the first of its shops in 1939, Beck and Doyle were the extract suppliers. Grandson Charley Beck still has the original Dairy Queen check (number four) framed and mounted in his office.

Virginia Dare was a spin-off from Garrett & Company, a North Carolina winery. Garrett was producing wine branded as "Virginia Dare" when Prohibition was voted in. Looking for a way to use up the alcohol it had in stock, the firm went into the extract business. Dr. Bernard Smith, a flavor chemist, joined Garrett & Company in 1919. He developed the flavor line and headed the Virginia Dare Extract Division. In 1923, Dr. Smith and a group of investors bought out the flavor and extract business, and Virginia Dare Extract Company was launched in Brooklyn, New York. Dr. Smith ran the business until his death in 1952, and in 1955 his son, Howard Smith Sr., took over the company.

Other companies made extract right from the start. Earl Baldwin Moffatt has no idea why his great-great grandfather, Henry Baldwin, started making vanilla in 1865 or how he got the information to make it, but make it he did, as probably one of the earliest of the extract producers in the United States. Henry's father was in the shipping trade, bringing the family from Scotland to West Stockbridge, Massachusetts, when Henry was about ten years old. He sold his vanilla to apothecaries and to fragrance companies as well as to the large hotels in the Hudson River Valley.

Henry's son, Charles, was a pharmacist with a degree from Columbia University. He took over the business as a young man and launched it as a bona fide enterprise in 1886. His formula was approved by the government in 1888. He made his vanilla with Madagascar beans, using approximately 100 pounds a year; the beans arrived by ship in small parcels wrapped in a piece of oilcloth.

Charles moved a small building from a local quarry onto his father's working farm to use as his lab. He contacted a bottle broker in Philadelphia, bottled the extract, and sold it from the back of a horse and wagon, traveling through the Catskills in the Hudson Valley. He had a set price no matter whether he was dealing with a restaurant or a woman at her doorstep.

Charles's two sons, Earl and Arthur, took over the business as well as the family farm and ran both together. Arthur took care of the farm and raised turkeys. Earl, after a stint as a medic in World War I, returned to West Stockbridge in 1921 and moved the extract business into a vacant warehouse that was once a tinsmith's shop. As the business grew quickly, Earl bought a percolator so that he could produce extract in twenty-five gallon batches instead of five: the percolator is still in use on the family farm more than eighty years later.

John A. Adams was a Michigan pharmacist who began selling Adams Extracts in 1889 in Michigan. In 1905, he moved his family to Beeville, Texas, to escape the harsh northern winters and set up what would turn into a very successful flavor business. The business remained in the family for four generations before being sold, and it has remained as Adams Extract Company under new ownership.

The family story goes that Adams's wife was frustrated by most extracts as they nearly always carried the disclaimer "Do not bake or freeze," which didn't provide her with a reliable way to flavor baked goods and frozen desserts. Hearing his wife's complaints, Adams announced that he could produce a better vanilla than any that she had tried. Working with just $6.71 worth of materials, he created the formula that would make his business famous. Mrs. Adams whipped up a cake with the experimental vanilla extract. Thrilled with the flavor, she announced, "John, this is the best flavoring I have ever used," to which he replied, "Well, that's old man Adams's best," and a new product was launched.

John's sons, Fred and Don, worked with their father, bottling and labeling the extract at night, and selling it door-to-door during the day, offering a money-back guarantee. In 1917, Fred Adams bought the company from his father. He built a two-story building at the corner of San Gabriel and Twenty-second Street in Austin, Texas, and moved the company to the new facility in 1922. His son, John G. Sr. (the recently retired president), grew up in the family home just around the corner on Twenty-third Street.

John G. says, "I started working in the business when I was five years old. My father felt that if you're old enough to go to school, you're old enough to work. I made a nickel an hour filling 1-gallon jugs of alcohol from 55-gallon drums. By the time I was in junior high, I was making all the extracts. When I was fifteen, my father took the rest of the family on a summer vacation while I stayed behind, and for three months I ran the business. I wrote him every day and he wrote back, giving me advice."

Lochhead Manufacturing opened its doors in 1918 in St. Louis in an unusual twist on the common trend of moving businesses from east to west. Angus Lochhead's family had emigrated from Paisley, Scotland, to Ogden, Utah, in the 1800s. Angus thought his chances for success were better if he traveled east to the center of the United States for the best opportunities in sales, so he moved to St. Louis where he worked for an extract producer, selling products in rural areas out of a horse-drawn wagon. He soon tired of being on the road three months at a time— a lifestyle that kept him away from his growing family—so in 1918 he began his own company. Although the family has continued to produce a variety of flavors and extracts, vanilla has always outsold every other flavor by a ratio of at least nine to one!

Dr. Richard Stelling, a Greensboro, North Carolina, physician, worked his way through medical school at the University of Georgia, selling food flavorings. When he set up his medical practice in the early 1920s, he continued to experiment with flavors. He became good friends with life insurance agent, Kermit L. Murphy Sr., and they became partners, selling their products to bakers in their spare time. By 1947 they had a new plant, with Murphy running the business and Stelling serving as a supervisor.

In 1884, when Conrad Frederick Sauer's, a young pharmacist, realized that flavoring extracts were a large part of the wholesale and retail drug business, he decided to prepackage the flavors and extracts and sell them to grocery stores.

On October 13, 1887, his twenty-first birthday, Sauer's founded Sauer's at Seventeenth and Broad Streets in Richmond, Virginia. It was the first company in the country to provide pure flavoring extracts in 5- and 10-gram bottles; they sold for 15¢ and 25¢, respectively. Sauer's wife, Olga, assisted in the plant, often coming in at night to help make the extracts.

The companies that produced the extracts generally didn't travel outside the country to get their vanilla beans, instead depending on the big vanilla brokers for their supply. Mexico had representatives in the United States, and buyers could purchase easily from them. For Indian Ocean beans, it was necessary to buy from Europe, primarily France. One of the old companies, Aust und Hachmann, was in Germany and is still very active in the industry.

In the late 1800s, Heinrich Georg Aust and Rudolph Hachmann

became partners in the spice trade. Rudolph had lived for two years in Réunion and was passionate about spices, but by 1910 he and Heinrich Aust decided to focus only on the lucrative European vanilla market. They neither owned nor operated plantations, instead purchasing their beans exclusively from the traders in Réunion in the early days. Their business was located in the center of Hamburg, near the family home where Rudolph had grown up, and where his father had worked as a lawyer and served as mayor of the city. When Aust died, Rudolph

An early ad for Sauer's vanilla

bought his shares of the business from his widow, but as their business name was synonymous with vanilla in Europe, it remained the same.

In the 1920s, Réunion's vanilla supply began to taper off, and Rudolph expanded the business by purchasing in Papeete, Tahiti, from the Chinese traders who cured and dried the vanilla on the outer islands, then brought it to the main port for sale to the Europeans. While the United States didn't trade in Tahitian vanilla until much later, it was quite popular in Europe, and Rudolph purchased forty to fifty tons of Tahitian beans a year, supplying vanilla to Poland, Hungary, and Russia as well as Western Europe.

Alfred Zink and William Triest joined as partners in their

vanilla business also in 1930. Both of their families had been in the trade involved mainly in Réunion and, to a lesser degree, in Madagascar, working out of New York. They launched their business in Philadelphia strictly as buyers of beans, purchasing from Mexico as well as the Indian Ocean islands. Their focus was mainly on the U.S. market.

The buyers provided the guarantee of quality beans and absorbed the risks involved in receiving shipments of beans from overseas ports. Mildew and spoilage, beans of a poorer quality than the samples, and robbery of entire shipments made their business complicated, but they were well compensated by those who depended on them for the quality of beans they needed to produce the extracts for which they were famous.

PROHIBITION

A seemingly unrelated event in American history also favorably impacted the vanilla industry. In 1920, Prohibition was instated nationally. For the next thirteen years there was a boom in the sales of coffee, soft drinks, and ice-cream sodas. Hotels installed soda fountains where bars once had flourished. Desserts took the place of after-dinner drinks, and candy bars were substituted for beers. Hershey Bars, Milky Way, O'Henry, Mr. Goodbar, Babe Ruth, Charleston Chew, and Peter Paul Mounds and Almond Joy cost a nickel, and boxed and tinned chocolates manufactured by Russell Stover, Whitman's Sampler, and Almond Rocha, to name a few, sold very well in the 1920s. While Milton Hershey went bankrupt several times early in his career, by 1925 his company had gross sales of $60 million a year.

By the mid-1920s, sugar consumption had soared to 106 pounds per capita up from 65 pounds in just twenty years! Granted, some of that sugar went into "moonshine," and illegal bootlegging was big business, but there was no doubt that sweets were everywhere, and the majority of them contained vanilla.

It was during Prohibition that the Bureau of Alcohol, Tobacco and Firearms (ATF, now known as the Bureau of Alcohol, Tobacco, Firearms and Explosives, yet still abbreviated as ATF) started to regulate the vanilla industry. Alcohol was necessary to create tinctures and extracts, which constituted 35 to 50 percent of the product. In order to obtain alcohol for extracts or medicinal purposes, it was now necessary to be bonded and registered with the ATF, and to account for every ounce of alcohol purchased. Further, anyone working with alcohol was required by law to keep all alcoholic products under lock and key. Ray Lochhead of Lochhead Manufacturing remembers the family's stashing their alcohol into the company safe before closing their plant each evening.

No matter how much the ATF controlled the manufacturer's use of alcohol, the reality was that pure vanilla extract ranged from 70 to 100 proof. For the secret drinker as well as anyone who wanted a "nip," vanilla was legal, easy to obtain, and just as easy to hide. As vanilla extract could be purchased at the drugstore and grocery, as well as via the door-to-door salesman, it wasn't difficult to get plenty of vanilla for making a *lot* of cookies and ice cream.

Ironically, "the noble experiment," as Prohibition was also known, was an abysmal failure. Anyone who really wanted a drink could find one, but when the law was finally repealed in 1933, soft drink, coffee, and ice-cream soda sales plummeted, adding credence to the old saw, "candy is dandy, but liquor is quicker."

EARLY ADS FROM
McCORMICK & COMPANY

In the 1920s and 1930s, McCormick put out recipe booklets to teach homemakers how to use their various products. Here are a couple of examples of these early ads as well as a fudge recipe made the "old-fashioned" way.

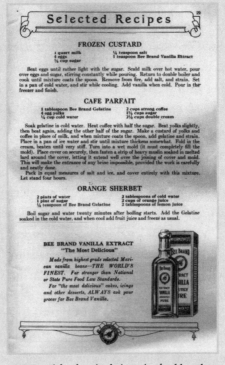

McCormick advertised via recipe booklets that provided customers with new ways to use vanilla while also picturing the company's product to ensure that customers remembered the brand.

POOR ECONOMY

The crowning success of cookery is the achievement of an enticing flavor in foods. If a housewife were baking a cake, almost instinctively she would insist on purchasing the finest butter, eggs, milk and all the other ingredients which a particular recipe might require. However, when this same housewife purchases flavoring extract, she is very likely to order a 'bottle of vanilla' and give the matter no further consideration. The proportionate cost of the flavoring extract which is used in cake never exceeds 2 to 5 percent of the cost of all the other ingredients of the recipe. Yet a truly delicious flavor is often entirely lost because the housewife uses an imitation or a pure extract of inferior quality. A wise purchaser will know that Bee Brand Vanilla Extract is pure and is noted for its 'highest quality' and mellow, delicious flavor. She will then insist upon purchasing only this particular brand and will, therefore, not ruin a large amount of first class food material with an inferior flavoring."

BEE BRAND VANILLA EXTRACT
"THE MOST DELICIOUS"

Made from highest grade selected Mexican vanilla beans—THE WORLD'S FINEST. Far stronger than National or State Pure Food Law Standards. For "the most delicious" cakes, icings and other Desserts, ALWAYS ask your grocer for Bee Brand Vanilla.

SMITH COLLEGE FUDGE (BEST OF ALL)

¼ cup butter

1 cup white sugar

1 cup brown sugar

¼ cup Karo or any other syrup

½ cup thin cream

3 squares (3 oz) Baker's chocolate

1½ teaspoons Bee Brand Vanilla

MELT BUTTER over slow heat. In another vessel mix sugar, syrup, and cream. Add this to butter, and bring to the boiling point, stirring constantly. When mixture is boiling throughout, add chocolate grated or melted over hot water. Stir steadily, and cook to soft ball stage. Remove from fire, and stir until mass begins to thicken (about 2 minutes). Stir in vanilla and pour in a greased pan. Cut in squares when partly cooled.

Synthetic and Imitation Vanillas

While vanilla certainly basked in the limelight as the "queen of flavors," there were also many impostors and pretenders to the throne. Despite the increase in production of vanilla beans after the 1840s, they were not as affordable as flavors such as lemon or peppermint, so it was inevitable that chemists search for ways to reproduce vanilla synthetically. In 1875, Ferdinand Tiemann, a Berlin chemist, patented a process for making synthetic vanillin, creating his product from coniferin, the glucoside that gives pine trees a subtle vanillalike smell. In 1891, a French chemist, by the name of De Taire, extracted vanillin from eugenol, which occurs in the oil of cloves. It was sold for $12 an ounce and was used as commercial "vanillin" for a long time. A third synthetic vanillin was created from coal tar or the by-product of wood pulp, sulphite liquor.

A fourth product used to enhance the flavor of synthetic vanilla was coumarin. Coumarin is a sweet, herblike fragrance reminiscent of newly mown hay or a freshly cut meadow. It is found in a large number of plants, most notably tonka beans *(Dipteryx odorata)*, clover, and sweet woodruff. While none of the synthetics matched the flavor and fragrance of the true vanilla, the combination of coumarin with the synthetic vanillin definitely gave it a familiar, vanillalike flavor, and the fragrance of coumarin filled the kitchen with an agreeable odor. Hamilton's imitation vanilla extract, Flavex, containing vanillin, coumarin, vanilla, and artificial flavor, assured consumers that it "will not bake out," a phrase repeatedly used by manufacturers of synthetics.

A 1950s advertisement from Watkins Company

Coumarin was also useful in masking the flavor of milk that had begun to "turn." Small dairy farms were often located near the rail lines in the late 1800s and into the 1900s, and their milk was brought to the nearest station in large tin cans. The slow-moving "milk trains," as they were known, stopped at every station and flag stop to collect the fresh milk each day, a process that involved considerable hours from pickup to delivery in the city. In the cooler northern states, the lag time of milk transport in unrefrigerated cars usually wasn't a big issue, but it took its toll in the South where the weather was hot much of the year. As a result, coumarin sales in the southern states was big business, especially in the ice-cream industry.

While imitation and synthetic vanillas were certainly cheaper, they were inconsistent and varied in strength, making it challenging for the homemaker. One teaspoon of pure vanilla extract wouldn't measure up to one teaspoon of double-strength imitation, but it wasn't necessarily obvious from the label that this was the case.

The U.S. Food and Drug Administration (FDA, known also as the Food, Drug and Cosmetic Administration for part of its history) was still in its early years, and there were so many serious violations in the food industry that they could hardly keep up with complaints about the contents of products labeled *imitation* or *synthetic*. Nevertheless, by the 1930s, they were doing their level best to control vanilla that was sold as pure but was actually synthetic. The following excerpt from the FDA addresses this issue:

> 1938: *A complaint from the assistant to the quartermaster supply officer at Fort Sam Houston in Texas led to the seizure of more than 500 bottles of a product labeled "Vanilla Extract" but which contained artificial color and little, if any, true vanilla. FDA noted that "fortunately, [the product] had not been paid for."*

More than likely the product came in from Mexico where label laws were never enforced, and where cheap synthetics developed a strong foothold in the industry. Merchants and sellers in border towns and tourist destinations took advantage of Mexico's reputation for fine vanilla beans, and passed cheap synthetics off as the "real deal." American vanilla industry leaders as well as the *beneficiadores* and importers from Mexico protested the sale of synthetics with little success, as they continue to remain popular in the Mexican marketplace today.

An interesting side note involves the Ontario Paper Company. In the 1930s, they had been dumping sulfite liquor into local streams, causing serious pollution problems. When they discovered that this effluent from paper pulp could be used for synthetic vanillin, they suddenly had a partially biodegradable solution that was also profitable with the commercial baking industry. It went over well, moreover, with manufacturers of rubber and other strong-smelling goods, where vanillin has been used to mask otherwise disagreeable odors.

NATURAL AND SYNTHETIC COMPOUNDS

*T*he *King's American Dispensatory,* 1898 edition, was used by druggists and chemists for making compounds containing natural and synthetic vanilla. For anyone interested in knowing more about the chemical components of natural versus synthetic vanillin, this is how it was analyzed by medical chemists. They also talk about adulterants that were applied to vanilla beans to give them a more fragrant odor or make them appear better in quality. Note the following:

Chemical Composition: The fragrance of vanilla is due to crystallizable *vanillin,* and a small quantity of a balsam, both of which are developed during the curing process. The presence of an odorous resin tends to impair the quality of the bean, according to its quantity. (For a complete analysis of vanilla beans, see W. von Leutner, *Jahresb. der Pharm.,* 1872, p. 36, from *Pharm. Zschr.* f. *Russland,* 1871.) The "frost" which forms upon vanilla beans, on storing, was formerly believed to be benzoic acid, until Gobley [*sic*], in 1859, pointed out its distinction from the latter, and named it *vanillin*. He obtained it by treating an alcoholic extract of vanilla with ether, and recrystallizing the ether extract from hot water with the use of animal charcoal.

VANILLIN ($C_8H_8O_3$) occurs in long, colorless needles, melting at 81°C. (177.8°F), subliming at a higher temperature, and boiling in an atmosphere of carbon dioxide gas, without decomposition, at 285°C (545°F). It is little soluble in cold water (198 parts), much more soluble in boiling water (11 parts), and crystallizing upon cooling. It is easily soluble in ether, alcohol, and chloroform, very little soluble in low-boiling petroleum ether. The researches of Tiemann and Haarmann (1874–76) have shown vanillin to be *methyl-proto-catechuic aldehyde*, or, more exactly, *meta-methoxy-para-oxy-benzoic aldehyde* (C_6H_3[OH].[OCH$_3$]. CHO). Thus it is closely related to *piperonal* (C_6H_3[OCH$_3$].[OCH$_3$].CHO), of heliotrope odor (see *Piperonal*). These authors prepared vanillin synthetically from *coniferin* ($C_{16}H_{22}O_8$+2H_2O), A glucosid occurring in the cambium sap of coniferous trees; when treated with the ferment emulsin, it becomes hydrolyzed into dextrose and *coniferyl alcohol*, or *oxy-eugenol* ($C_{10}H_{12}O_3$), which, upon oxidation, yields vanillin. The latter is now prepared synthetically by oxidation of *eugenol (see* Oil of Cloves and diagram, by Prof. V. Coblentz, *Journal of Pharmacology*, 1898, p. 37). Or, it may be obtained from other similarly constituted compounds—e.g., *creosol, guaiacol, caffeic acid*, etc. Owing to its being an aldehyde, vanillin enters quantitatively into a crystallizable, ether-insoluble compound with sodium bisulphite (SO_3HNa), from

which vanillin may be regenerated by treatment with diluted
acid (Tiemann and Haarmann). Another interesting aldehydic
compound of vanillin is that with ammonia, which permits the
quantitative separation of vanillin from coumarin, the aromatic
principle of the tonka bean. "If vanillin be dissolved in pure,
dry ether, and dry ammonia gas be passed through the solution,
the aldehyde-ammonia compound of vanillin will be precipi-
tated in almost quantitative proportions. . . . Coumarin, on the
other hand, remains wholly (and unchanged) in the ether solution" (Wm. H. Hess and A. B. Prescott, *Pharm. Review,* 1899,
p. 7). By oxidation, vanillin forms odorless, volatile *vanillic
acid,* melting at 212°C (413.6°F). An alcoholic solution of
vanillin produces greenish blue with ferric chloride; an aqueous
solution produces a permanent blue with the same reagent. It
dissolves in sulphuric acid with yellow color.

The quality of commercial vanilla beans does not necessarily depend on the quantity of vanillin they contain; thus Tiemann and Haarmann found, in Mexican vanilla, 1.32 to 1.69
percent, while Bourbon yielded from 0.75 to 2.9 percent, and
Java vanilla from 1.56 to 2.75 percent of vanillin. Denner (1887)
obtained 4.3 percent from vanilla cultivated at Marburg (Flück-
iger, *Pharmacognosie des Pflanzenreichs,* 3d ed., 1891). West Indian vanillons contained 0.4 to 0.7 percent of vanillin, together
with a liquid aldehyde, probably benzoic aldehyde; when both
are in prolonged contact with each other, an odor resembling
heliotrope will be developed.

BENZOIC ACID, dusted over vanilla beans, with fraudulent
intent, may be recognized, according to Messrs. Schimmel & Co.

(1888), by abstracting the crystals with sodium carbonate, adding sulphuric acid and metallic magnesium or zinc; if the crystals are benzoic acid, the odor of oil of bitter almonds (benzoic aldehyde) will then be developed. Vanillin is also a constituent of many other vegetable products, such as Siam benzoin (Balsam of Peru, see H. Thoms, *Archiv der Pharm.*, 1899), the sugar beet, asparagus, several kinds of wood, the husks of oats, etc.

Related Plants: A plant of the distinct genus SOBRALIA, collected by Prof. Rusby in the Andes, produces a pod which develops the odor of vanilla upon maturity (see *Jour. of Pharmacol.*, 1898, p. 29); likewise, the flowers of a certain orchid, growing in Switzerland, yield considerable quantities of vanillin.

THE VANILLA PLANT, or Southern vanilla, is the *Liatris odoratissima*, Michaux. The odorous principle of its leaves is coumarin (see Charles Falkenhainer, *Amer. Jour. Pharm.*, 1899, p. 133; also see Liatris).

A similar odoriferous plant is *Angraecum fragrans*, Du Petit-Thouars, known in Mauritius and Réunion as *faham*. Its odoriferous principle is coumarin; its odor is that of vanilla, tonka, and melilot combined.

VANILLA AND THE
PERFUME INDUSTRY

Until the mid-nineteenth century, fragrances were limited to floral and spice blends that could be created from natural plant extracts and resins. Potpourri, loose crushed flowers, and perfumed "toilette waters" made with roses, lavender, and other common flowers were standard fare. Fragrances were mostly purchased from drugstores and produced by the chemist or pharmacist.

Then, in 1867, perfumes and soaps were showcased at the Paris International Exhibition in exhibits separate from the pharmacy section, thereby establishing a new commercial arena for fragrances. Even more significant was the production of the first synthetic fragrance, coumarin, in 1868, followed twenty years later by musk, vanilla, and violet. By the early 1920s, there were many hundreds of synthetic fragrances—the first perfumes unsuitable for medicinal use.

Perfume defined the modern woman of the upper and middle classes. Chanel No. 5 was the first fragrance to enter the marketplace that was created entirely from synthetic aldehydes, making its fragrance far stronger than anything available before. As the aroma of synthetics did not easily diminish due to humidity or perspiration, this shift in perfumery opened the doors for a new image of independence and eroticism for urban women. As scientists determined how to create synthetic aldehydes and benzoic- and balsamlike aromas, as well as piperonals such as heliotrope, new fragrances incorporating vanilla as a predominant, secondary, or base note came on to the market. Often referred to in the trade as "oriental," these fragrances have always reflected the deep, smooth notes of vanilla.

In 1889, Guerlain launched Jicky, an oriental fragrance uniquely modern among its contemporaries and the symbol of a new trend. Jicky contained a fresh and aromatic top note with hints of lavender, bergamot, and rosemary to blossom into a middle note of rose and jasmine. The woody end note (the industry term for the last impact of a scent) with touches of tonka bean and vanilla brought softness and character to this pioneer among modern perfumes. Jicky was the first "abstract" perfume to come on to the market as it didn't evoke flowers or a particular specific fragrance.

Caron introduced Narcisse Noir in 1912, and Molinard brought out Habanita in 1921, again all three oriental perfumes with vanilla as strong secondary notes. But it wasn't until 1925 when Guerlain launched Shalimar that vanilla emerged as a dominant aroma in perfumery. Shalimar was the first perfume to contain vanillin ethyl, an artificial molecule smelling like vanilla and marked by an overwhelming intensity. It remains the epitome of the oriental profile.

Legend has it that Jacques Guerlain created this perfume as a tribute to the legendary love story between Mumtaz Mahal and Emperor Shah Jahan in the Shalimar ("home of love") Gardens of Kashmir. When Mumtaz Mahal died, her devastated husband created the Taj Mahal in tribute to their eternal love. Whether this story is fiction or fact, Shalimar has certainly endured the test of time and continues to be popular today.

The last of the truly famous vanilla-based perfumes of the early twentieth century was Vol de Nuit, created in 1933 by Guerlain and named after Antoine de Saint-Exupéry's most famous novel, which tells the story of the early days of airmail when each flight was an adventure. Described as a precious multifaceted fragrance, Vol de Nuit contained citrus and floral top notes, sandalwood and spice, and a bold end note of vanilla.

Popular as these modern fragrances were, they were not yet within the reach of working class women or women living in rural America. Instead, these women relied on the bottle of vanilla extract, which they dabbed behind their ears or on their wrists, and sprinkled on their handkerchiefs. It wasn't until much later in the century that affordable vanilla fragrances were available to everyone.

VANILLA AS MEDICINE

Until the advent of modern antibiotics, which became available in limited quantity during World War II, there was little that doctors could do for people sick with wasting diseases such as tuberculosis, long-term chronic illnesses, or debilitating illnesses such as influenza or scarlet fever. It was up to pharmacists and family members to care for the ill as well as possible, usually with patent or home remedies that eased the discomfort of symptoms, and with nutritious foods. Vanilla remained in the American pharmacopoeia until 1916 and in other medical annals until the 1920s as an aid for stomach distress, a stimulant, and as a calmative for hysteria. Even after vanilla was long forgotten in the medical journals, prudent druggists dispensed bottles of Coca-Cola syrup for children suffering from gastrointestinal viruses. Even today we often reach for a Coke or Pepsi to help calm queasiness, usually unaware that the vanilla it contains is partially responsible for settling the stomach.

INVALID COOKERY

A very typical example of advice for the ill and infirm comes from *The Settlement Cook Book*, a book that generations of women relied upon as it dispensed tips and helpful advice on a full range of topics related to the home. The lead page tells us that it contains "Tested Recipes from The Milwaukee Public School Kitchens, Girls Trades and Technical High School, Authoritative Dietitians, and Experienced Housewives." The following advice was from an edition published in 1947.

With regard to serving food for people who are ill, it says:

In preparing food for an invalid the following points should be kept in mind:

The food should be served in the most pleasing manner possible. It should be served in small quantities, suit the digestive powers of the patient, and satisfy hunger or furnish needed strength. In a severe illness the doctor prescribes the kind and amount of food to be given. In long and protracted illness, it is necessary to take nourishing foods in small quantities at frequent intervals.

Use the daintiest dishes in the house. Place a clean napkin on the tray, and if possible, a fresh flower.

Serve hot food hot, and cold food cold.

Remove the tray as soon as the food is eaten, as food should not be allowed to stand in a sick room.

CARAMEL JUNKET

2 cups milk

⅓ cup sugar

⅓ cup boiling water

1 junket tablet

few grains salt

1 teaspoon vanilla

whipped cream, sweetened and flavored

HEAT MILK UNTIL LUKEWARM. Caramelize sugar, add boiling water, and cook until sirup [*sic*] is reduced to ⅓ cup. Cool and add milk slowly to sirup. Reduce junket tablet to powder, add to mixture, with salt and vanilla. Let stand in warm place until set, then chill. Cover with whipped cream.

RICE CREAM

1 cup hot rice, cooked in milk

1 tablespoon gelatin, soaked in 3 tablespoons cold water

2 tablespoons sugar

¼ teaspoon salt

1 teaspoon vanilla

1 cup heavy cream, whipped

DRAIN RICE, add gelatin, sugar, salt, and vanilla. Mix thoroughly. Cook, fold in cream, mold, or pile in dessert glasses. Serve with any sauce suitable for ice cream or, if in small glasses, pour over maple sirup.

Cookbooks, housekeeping guides, magazines, and health journals written with the homemaker in mind dispensed advice on how to care for sick and feeble family members through the preparation of healing and strengthening foods. Milk, cream, and eggs were sources of digestible protein, so custards and puddings thickened with eggs, cornstarch, tapioca, or rennet were highly recommended. For those competent in the kitchen, cookbooks offered a plethora of recipes, but by the late 1920s packaged custard and pudding mixes could also be found on the shelves of many local grocery stores. Whether the two came homemade or packaged, plain or enhanced with fruits, coconut, chocolate, or almond, the modern homemaker intuitively knew to add a teaspoon of vanilla extract after removing them from the fire. And when the baby was colicky or children were tired and fussy, a few drops of vanilla were often added to the little ones' milk to calm them down and encourage them to drink a beverage itself known to calm and soothe. Though vanilla became a forgotten medical cure for decades, we will see that late in the twentieth century it would be rediscovered and its use in medical application would again be explored.

VANILLA THRIVES
WORLDWIDE

With Réunion's great success in the early years of commercial vanilla-bean production in the Indian Ocean, Mauritius, the Seychelles, the Comoro Islands, and Madagascar soon followed suit. It quickly became clear that vanilla growing was a moneymaking proposition, perhaps a wiser choice than sugar and some of the other tropical products. The exporters' target market was Europe, where vanilla was certainly in demand, and Paris was the hub of the vanilla commodities market exchange.

Madagascar grew vanilla as early as the 1840s but it lagged behind Réunion in production. In 1900, Madagascar only produced approximately 15 tons of vanilla, but by 1915 their crop had grown to 233 tons, and by 1929 they produced 80 percent of the world's vanilla.

Other island countries, such as Tahiti and Indonesia, where vanilla also arrived early but wasn't immediately utilized as a cash crop, suddenly emerged on to the market in the latter years of the nineteenth century and early years of the twentieth. In tracing vanilla's travels to the tropical islands where it became important, we will begin with Tahiti, a legendary and exotic group of islands synonymous with paradise in the nineteenth and early twentieth centuries, and which still remains a hallmark of tropical romance and beauty.

TAHITI

The Society Islands are no more than a handful of the thousands of islands and atolls that comprise Polynesia, south of the equator in the middle of the South Pacific. Originally a cluster of volcanoes and volcanic uplifts from the ocean floor, they have been worn away by wind and water and time until now they are lush, verdant islands with sharp pinnacles and mountains that begin nearly at the sea and stretch up to balance the clouds that gather on the high edges of the precipices. Trade winds blow continually. Reefs surround most of the islands, providing sheltering bays that fairly burst with brilliantly colored tropical fish and corals. The islands exemplify paradise, warm and lazy and layered, with the history of people who thrived on music, dance, art, and the sea.

Tahiti is the principal island, home of Papeete, the islands' capital, where vanilla first arrived with Admiral Ferdinand Hamlin in 1786 and was planted in the governor's gardens. The vanilla grew there, thick stemmed and wide leaved, with no one particularly interested in, or even aware of, its potential value until the arrival of Catholic missionaries in the latter years of the nineteenth century.

Traditional culture was built around myth and animist beliefs, music and dance, and the arts of boat building and decorative tattoo. Life was easily sustained through fishing and the gathering of foods that arrived on the islands in dugouts with the first settlers, by ocean passage, or in the guts of migrating birds. Settlers first arrived from the islands to the east, originally from Southeast Asia. The Polynesians had legendary navigational skills, and boat building was a high art form creating a lot of cross-island travel and considerable migration in the early years. Until the arrival of the Protestant missionaries, traditional life prevailed. Provided with the basic necessities of life, the people saw no need for complex systems of trade or elaborate material culture.

But according to Dorothy Levy, Tahitian genealogist and cultural historian, by the time of the arrival of the missionaries, the islands were wracked with intertribal warfare at a level where everyone's nerves were frayed. Human sacrifice was practiced and had created more pressure than the culture could handle, and the islanders were ready for something to arrive that would rescue them from the complicated circumstances that had evolved.

There was a legend and prophecy of a great white bird arriving to help the Tahitians. The white bird took form in the white sails of the missionary boats. The Tahitians valued structure and laws, so they essentially threw themselves at the feet of the missionaries and accepted whatever they said. Having the church intervene was, in some ways, a relief for the indigenous people, and the church remains an enormously powerful institution within the islands. This isn't to say that the missionaries had the best interest of the Tahitians at heart, as they methodically dismantled or destroyed much of what was also beautiful about the islanders' traditional culture. Fortunately, the true Polynesian spirit has prevailed.

It's uncertain precisely when commercial vanilla growing became part of the island culture, but it was first established by the French Catholic missionaries, some of whom were previously based in the Indian Ocean islands where vanilla had taken hold.

A Tahitian vanilla orchid. Note the difference in appearance from the Vanilla planifolia. *It has a wider, more open flower and is of a somewhat creamier color.*

What is known is that the vanilla of Tahiti was significantly different from the vanilla found in Mexico and the Indian Ocean, and has therefore often been considered native to Tahiti. In fact, it arrived from the Philippine Islands where the Spanish had a plant laboratory where cross-pollination and early genetic engineering modified plant species or created new ones. The earliest variety of what is now known as *Vanilla tahitensis* was created in the Philippines. The beans were small and fat, an apparent cross of *Vanilla tahitensis* and *Vanilla pompona Schiede.* From Papeete the vines were taken to the islands of Huahine, Raiatea, Moorea, and Tahaa, where early plantations were established.

The missionaries taught the local people how to cultivate, cure, and dry vanilla. As the church was well established before vanilla was introduced, all traditional praise and spiritual beliefs had been thoroughly repressed. Except for offering church blessings of the crops, observing anything traditional that was outside the dictates of the church was taboo. As a result, vanilla has always been a cash crop without a spiritual association.

Tahitians sang songs in the fields as they cultivated, pollinated, harvested, and cured vanilla. Hymns and religious songs replaced traditional music, but the music maintained the rhythm of the work in the hot sun. The children were encouraged to "sing for the vanilla beans." Perhaps it was a way to keep them less wild and happier while working alongside their parents or friends. As recently as twenty years ago, the children still sang in the fields. One young man remembers singing "The Mountain" and "Tahiti Nui" while working in the fields. He said that no one seems to sing any longer; it's strictly a cash crop now.

False coffee bush *(Breynia oblongifolia)* was used as a traditional tutor as was *Purau* (no translation, unfortunately). Other bushes and trees were used as well. Unlike the tutor trees in Mexico, Tahitian tutors were (and still are) cut to 6½ feet (about 2 meters). The vines were looped several times around the tutors, making them accessible for pollinating and picking.

The vanilla was pollinated or "married" with a bamboo stick, though adults often used a long, vanilla-stained and scarred thumbnail. A Tahitian, Ruth Chisaka, said that her mother was a champion in the informal pollinating contests held on the plantations in Huahine, adding, "Not only would you move quickly but also very carefully. If you weren't delicate at marrying the vanilla, it would damage the flowers. So the children were told by the adults that the vanilla 'tree' would eat you back if you weren't careful."

In the "old days," the Tahitian children usually remained segregated in groups of boys or girls when they worked on Tahitian plantations. However, when they worked for pocket money on the

Chinese plantations, the boys and girls worked together to "marry" the vanilla.

THE ARRIVAL OF THE CHINESE

In the early years of the twentieth century, Chinese men from small villages in the Canton province headed south and west in small seaworthy junks in search of better opportunities than existed at home. The trip to the Society Islands took two to three months, with the boats maneuvering past Australia and on to the South Pacific. The men, often related or from the same villages, established themselves with work and, later, a business; then they returned home for family members.

The Chinese worked hard. They usually started at the bottom of the economic ladder, working as laborers in the fields. Frugal and diligent, they then set up their own businesses, curing and drying the Tahitians' beans, running small grocery and supply stores, or finding another niche within the community where there was a need. Their community was small but close-knit, and they all shared their secrets and discoveries about the vanilla they were growing or drying. Within the period of a generation, they established themselves as the curers, driers, and intermediaries in the vanilla industry.

During the peak years of vanilla production in Tahiti, both Chinese and Tahitians grew vanilla, but very few Tahitians cured and dried their vanilla themselves, instead bringing it to the towns where the Chinese had their stores and cement slabs or special roofs where the vanilla dried. Those who did cure and dry their vanilla usually sold it to the Chinese who, in the early days, took the vanilla to the port in Papeete where the European traders would come to purchase the crop. Later, when vanilla was not as large a commercial venture, some traders ventured out to the island of Raiatea where the largest family brokerage business was now run by Madame Jeanne Chane. A few buyers even traveled to Tahaa, the center of the growing region, to negotiate directly with the growers.

MADAME CHANE:
THE EMPRESS OF VANILLA

Madame Chane is a soft-spoken, slightly shy woman, who wears local "mama" dresses and looks like a shopkeeper and grandmother, not a woman who runs the Tahitian vanilla industry. Appearances aside, Madame Chane is probably the single most powerful person in the Tahitian vanilla trade. She knows the business inside out, sets the prices, and negotiates vanilla futures. As she says quite truthfully, "I've been in the vanilla business my entire life."

Jeanne's grandfather, Chan Woun Kim, and eleven other men sailed to the Society Islands in a small boat in 1918, leaving their families behind in a tiny village in Canton province. It was a six-month journey, traveling via Australia. They first settled in Papeete, but after two months Chan Woun Kim moved to Raiatea and later to Tahaa. He established a small market to provide a year-round cash stream, then started buying green vanilla and drying it. The men shared with one another their secrets and discoveries about the vanilla they were cultivating and drying. Jeanne's grandfather worked hard for six years before saving enough money to send for his wife and twenty-four-year-old son, Chan Fook Wan. The son was predestined for the vanilla business. His father bought land in Tahaa and became a grower; Fook Wan cured, dried, and sold the beans. He married the daughter of another immigrant family and continued building his father's vanilla dynasty.

Jeanne was the seventh in a family of eleven children. She remembers as a two-year-old child holding her mother's hand as they crossed the threshold of their family business in downtown Uturoa for the first time, the same store where she still does business today. It was as if she arrived at the tender age of two and never left. "I lived vanilla right up to today," says Jeanne.

Chan Fook Wan bought from many growers on Raiatea and Tahaa. The freshly picked vanilla arrived in big flour sacks. All the children worked in the family business from the time they turned five. The children sorted the black beans (which they referred to as "chocolate") from the yellow. If the beans were black, the children rinsed them in water and put them in the sun to dry. If the beans were yellow, the children put them into a big box to cure until they turned black. "Another of our tasks was to massage each vanilla bean *every* day," says Jeanne. "We all did it, and we visited with each other after dinner while we made the vanilla beautiful."

The children were paid five francs a day for their work. It served as pocket money for them but was also designed to teach them that when you work, you earn money and buy what you need with it. It created a strong work ethic in the children, an ethic to which Jeanne attributes her success.

Jeanne attended Chinese school for five years in addition to going to regular school and working with her family. In the late 1950s, she assumed responsibility for the family business, buying the fresh beans, overseeing the drying, and selling them to the big buyers who came to the islands looking for vanilla. She never married. "Why should I marry?" she says. "I had my own money. I didn't need a man to take care of me." She remembers that in 1959 20 tons of raw vanilla came through their business: "It was a mountain of vanilla. We never hired workers from outside the family; everyone worked. No matter how much time it took, there we were, working!" Despite the hard work and long hours, Jeanne Chane achieved a great level of independence and satisfaction in carving out an important niche for herself in vanilla.

Jeanne is the only family member in her generation still in vanilla, and none of the younger generation has chosen vanilla as a livelihood: "There is much less emphasis on vanilla in the islands now. The young people don't want to grow it, as it's hard work. They would rather grow [the fruit] noni, as it's a fast cash crop and much less complicated." Jeanne laments that the focus now in the islands is on noni and black pearls. She says, "The beast to go after" is vanilla, as it is a food product. Her nieces and nephews disagree. "They tell you that growing vanilla is boring."

Jeanne persists in her work. She shows off the cement slabs she inherited from her grandfather, a symbol and reminder of the continuity of her family's livelihood, created on an island so very different from the land of her ancestors. But life sometimes has a way of drawing us back to our ancestral roots, she says:

"Do you know, a delegation of eight people came here from Hainan to beg me to go to China to help them grow Tahitian vanilla? They told me they will treat me like royalty to help them. I am already the queen here and so I must be the queen there as well.

"I didn't say no to them. I said I would go with them but I would not be able to help them. Think about it. If I go there, I will help make the vanilla of Tahiti go under, as it is cheap there. There are six generations of my family in vanilla. If I go, I will pull the carpet out from under them. I will not become Judas!"

Although Jeanne is unwilling to assist the Chinese, her face lights up as she tells the story. She's proud of the attention and acknowledgment of her skill and experience, as well she should be—she's made it in a world dominated by men. In fact, in the Tahitian department of agriculture offices there is a poster with Jeanne Chane on the front, advising the younger generation that "if you want to be successful, be like Jeanne Chane. Work hard and stay with it, and you will succeed!"

Despite her stature in the industry and her considerable financial success, Jeanne Chane continues to live simply and frugally. Born during the Great Depression, of a family who worked hard for a living, she has not forgotten her humble origins. Regardless, she's quick to say, "I am more than the queen of the vanilla—I am the *empress*. No one has lived vanilla as I have. I must be the empress." When it comes to knowledge, hard work, and experience, she deserves the title hands down!

The Tahitian Vanilla Growing Process

Tahitian vanilla is grown the same way as Bourbon and Mexican vanilla, but it has different needs and very different methods of curing and drying. At first, only the small Tahiti beans were produced, but soon they were crossbred with Bourbon vanilla from the Indian Ocean islands. Over time, the newer plant stock was refined until finally there were five varieties of *Vanilla tahitensis:*

- TAHITI: Small and fragrant, and the first vanilla to arrive in the Society Islands.
- HAAPAPE: Now the most common variety of vanilla grown in the islands. Its leaves are long, with a deep groove running down the center. Haapape grows fast and well and produces nice-quality beans.
- REA REA (YELLOW): This vanilla has the most fragrant aroma. It flowers later in the season than the other varieties. The pods become yellow within three months, but they are not mature until ten months after pollination. The pod will be the same brown color as that of the other beans when they are ripe. A vigorous plant with good flavor and taste, the Rea Rea bean tends to be larger than the other varieties.
- PATATI: The vine of the Patati grows in a slightly irregular shape. It has smaller leaves and pods than the traditional vanillas and isn't a very good commercial variety.
- PARAHURAHU: Has unusually long leaves and very large pods. It is generally not used commercially.

. . .

ALL TAHITIAN vanilla varieties are low in vanillin with between 0.2 and 1.8 percent vanillin content. While low in vanillin, they contain large quantities of anis aldehyde and heliotropin, giving the vanilla a very floral fragrance and fruity, cherry, pruney, and licoricelike flavor notes.

Originally, the vanilla vines took three years to produce their first flowers. Now, with new compost technology, the vines flower in two years and sometimes as early as fourteen months. The growers don't marry all the flowers. Usually only six or seven are pollinated on each vine so that the plant won't be stressed and the beans will grow healthy and large.

Pollinating begins between 5:30 A.M. and 6:30 A.M. This way the pollen hasn't been "melted" (damaged) by the sun's heat. After 11:30 A.M., all pollinating stops as otherwise the pollen will be no good. Pollinating takes place from late June through August. Families pollinate with the stem off a leaf of the tutor tree, toothpicks, twigs, or long thumbnails.

Harvest occurs almost exactly nine months after the flowers are pollinated. Beans are not harvested until they are ready. And this is where the process between the *planifolia* and the *tahitensis* differs. "Ready" for Tahitian vanilla is when the beans have turned golden brown, not just at the tips, but throughout the entire bean. Windfalls (beans that have fallen early) and any beans that aren't evenly colored are placed in the sun until they darken. The beans are then washed, dried off, and placed on mats in the shade, where they will begin the drying process. The time frame for the drying and conditioning process is three months for the little beans and up to six or seven months for the big beans.

The drying beans are placed in the sun for two hours each day (in some places, every other day) until the beans are nearly too hot to touch. Then they are wrapped in muslin sheets and moved inside until the next day. Traditionally, each bean was massaged every day. While the beans aren't massaged daily now, they still are massaged at least a dozen times during the drying process. Tahitian beans never go through a scalding or heating stage to "kill" the enzymatic process. They are strictly sun-dried, rested, massaged, and conditioned. Some families condition the beans in large wooden crates; others use racks to complete the drying cycle.

Most Chinese no longer grow vanilla. Tahitian families and mixed-marriage families continue to grow vanilla, but the plantations are smaller. From the 1920s through the 1960s, vanilla was big business in Raiatea, Huahine, and Tahaa, with as much as 150 tons of cured vanilla exported from the islands. Slowly the process diminished, as children grew up, went to college, and entered other professions. This was especially true in the Chinese families. Noni fruit *(Morinda citrafolia)* became a preferred crop with many Tahitian families as it produces within seven months of planting, requires minimal labor, can be harvested every three weeks, and has a ready market for the production of noni juice, a very popular product considered to have strong healing properties. Black pearls have also become big business in Tahiti. The outer islands have the pearl beds and the pearls fetch a handsome price, making them a desirable "crop." At one time, 160 tons of dried vanilla were produced in the islands yearly. Now it's down to roughly 4 to 5 tons. Several locals have said that Tahitians are famous for starting things but not very good at staying with them. As vanilla is such an intensive crop, and as they can get a lot of money for noni without doing anything, why bother growing vanilla? Other families have valued the tradition of vanilla and keep growing it despite the problems they face with weather conditions and fungus.

HANOA PLANTATION

The government ministry of agriculture is aware of the need to increase the production of Tahitian vanilla, as demand is far greater than supply (though in recent years, Papua New Guinea has become a large producer of *Vanilla tahitensis*). They are experimenting with plants, compost, and methods of shed-house production to improve both quality and quantity. The best density of plants, the choice of compost, and virus control are of great interest to the researchers. There are agricultural stations on several of the main islands, including the Hanoa Plantation on Raiatea, which sits up from the highway on a verdant strip of land studded with palms, bananas, and hardwoods. Bordering the facility is a technical high school where students learn basic farm management and techniques for the cultivation of bananas, pineapples, papayas, vanilla, taro, sugarcane, and other crops. The school has a relaxed attitude about agriculture, and their plants joyfully grow wild in all directions in the warm, rainy weather. On the government side, the crops are uniformly planted and carefully maintained, providing an amusing contrast to traditional Tahitian lifestyle, and the French bureaucracy.

There are several 1,000-meter-long shed-houses, each containing four hundred supports for the plants. Some of the supports are made of concrete, and others are of wood. On the islands there are no chemicals available to protect the wood from rot, so it's uncertain how long the wood supports will last. This is an experiment in itself, as all the materials for the growers' work come from France. Over the next few years they will determine the most cost-effective way for growing shed-house vanilla.

During periods of heavy rain, water collects around the plants and triggers fungus, causing deformed flowers. Workers pick off fungus-infected leaves and vines. Because Tahitian vanilla has a high moisture content, it is naturally susceptible to virus, even when grown in optimal conditions. "One thing we are studying is whether vanilla grown in such close quarters suffers from many more viruses than vanilla that grows on traditional plantations," says Michel Grisoni, a plant virologist and specialist in vanilla. "If so, we need to learn ways to combat this."

One advantage of shed-house production is that plants are more protected from the cold than on traditional plantations. This is a consideration as Tahitian vanilla dies when the temperature drops below 14°C (60°F).

Another area of the plantation contains hundreds of small plants that look like small cuttings of a decorative vine. "This is what vanilla grown in vitro looks like," Michel explained. "In vitro literally means 'in glass.' Until fairly recently it was extremely difficult to grow vanilla from seeds, and even now it takes a very long time for the plants to develop enough to produce." Asked if this is how Tahitian vanilla has got to other countries, Michel said, "Absolutely. The French government has had a ban on vanilla vines leaving Tahiti, so people start the vanilla from the seeds inside the beans which, of course, they cannot ban."

MODERN TAHITIAN
PLANTATIONS

There is a new generation of growers who use modern technology to grow Tahitian vanilla. La Vanillère is a prime example of the modern Tahitian plantation. Situated in a breathtaking, rain-swept valley with massive volcanic outcroppings as a backdrop, La Vanillère sits on a knoll with a view of the water in the distance. After purchasing the land, three partners, young men who have maintained their day jobs, developed this plantation. They gathered vanilla vines that grew behind the property in the mountains. Probably abandoned from an earlier venture, the wild vanilla was hearty and well adapted to the local environment.

La Vanillère has four large greenhouses. The plants grow in long, narrow beds bordered with cement, with gravel walkways for drainage. Instead of using tutor trees or cement posts, the owners have created tutors from compost wrapped with chicken wire and shaped into poles. The tutors stand 6½ feet high, and the aerial roots grow into the compost tutors. The greenhouses are covered with shade cloth and house about four hundred plants each. Because of the compost tutors, the vanilla feeds off the compost as it grows. As a result, the vanilla has unusually thick vines, and the orchids bloom far earlier than on a traditional plantation. Because of the proximity of the plants, the workers can pollinate two to three thousand plants a day. The partners anticipate harvesting a few tons from each greenhouse once the vines are mature, with each plant producing several kilos (approximately 12 lbs) of green beans. The goal of La Vanillère is to produce a small premium-quality crop. And, although the partners' initial investment was considerable, shade-house vanilla is far less labor intensive and provides a far higher yield than traditional plantations.

The three men represent a growing shift in the way vanilla is grown in Tahiti. One of the partners is of Chinese heritage; his family has been in Tahiti for several generations. A banker, he's interested in the economic future of Tahitian farmers. The other two men are originally from France and, typical of many Europeans, are interested in ecologically sound, organic products. While Tahitian vanilla has traditionally been more expensive than *planifolia*, there is certainly a demand for its unique fruity and floral flavor. Therefore, vanilla will continue to grow in Tahiti, though probably there will never be a return to the old days when everyone grew it.

MEDICAL AND CULINARY USES OF TAHITIAN VANILLA

Tahitians have a great interest in the medicinal uses of plants. When vanilla became a cash crop, the locals soon realized its astringent value for treating eruptions and infection on the body. The vanilla leaf was broken and placed directly on the wound to draw pus to the surface so that the area could be cleaned and heal. Islanders also used it to treat powerful bites from a local centipede. *Monoi* (coconut) oil is a Tahitian favorite for keeping the skin smooth and moist. Vanilla is often mixed into the oil for its refreshing, fragrant scent.

Despite the French presence and influence on Tahitian cuisine, vanilla would have become a part of Tahitian culinary culture on its own as the locals make full use of the many flowers, leaves, fruits, greens, and vegetables that have found their way to the Society Islands. Once vanilla was cultivated commercially, families created their own extracts, using rum and allowing the fragrant Tahitian beans to remain in the liquor indefinitely, adding more rum as necessary. The rum also flavored alcoholic drinks such as Planter's Punch and other exotic beverages that have become popular in the tourist market.

Vanilla beans were put into grenadine syrup and other fruit drinks, in coconut milk and homemade punches, and in coffee and tea. Vanilla was also included in luscious fruit jams, cake batters, coconut ice cream, rice pudding, banana *poe* (an island food made from manioc flour), and other sweets. As the local diet depends on the fine local fresh fish, everyone has a recipe for mahimahi in vanilla cream.

PAPAYA CHICKEN AND BANANA POE

The small, sweet papayas of the islands are abundant and delicious. Papaya is used interchangeably as a fruit and a vegetable in Pacific and Asian cuisine. Use a ripe, but firm, papaya for this recipe.

PAPAYA CHICKEN WITH VANILLA-SCENTED COCONUT MILK

1¾ cups coconut milk
½ teaspoon sugar
1 Tahitian vanilla bean, split lengthwise
1 firm papaya

3 tablespoons olive oil
4 chicken breasts, cut into ¾-inch cubes
1 medium onion, chopped
salt and pepper to taste

IN A SAUCEPAN, combine the coconut milk, sugar, and vanilla bean, and bring mixture almost to a boil. Remove from stove and allow to steep.

PEEL THE PAPAYA, remove the seeds, and cut into thin slices.

HEAT OLIVE OIL in a large skillet, add chicken, and cook until nearly done. Add chopped onion and cook until the onion is translucent, about 5 minutes. Add the papaya slices, salt and pepper to taste, and cook another 5 minutes.

WHILE THE CHICKEN mixture is cooking, remove vanilla pod from coconut milk and scrape the seeds into the liquid.

TRANSFER THE CHICKEN-PAPAYA mixture to a serving platter. Add coconut milk to the skillet and cook over medium-high heat until milk boils and sauce reduces slightly. Pour over chicken mixture and serve over hot rice.

SERVES 4

BANANA POE

Manioc root is used a lot in traditional Pacific Island cuisine. It's filling, nutritious, and easy to digest. Banana *poe* is so popular that it's sold premixed in boxes in the stores.

Manioc is also known as yucca in Latin American cultures. In European and American culinary traditions, manioc is known as tapioca pearls. In poe, manioc starch is used. It can usually be found in specialty food stores, Asian markets, and sometimes places where bulk foods are sold.

  5 large, ripe bananas (about 2⅔ lbs)
  6 cups water
  ½ Tahitian vanilla bean, sliced open lengthwise
  ¾ cup manioc starch
  1 cup coconut milk or light cream
  ⅔ cup sugar

PREHEAT OVEN TO 300°F. Peel the bananas, cut into large slices, and place in a large saucepan with the water and vanilla. Bring to a boil and cook 15 minutes. Drain the fruit, setting the vanilla bean aside.

PUREE THE COOKED BANANAS in a food processor. Add the starch and scrape vanilla seeds into the mix. Mix thoroughly so that the mixture is smooth and creamy. Fill a greased casserole dish with the poe, and place in oven for 30 minutes.

REMOVE POE FROM OVEN and cut into small pieces. Serve with the coconut milk or cream and sugar.

SERVES 6 to 8

Despite the fact that vanilla is no longer a major cash crop in Tahiti, its cultural significance can still be found in many ways. In the beautiful Museum of Tahiti and its Islands in Punaauia, there are early records kept by Mormon and Catholic missionaries that talk about the vanilla trade, and vanilla is certainly represented there as an important part of Tahiti's heritage.

In recent years, traditional dance and music have made an enormous resurgence in the Society Islands. One of the museum docents, a Teraitua, was the first Tahitian to play the traditional drum in the church. He fought for this for a long time. He said that the first time he saw girls dancing in the Catholic church, tears poured from his eyes. He saw it as an acknowledgment that Tahitians were recognized for their traditional beliefs and honored as equals. In tying in vanilla with the tradition of song and dance, costume makers often include a piece of vanilla in the headpiece or waist of the costumes. During times when vanilla isn't tremendously expensive, it may also be woven into bracelets. Vanilla can be found at the many stands and small shops that line the first streets of the ports where cruise ships berth, and tours of vanilla plantations are a popular destination point for tourists. In the great market in Papeete, along with the vanilla that is sold, there are woven containers used to present the Tahitian beans as special gifts to friends and family. But the most telling comment about vanilla's economic and cultural value in Tahiti can be seen on the 20-franc piece, a silver coin traded daily throughout the islands. The "head" side of the coin says "République Française" and portrays the head of a warrior. The "tail" side of the coin represents the *true* French Polynesia: pictured on the coin are breadfruit, pandanus leaves, tiare blossoms (Tahitian gardenias), *and* a bunch of vanilla beans.

VANILLA

INDONESIA

Indonesia, the world's largest archipelago, is located in Southeast Asia, between the Indian and Pacific Oceans. It is comprised of nearly 18,000 islands, a third of which are inhabited. While there are several primary ethnic groups—the Sundanese, Madurese, Javanese, and Coastal Malay—Indonesia is a country of more than five hundred distinct tribal groups. Bahasa Indonesia is the official national language, but each tribe has its own language or dialect, sometimes tied to Bahasa Indonesia, sometimes not.

During the Pleistocene epoch, Indonesia was part of Asia; when the ice age ended and the sea levels rose, the archipelago was created. In addition to the indigenous Asians who first inhabited the islands, people from mainland Asia migrated early to the islands as did Indo-Aryan migrants from the subcontinent of India. At the beginning of the Christian era, Indians came from Gujarat state, bringing with them both Sanskrit and the Hindu religion. Hospitable trade relations between the two regions were established, with each providing the other with a wealth of products ranging from foods and spices, to textiles and precious metals. Java was known as the "rice island" and Sumatra, the "gold island."

In addition to Indian Hindu culture, Indian Buddhism was introduced during the same time period. The islands that now comprise Indonesia were not a unified group but, rather, a series of many kingdoms and animistic tribal groups. By the 1300s, an enormously powerful Hindu kingdom had emerged in Java that extended beyond modern Indonesia to as far as Vietnam and the Philippines. It was also during this time that Moslem traders from Persia and Gujarat state in India came to the islands, and slowly Islam took hold, and the Hindu kingdoms gradually retreated as Islam spread through many of the islands.

Marco Polo was the first European to visit Indonesia, arriving in 1292. But it wasn't until the early 1500s that the Portuguese traveled here in search of spices, with the Spaniards following close behind. The Molucca Islands, famous for their cloves, pepper, nutmeg, and other spices, were conquered by the Portuguese and Spanish, and Christianity replaced Islam. The Dutch arrived next, conquering many of the islands and establishing the Dutch East India Company in 1602. They created a lucrative spice business, amassing great wealth for themselves, unfortunately at the expense of the native peoples.

The British established themselves temporarily during the Napoleonic Wars, but the Dutch regained control in 1815. The tumultuous battle for control of Indonesia continued, with the Dutch suppressing rebellions and uprisings and maintaining a strong hold. In 1942, the Japanese overthrew the Dutch and occupied the islands. Indonesian nationalists fought for control of their islands and finally, in 1945, founded the Republic of Indonesia. The infant nation was quickly attacked by both the British and the Dutch, and it wasn't until 1950 that the unitary state of the Republic of Indonesia was restored. Since that time, there has been ongoing political unrest between the islands within the republic, as the struggle for stability continues.

This brief historical overview exemplifies the incredible blend of cultural and religious influences within Indonesia, and the subsequent development of extraordinary art, music, dance, textiles, wood and silver work, and ritual that is the complexly woven tapestry of Indonesia. It also helps to explain the difficulties Indonesia has faced in its struggle to become a united country.

Little wonder that Indonesia has been fought over for centuries: it is a stunningly beautiful country, which still contains one of the largest rain forests in the world, boasts a lush tropical climate, rich alluvial and volcanic soil that easily supports coffee, tea, sugar, spices, tobacco, exotic hardwoods, rubber, palm oil, and a full array of tropical fruits; it has mineral resources in tin and copper; and the islands are surrounded by palm-studded beaches and enviable coral reefs that harbor an abundance of fish. In short, Indonesia has been both blessed and cursed. But ever determined, the Indonesians have three words that sum up both their diversity and their interest in uniting for the common good of all: *adat, budaya,* and *pancasila.*

Adat is an Arabic word that means "tradition." It is used to define the individual cultures of the people of each island. *Budaya* represents the overall culture of the people of Indonesia. *Pancasila* comes from "pancha," the number five in Sanskrit, and means "five pillars." It represents the united ideology and philosophy of Indonesia: belief in God Almighty; belief in a humanity that is fair and balanced; belief in the unity of Indonesia; belief in the leadership of guided democracy of the people; and belief in the right of social justice for all.

In 1817, Professor Casper Georg Carl Reinwardt, a German who had immigrated to Holland, was appointed to the position of director in agricultural business, arts, and sciences on Java and its neighboring islands. He was interested in investigating the plants that were widely used by the Javanese for domestic and medicinal purposes. Professor Reinwardt decided to gather all these plants in a botanic garden now known as Bogor, and then called Buitenzorg (translated as "without a care"). He also collected plants and seeds from other parts of the archipelago, and the botanic garden would eventually make Bogor a center for the promotion of agriculture and horticulture in Indonesia. And it was here that vanilla was first introduced in 1819. Although the plant flowered in 1825, it did not produce beans.

In 1830, Johannes Elias Teysmann, a Dutch gardener, became curator of the Buitenzorg Botanic Garden and spent more than fifty years developing the garden, introducing plants from throughout the archipelago. In 1846, Teysmann first began the systematic cultivation of vanilla in Indonesia, giving birth to "Java vanilla." The vanilla was grown largely in central Java, and was known for its characteristic smoky flavor and its high vanillin content. Teysmann also introduced many other valuable plants to Indonesia, among them quinine, cassava, and palm oil. The Bogor Botanic Gardens are located about 35 miles (60 km) from Jakarta in Western Java; they have remained a popular tourist destination to this day, and most certainly contain healthy specimens of Java vanilla.

Around 1830, Governor Johannes van den Bosch introduced *cultuurstelsel,* a cultivation system in which the native Indonesians were forced to cultivate certain agricultural products for export. These included pepper, cloves, nutmeg, tobacco, sugar, and coffee. Vanilla apparently was not one of the enforced crops, perhaps because it is much more labor-intensive and yields less than these other agricultural products. As it wasn't under production until 1846, it was not a major player in the economy. Its value was considerable, however, and the problem of theft of Java vanilla led to a history of early harvest and poorly dried beans. Nevertheless, it has been used in Europe and the United States since the latter part of nineteenth century as its distinctive flavor adds depth and nuance to extract blends.

JAVA VANILLA

Until the late 1960s, vanilla (or *vanilie,* as it is often called through-out Indonesia) was grown exclusively in Java, in central eastern Java near Temanggung, and later, western Java. Production was never enormous, but vanilla certainly added to the agricultural exports, with an average of about 60 tons of dried vanilla for export by the 1960s.

The dadap tree *(Erythrina lithosperma)* has been the traditional tutor throughout Indonesia. It grows quickly and easily, taking root from a simple cutting of a branch pushed into the rich soil. It grows tall and provides the correct amount of shade for vanilla. Additionally, its spines are ideal for use in pollinating the vanilla flowers, and the leaves of the dadap contain medicinal value.

Two smaller trees, members of the legume family, are occasionally used as well: the lead tree (*Leucaena leucocephala,* also called palang) and the pigeon pea (*Cajanus indicus Spreng,* more familiar as "dhal" or "lentil" and called Lamtoro Gung). These plants provide fodder for livestock and legumes for humans in addition to offering support for vanilla.

As in most countries, the pollination is considered the "marriage" of vanilla. Throughout Indonesia it is known as *kawin, kawinkan,* or *mengawinkan,* which more accurately means "coitus" (yet another example of vanilla's history as a very sexual member of the showy and sexual orchid family).

Because of the ongoing issue of theft, Java vanilla was usually dried on racks over smoldering fires. It's unclear whether or when the technique of blanching the beans was introduced to Java, but it is now a method used throughout the islands and is called *rebus* or *masak,* meaning "to boil" or "to cook."

Initially, the Dutch were in charge of vanilla production in Java and were skilled at curing and drying vanilla. When the Dutch lost political control and left the islands, the Indonesians were faced with the task of curing and drying the vanilla with fairly disastrous results at first. Later, the Chinese became the middlemen in Java, who then cured the vanilla before selling it to exporters. Because vanilla was never a major crop in Java and because it has only been a major cash crop in the rest of Indonesia since the 1970s, the word "vanilla" has not been incorporated into local slang to mean money, nor is there a history of using vanilla in barter as money.

Bali

Vanilla came to Bali sometime between the very late 1960s and 1975, beginning in the Pupuan region. It was so enthusiastically embraced by the local farmers that the expression *bebek bebek* (which, literally translated, means "leading ducks down the rice paddy") was used to describe how the Bali farmers took to vanilla.

Bali's geography and ecology are influenced by a towering range of volcanic peaks that dominate the land, dividing the small island from the east to the west. These volcanoes have created its landforms, periodically regenerated its soils, and helped to produce the dramatic downpours, which provide the island with life-giving water. The Balinese are very in tune with the forces of nature, and the island's many volcanoes, lakes, and springs are considered by them to be sacred. It is due to this range of volcanic mountains that the north side of the island is a bit drier and more conducive to drying the vanilla, whereas the southern part of the island is wetter and better for growing vanilla, cloves, rice, and other staple crops. A violent eruption of Mount Agung in 1963

Vanilla beans "cooking" in a large metal pot.
Note the Hindu offering at the side of the pot.

BALINESE AGRICULTURAL RITUALS

Balinese culture is filled with ritual and celebration, with offerings of food and flowers placed in honor of God and the
elements that touch the people's daily lives. For the farmers
there is a ceremony called *mecaru* to purify the land and to prepare it for planting. Although a lower priest will perform the

ceremony, a high priest chooses the auspicious day, and preparations begin at least one week before the ceremony.

The purification offering is called *baten caru,* and consists of rice, flowers, fruit, the leaf of a young coconut palm, coconut shells, and a Chinese coin. *Mecaru* is held at noon so the "black spirit" can attend. This is important as the intention is to chase the "black spirit" away.

The priest asks God to please protect the land for the farmers and beseeches God's assistant, the black spirit, (naming a particular person or people in particular) to leave the land. This is all said in Sanskrit.

After the priest has offered prayers, the people pray to God, telling Him their plans for planting and asking protection for their business and crops. Next, each individual makes a request in the following manner:

- A prayer offering with no flower
- A prayer with a yellow and white flower, asking for the god of the sun to bring power
- A prayer with a black (although usually blue is used), yellow, and red flower, representing the trinity of the gods Vishnu (black), Siva (yellow), and Brahma (red). "In the trinity, God is stronger. You are kind to people, and now, please, protect me while I plant *vanilie.*"
- A prayer with a flower that is yellow and white or red and white. This prayer is to the ancestors (mother, father, etc.) to, please, be kind and provide protection and assistance.

• Finally, a prayer without a flower: "Thank you, God. I believe you will help me and listen to my needs."

A special mantra will be said at this time but also anytime protection is needed. Again, this is in Sanskrit: "Please, keep me away from somebody who wants to disturb me. Allow only kind people to come to me."

Once the prayers are completed, the priest uses holy water, which has been prepared earlier in the ceremony, by talking with God during the ceremony blessing. Holy water is sipped three times, and rice is eaten in three pieces as a symbol of the trinity.

A small purification ceremony is performed every year, a medium ceremony every five years, and an elaborate ceremony every ten years in honor and protection of the land.

Once the crop has been successfully harvested, there is a success ceremony to give thanks to God. This ceremony is usually held in the house temple or out in the rice fields in a temporary temple created for the ceremony. Holy water is sprinkled on the trees and garden, and prayers and offerings are made. If the sale of the *vanilie* has been lucrative, there may be a family celebration as well, with special foods to mark the day.

There is also a plantation ceremony held every six months. It's not specific to any one crop but for the entire plantation. Known as *tumpek ngatog* (thanks-giving), this is a small family ceremony, often led by a lower village priest.

showered the mountain's upper slopes with ash and debris that slid off as mudflows, killing thousands of people. Refugee farmers from this region of Bali relocated to western Lombok (known as

Sorting vanilla in a warehouse in Indonesia

Lobar), planting cloves, coffee, and cacao, and, after vanilla was introduced to Bali, they, too, began to grow it.

The Bali Hindu culture (which also exists in western Lombok and small areas of some of the other islands) is one of ritual and an honoring of life's many forms and cycles. As a result, more than in any other country where it has arrived as an agricultural crop, vanilla has been included in traditional rituals during its planting, growth, and harvest cycles.

Vanilla continued to be a popular cash crop in Bali until the early 1990s. In fact, in the 1980s, Bali produced two-thirds of Indonesia's vanilla, which, by now, rivaled that of Madagascar in quantity and was a major player in the vanilla industry. But because vanilla is so labor-intensive, and because tourism became a very successful and lucrative industry in the 1980s, the Balinese slowly changed focus, attracted to the new money coming into the island. At the same time, fusarium, a fungal root disease that kills the plants and spreads quickly to healthy plants, struck some of the primary vanilla-growing areas. Once in the soil, fusarium is nearly impossible to stop, and it spread quickly through Bali. When the world prices for vanilla plummeted in 1994, many farmers gave up and returned to growing coffee, pepper, and cloves. Bali now only produces approximately 150 metric tons of green vanilla a year.

SUMATRA, SULAWESI, AND FLORES

In the late 1980s, the Berastagi area (also known as the Karo district) of northern Sumatra and the Lampung province in southern Sumatra became substantial producers of vanilla. The ethnic Karo Batak people, living in the highlands of northern Sumatra, are known for their skill as vanilla growers. Their religion is similar to Bali Hinduism, complete with traditional rituals and blessings of the crops. The quality of their vanilla was exceptional, and their climate allowed for two crops a year. In the late 1980s and early 1990s, they had enormous harvests. Unfortunately, fusarium struck in the mid-1990s, and production dropped to less than 50 metric tons of green vanilla a year. The ethnic Muslim south Sumatrans and Javanese transmigrants also produced significant vanilla crops in the late 1980s and early 1990s.

The tip of northern Sulawesi in the area of Minado, comprised of the ethnic Christian Minahasa and Muslim Gorontalo as well as Muslim transmigrants from Java, was a very productive vanilla region from the late 1980s to the mid-1990s. The terrain is extremely mountainous with rich volcanic soil and extensive lakes and rivers. Crops thrive in both the highlands and lowlands. The Minahasa are a very prosperous people, who hire laborers to manage their well-tended coconut, clove, and banana plantations, and their vanilla was also known for its fine quality. Nutmeg, sago palm, and other cash crops thrive here, and the region is also famous for its beautiful hardwoods, diverse orchid species, and fauna and flora unique to this area of Indonesia.

Then, in the mid-1990s, both Sulawesi and Sumatra were hit hard by the El Niño/La Niña climate shift, causing disastrous droughts and forest fires that covered the islands in a thick brown haze. While all of Indonesia has both a wet and a dry season, these particular islands were devastated by the shifting weather pattern, as the rain did not return for two years. Although some vanilla is still grown here, it is only a small percentage of what was produced ten years earlier.

The newest region to produce vanilla is the island of Flores located in the east Nusa Tenggara province, southeast of Bali and northwest of Australia. Controlled by the Portuguese until the late 1970s, this area is largely Christian. Also known as the Lesser Sundas, the three main islands are Flores, Sumba, and Timor, from which comes the term "Flobamor." The geology of the area is largely an extremely rugged mixture of volcanic and limestone rock, and there is the lowest rainfall in Indonesia here. These islands are among the poorest in Indonesia, with bare subsistence living for many of their inhabitants. But there are pockets of forests, greater rainfall, and therefore the possibility of agriculture, and Flores is now the largest producer of vanilla. Hopefully, vanilla will help to raise the local standard of living.

Throughout Indonesia the vanilla plantations are small, with farmers tending their own individual plots. Because of the ongoing problem of theft, it is common for farmers to build small huts or lean-tos in their fields, and to sleep in the huts, machetes by their sides, from the time when the beans appear until the vanilla is ready to harvest. Usually these huts are within walking distance of their homes in the village. Additionally, families have guard dogs on their property to alert them to potential robbers.

Most vanilla growing and selling is done cooperatively as a way to protect the growers' investment. If everyone harvests at the same time, it's harder to have the beans stolen. And if everyone has beans and one farmer has his stolen, it's easier to track down who committed the act. Until harvest, farmers aren't inclined to leave their property for fear of robbery. By choosing a day when everyone harvests, it's much safer for the entire community.

The other advantage to being part of a cooperative is the fact that, as a group, they are likely to get a better price. Indonesian collectors travel throughout the countryside in big trucks. Farmers gather together as much as 10 to 20 tons of green vanilla, which is then sold as a lot to the collectors. There is a five- to six-day window in order to gather the beans, so collectors are very busy at the time of harvest.

Some of the villages in Flores are very remote. The farmers there are able to cure and dry their own beans, but this is not to their advantage, as they don't have the leverage to get the best prices. As a result, many farmers in the more remote areas take their green beans to the small Chinese stores nearest them and receive store credit for them. The Chinese then sell the beans to the collectors as they come through the region.

The potential for vanilla growing in Indonesia is tremendous. The climate is consistent enough in many of the islands to allow for greater production, cheap labor is readily available, and the people are accustomed to selling their vanilla collectively. It remains to be seen if this potential will be realized in the coming years.

MEDICAL, ARTISTIC, AND CULINARY USES OF VANILLA

It appears that no one has ever tapped into the use of vanilla for medicinal purposes in Indonesia. Given that, except in Java, vanilla is a relatively new crop, this isn't surprising. There is certainly an ample supply of medicinal plants long established in the islands, so there hasn't been the need to explore vanilla's use in curing.

The Balinese growers embraced vanilla in their cuisine as soon as it became a cash crop, and they have used vanilla in a number of unique and creative ways in value-added products for the tourist market. Spas in Bali abound, and vanilla can be found in soaps, candles, lotions, oils, and scrubs. It is also used in aromatherapy. Vanilla bean pieces can also be found adorning a variety of handicrafts, and during the crop's heyday, paintings depicting vanilla were popular. Today it's much more likely that vanilla will be featured in some entrées and in desserts at the lovely tourist hotels along the coastline or in Ubud. If vanilla becomes a major cash crop again, perhaps some day it will earn its place next to Indonesian coffee, where the expression "cup of Java" was coined.

Despite problems with weather and disease, Indonesia has the potential for remaining a major producer in the world vanilla market. During the years of crisis (2000–2004), farmers have responded to the problems of theft and demand by harvesting their vanilla too early, thus compromising quality but protecting themselves by having a crop to sell, albeit of less than premium quality. Desperate extract producers have been willing to purchase vanilla to meet the current U.S. Food and Drug Administration (FDA) requirements with whatever is available. ForesTrade and Tripper, Inc., are two companies that are actively involved in projects in

RICE PUDDING FROM MURNI'S

Murni's Warung is a popular restaurant in Ubud, Bali, that has fed locals and tourists alike since the 1970s. The restaurant itself sits next to a river and is three stories down from street level. It's beautifully decorated and serves excellent food. This is a rice pudding typical of Indonesia that owner Murni serves.

1–1½ cups black glutinous rice
5 cups water
1 pandan leaf (when available)
½ cup thick palm sugar syrup
½ teaspoon salt
½ teaspoon vanilla
1½ cups fresh, thick coconut milk

SOAK RICE IN WATER for 5 minutes and drain. Place water and rice in a heavy pan and bring to a simmer. Add pandan leaf and palm sugar syrup, and simmer over medium heat for about 30 to 40 minutes, or until most of the liquid has evaporated.

ADD SALT AND VANILLA, remove from heat, and allow to cool.

PLACE IN BOWLS, top with coconut milk, and serve at room temperature.

SERVES 10

NOTE: The amount of water used and cooking time required may have to be adjusted according to the quality of the black rice. This dish can be stored in the refrigerator for several days, but do not add the coconut milk until served.

VANILLA IN TRADITIONAL CAKES AND STEAMED DISHES

Jaja abug is a cake made with rice flour, coconut, sugar, salt, vanilla extract, and enough water to bind the ingredients. It is steamed, then cooled, before being cut into small pieces and served on banana leaves. *Jaja abug* is served at all special ceremonies.

Kaliadrem is a fried cake made with rice flour, coconut, water, red sugar (probably unrefined), salt, and vanilla. This is a flat, oval-shaped cake with a hole in the center, similar to a Western doughnut. *Kaliadrem* is usually fried in coconut oil, ideally from the oil of a small coconut called *kelapa sawit* from the island of Kalimantan.

Jaja uli is made from the same ingredients as *kaliadrem* but without sugar. It is a heavy dough that sits overnight and is then thinly sliced. The slices are dried for two days, then placed in a container until ready for use. They are fried until crisp and served at every ceremony. Sometimes colored sugar is sprinkled on the fried cakes.

Tape is a fermented rice dish made from glutenous rice, fermented cooked black rice *(ragi)*, and a small amount of vanilla extract. The ingredients are steamed until cooked, then cooled on a big plate. The rice is packed into banana leaves for two days. *Brum,* a fermented rice liquor, is drained from the *tape* and used as a drink, and the *tape* is served. Another steamed specialty is *apem,* made with rice flour, white sugar, water, and vanilla.

In addition to flavoring baked and steamed foods, vanilla is occasionally added to *sambals,* a fiery hot condiment that is served with meals. *Sambals* may contain fruits or vegetables, and are sometimes sweetened, but always contain chilies.

Indonesia, especially in the more remote regions, working with small farmers to develop vanilla plantations and to improve quality. Because of their experience with, and the tradition of, growing vanilla that began well over one hundred years ago, it will be interesting to see how Indonesia fares in the years to come.

RÉUNION

Réunion was the first island where vanilla was grown in the Indian Ocean. With Albius's discovery of artificial pollination, Réunion was in the perfect position to become a major producer. Vanilla replaced sugar as a primary crop in the 1850s and was such an important commodity that, more than 150 years later, vanilla from the Indian Ocean is still referred to as Bourbon vanilla, in honor of the country's brief legacy as the Île de Bourbon.

It was here in Réunion in the late nineteenth century that the process of dipping the newly harvested vanilla beans into near-boiling water was first developed. A quicker and, in some ways, more efficient method of stopping fermentation than oven curing or sun curing, this technique of "cooking" the vanilla quickly spread to Madagascar and the Comoro Islands, then on to Indonesia. In fact, in much of the world, this is the most commonly used curing process.

Réunion provided another term in vanilla jargon: canary tail *(queue de serin)*, which describes the best stage for harvesting the beans. The fruit is still green, but the base is canary yellow. Harvesting beans at this stage produces the finest-quality beans, which will have a full, rich aroma when dried. The beans were—and still are—harvested one at a time for peak quality.

Réunion was also the staging ground for many early experiments to determine the best density for planting vanilla, the best tutor trees (Réunion is one of the few places in the world that uses the Dracaena tree as a tutor), and the best methods of dealing with fungus and rot, two problems that plague vanilla plantations everywhere. There is still a French agricultural station on Réunion where the ongoing study of vanilla diseases and effective growing techniques continues into the present.

Unfortunately, the vagaries of nature have often taken precedence over the most carefully considered plans. While Réunion excelled in vanilla production for well over one hundred years, it is an island struck frequently with hurricanes. Fusarium has also swept through the plantations at various times, most recently in the late 1980s. Additionally, during the French colonial period, labor costs exceeded those of Madagascar and the Comoro Islands. While production of vanilla will very likely never die out completely, other crops have replaced it, just as vanilla replaced sugar.

Regardless, Réunion has celebrated its history as a major Indian Ocean producer with a small vanilla museum showing early pictures of the Bourbon vanilla trade, and vanilla spiced rum is an island specialty. Because Réunion has remained a French department, much of the current production of roughly 5 tons yearly goes directly to Grasse, the center of the famous French perfume industry.

MADAGASCAR

Madagascar, also known as "the great red island," is perhaps the most distinctly unique country in the world. It is filled with remarkable fauna and flora found nowhere else, and boasts a colorful history and gracious, welcoming people. That it also happens to be the largest producer of vanilla worldwide only adds to its fascinating and idiosyncratic character.

Located 250 miles (400 km) across the Mozambique Channel from southern Africa, Madagascar was one of the first landmasses to break away from mainland Africa, a circumstance occurring approximately 70 million years ago. For the past 30 million years it has remained cut off by the sea from the rest of the world. As a result, it is often considered a mini-continent. And due to the unique way that its plants and animals have evolved, it has created a remarkable botanical treasure, with eight out of ten plant species found on the island growing nowhere else but Madagascar, as well as lemurs and other animals and birds unique to the island.

Despite its early separation from Africa, Madagascar was one of the later areas to be colonized by humans. The first Malagasy (from the French Malagache for the inhabitants) were Malay-Polynesians who traveled across the Indian Ocean from Indonesia and Southeast Asia, roughly 1,500 to 2,000 years ago. Over time, others arrived—Africans, Arab and Portuguese traders, and British and French colonials who intermarried with the original settlers— eventually creating the eighteen clans, or tribes, of Madagascar. The early Malagasy brought with them the food crops of Southeast Asia, with rice grown in the style of the Asian-style terraces of their countries of origin, and Zebu cattle as the foundation of their diet. Influences from the Arabic Muslim tradition in the Comoro Islands and the east coast of Africa, as well as traditions from later immigrants, can be found, especially on the eastern coast of Madagascar.

Madagascar is the fourth largest island in the world, nearly 1,000 miles in length (1,600 km) and 350 miles (560 km) across at its widest point. Unlike the other Indian Ocean islands, it is not volcanic in origin, but rather crystalline bedrock everywhere but the west coast, which is sedimentary and covered with red laterite sandstone. Over the years of settlement, deforestation, and slash-and-burn agriculture, tremendous erosion has occurred. The eroded red soil eventually joins the rivers, creating great blood-stained waterways that eventually flow into the ocean, coloring the sea an intense red. If you're flying over Madagascar, it is easy to understand why it is known as "the great red island."

Vanilla is grown along the northeast coast of Madagascar in a tropical rain forest that extends around the northern tip of the island and is home to about 30 percent of the Malagasy. Despite the fact that each of Madagascar's tribes has its own customs and identity, and although the geography is varied, roads are limited and minimal outside the cities, and many areas are quite isolated. Also the Malagasy are united in a shared language, which is a mixture of the Indonesian/Polynesian language family, with Bantu, Arabic, French, English, and Sanskrit words introduced over the years.

They are also united in their spiritual belief in Zanahary, the creator, and their deep respect for their ancestors. The entire island is *tany masina*, sacred ground that acts as a vessel for holding all the ancestral bodies of the Malagasy. Christianity, which is practiced by about 50 percent of the Malagasy, is not in conflict with traditional beliefs.

Madagascar was appealing to early visitors not so much for its natural resources as for its location along the spice route. Arab trading posts were established around the tenth century along the northwest coast. The Portuguese arrived in the early sixteenth century, but ultimately settled along the African mainland. While other groups drifted in and out of Madagascar's coastal ports, it was during the early fifteenth century that the English became regular visitors, having recently established the East India Company.

In 1810, the British seized Mauritius from the French, and Radama I became king of the Merina, Madagascar's ruling clan until French colonial occupation in 1896. Over the years, the British and French continued to struggle for control of Madagascar, with the French finally wresting the island in 1896 in a political buy off between the two colonial powers. The French established a stronghold on the island and abolished the Malagasy monarchy. An efficient colonial administration was established, roads and railroads were built, and French was imposed as the primary language.

The Malagasy felt betrayed by the British, and the French did too little too late to win the support of the Malagasy, creating major internal tensions. By the late 1920s, the Malagasy Nationalist Movement focused on the goal of freedom and independence, a struggle that flared into a violent armed rebellion in 1947. In 1960, the Independent Malagasy Republic was formed, led by Phillibert Tsiranana, a Malagasy with strong ties to the French. In the late 1960s the economy stagnated, and by 1975 the French had pulled out of Madagascar. In 1972, striking students were joined by civil servants and peasants, demanding a government that better represented them. In 1975, Marxist Didier Ratsiraka came into power and, breaking off relations with France and nationalizing French enterprises, produced a charter of the Malagasy Socialist Revolution and renamed the country the Democratic Republic of Madagascar. However, without financial assistance to support the infrastructure and power struggles continually waged between superpowers for control of the African continent (including Madagascar) during the cold war, Madagascar has suffered tremendously, becoming one of the poorer countries in Africa despite its wealth of resources and valuable export crops such as vanilla. In 2002, there was a power struggle for the presidency, eventually won by President-elect Marc Ravalomanana. At the time of publication of this book, the government appears to be stable.

VANILLA IN MADAGASCAR

As early as the mid-eighteenth century, French botanists transported aromatic and medicinal plants between Madagascar, the Comoro Islands, and Réunion and Mauritius in the Bourbon Islands. Ylang-ylang, frangipani, patchouli, lemongrass, basil, cloves, pepper, and ginger became economically valuable agricultural crops to sell to Europe. Frangipani and ylang-ylang were grown specifically as aromatic oils for the French perfume industry. But it was vanilla, introduced to the east coast of Madagascar in 1840, that eventually became its most famous and profitable export, bringing notoriety to the great red island as the world's largest producer of the orchid of commerce.

When vanilla was introduced to Madagascar just before Albius discovered artificial pollination, it was planted in the tropical rain forests along the northeastern coast, but it was not a major commodity until the late 1890s when French occupation began. Once the French set up the industry, the crop was planted along most of the eastern coastline wherever there were French settlements. Combined with vanilla from the plantations of Mauritius and Réunion, 80 percent of the world's vanilla came from the Indian Ocean islands by the turn of the twentieth century. By 1924, Madagascar was exporting three hundred tons of vanilla, and by 1929 more than one thousand tons, exporting 80 percent of the world's vanilla from its shores alone. In fact, the town of Antalaha, located in the northeastern area where there's now a vanilla research station and where most of the island's vanilla is currently grown, was known early on as the "mecca of vanilla."

The eastern coast of Madagascar is a heavily forested, humid, and wet region. The lush tropical climate supports an enormous number of tree-dwelling orchids and many varieties of ferns, and the air is rich with frangipani, wild gladiolus, hibiscus, and, in the Nosy Be region in the northwest, ylang-ylang. The climate is ideal for growing vanilla, even with a relatively dry two-month period when the flowers are pollinated. The only drawback in this otherwise vanilla paradise is its susceptibility to cyclones, which can be fierce and deadly.

Initially, the majority of the vanilla was produced on small family plantations overseen by French and Creole colonists in eastern Madagascar. Their workers were indentured servants supplied by the French colonial administration. When slavery was outlawed in Madagascar in 1896, Malagasy workers were conscripted to work the plantations. The Malagasy had neither the interest nor motivation to work for the French on their plantations.

In traditional coastal culture, the forest provided all that was needed. Land was cleared, using slash-and-burn techniques, then terraced and planted with rice. Hard labor and money were anathema to local values of friendship and community. The workers' initial involvement in the vanilla industry was not by choice but through force.

The French had absolute control of the market, sending the vanilla to France where it was sold to the European market. Families of French and European heritage set up offices in the United States, and Madagascar vanilla came on to the American marketplace in the early years of the twentieth century. However, the vanilla had to be purchased through Europe, not directly from the Indian Ocean, until the 1930s.

The Betsimisaraka people of northeastern Madagascar have been the primary cultivators of the vanilla, first for the French and later on their own. The Betsimisaraka were originally a diverse group of clans who had immigrated to the eastern coast of Madagascar from Melanesia and mainland Africa. During the heyday of piracy, buccaneers and mercenaries from Britain, Europe, and the Americas came to the region, creating the Zana-Malata (mulatto offspring of foreign pirates and Malagasy women). In the early 1700s, Ratsimilaho, the son of an English pirate and Malagasy ruler, Queen Antavaratra Rahena, created a unified state, bringing together the various clans and naming the tribe Betsimisaraka ("those who stand together" or "the inseparable many"). The Sakalava ("those from the long valleys"), Antakarana ("those from the cliffs"), and Antaimoro ("those from the coast") tribes have also grown vanilla, especially when the vanilla-growing region was more expansive. Workers planted, cultivated, pollinated, and harvested the green vanilla and labored in the curing and dry-

VANILLA TATTOOS

Because of vanilla's intrinsic value, and because robbery has always been an issue, the French in Madagascar created an innovative method of protecting their vanilla crops. A wooden tool with thin nails affixed into the flat end was used to tattoo each bean roughly two weeks before harvest. Letters, numbers, and symbols were designed so that each plantation had its own unique branding. The brand was affixed into the green beans well enough so that even after curing and drying it was easy to determine where the beans had come from. This method of tattooing the beans has continued to the present, though when vanilla's value dropped dramatically in the mid-1990s, most farmers didn't bother to brand their beans. As most vanilla is now grown only on very small plantations, it's common to see the initials—and sometimes the name—of the growers branded on the beans rather than a tattoo that represents a large family enterprise.

ing houses. All curing and drying was overseen by the French or the Chinese, who came to Madagascar to build the railroads during the French colonial period, and who later became shopkeepers and merchants.

THE EXPORT MARKET

Beginning with World War I and through the Great Depression, French involvement in Madagascar's plantation system shifted.

*Tattooed vanilla beans from Madagascar.
The concept of tattooing beans was first
developed during the French colonial period
in Madagascar. Each bean is branded with
a unique design, initials, or the name of
the grower while the green beans are
on the vine. This technique is used to
later identify stolen beans.*

The Malagasy continued to cultivate vanilla on small family plots, individually or as an extended family, but with fewer French families overseeing production. In the 1930s, Robusta coffee became a major export, eventually replacing vanilla in some coastal areas. French traders still controlled the Malagasy market, exporting the vanilla to Bordeaux and Marseille, where it was then sold for transshipment to the United States and Europe, but the traders' involvement with cultivation was slowly phased out.

Louis Abel Champon was the first person to break the French monopoly of the Madagascar vanilla trade. He had come to the United States from Marseille in 1924 as an agent for his uncle whose company sold herbs, spices, and crude drugs. He left his

Women working with the vanilla beans in Madagascar

uncle's firm and went into business on his own in 1930 as
L. A. Champon and Company, adding essential oils and vanilla
beans to his line of spices and herbs. His bold move to purchase directly from Malagasy French and Chinese exporters so infuriated
the French brokers that he was told that if he dared to show his
face again in France, he would never return alive to the United
States. However, his business was very successful, and he handled
a substantial percentage of the imports from the Indian Ocean up
until World War II, selling directly to the dozen importers who
purchased Indian Ocean vanilla. Interestingly, he never once went

to the Indian Ocean islands, nor did he know most of the exporters except through correspondence and cable communication. The company is still active today, run next by his son Bernard, and now by his son Michael, both of whom have visited Madagascar regularly.

Dammann and Company, Inc., opened its doors in the United States in 1935. Pierre Dammann came from a family in Marseille, which had been in the vanilla industry in Europe for years and had a subsidiary company in Toamasina (Tamatave). By moving to the United States, he effectively made vanilla purchases for American manufacturers seeking Madagascar beans much easier.

A third company, Zink & Triest, opened in Philadelphia in 1930. Bill Triest had been a tennis professional, and Jack Zink was the son of one of Bill's earlier partners. Both men came from the New York area and had families that had been involved in the flavor business. The two set up business in Philadelphia and relied heavily on Louis Champon for their beans. They competed with McCormick to sell vanilla beans to extract manufacturers.

During World War II, Indian Ocean vanilla could not be shipped to Europe or the United States, initially because of the Allied blockade and later because of an acute shortage of shipping space. When transcontinental shipping resumed, businesses that cured and dried the local vanilla made direct connections with the United States. The French government supported this shift as the stock accumulated in Madagascar had reached 1,600 tons and there was reason for concern about the stability of the market.

The French Malagasy government, in an effort to control prices, set a minimum of $17 a kilo ($7.70 per pound) for top-grade beans; the U.S. importers responded by placing a virtual embargo on the country's vanilla. This continued until May of 1949 when price control was abolished and six hundred tons of low-quality beans were burned by the government as a precaution against price collapse.

The government attempted to stabilize the vanilla market with varying degrees of success during the 1950s. In 1954, the Station de la Vanille, part of the Institut de Recherches Agronomiques, was established in Antalaha to research the most effective methods for producing vanilla. In the early 1960s, the government established another aggressive campaign to control prices, and the U.S. importers again boycotted the country's vanilla, preferring to work directly with the exporters, and eventually the government backed down.

In 1964, the Vanilla Alliance (Unavanille) was formed, along with a rigorous system of production control involving export quotas and fixed prices. After the 1964 Saint-Denis conference, Réunion and the Comoros followed Madagascar in submitting their vanilla marketing to more rigorous control and in organizing cooperative systems and price-stabilization funds. Subsequent conferences convened by the government of Madagascar brought together representatives of vanilla planters, trades, and consumers.

Another reorganization occurred in 1966 with an interprofessional group consisting of all vanilla planters, processors, and exporters. Membership was to be compulsory and was to be governed by representatives of government ministries. The main objective of this tactic was to form insurance against crop failure, but annual stock fluctuations affected prices, and farmers were so isolated that it was impossible to organize all of them either as effective communal associations or for compulsory membership in a government-run program. Eventually, the government instated an export tax on all vanilla leaving the island, with the intention of using the money to benefit the country. While this would have been helpful to everyone, the lack of a solid infrastructure and mismanagement of funds meant that essentially nothing of value to the country was accomplished. Despite the riches gained from vanilla by middlemen and traders purchasing for resale, native growers barely survived on their income from green vanilla. The traditional forest was gone, and most families either grew or worked on plantations where cloves, cinnamon, rice, pepper, or lychee nuts were cultivated in order to supplement their income.

VANILLA GROWING IN SAVA

After the French left Madagascar in the mid-1970s, vanilla has been grown nearly entirely by local families. The majority of the island's vanilla grows in the northeastern corner of Madagascar in an area known as SAVA for the local cities of Sambava, Antalaha, Vohemar, and Andapa. Some vanilla is grown near the towns of Fenerive and Toamasina (Tamatave), then tapers off after Vatomandry and Mahanoro, where cloves, coffee, and rice are the primary crops. Vanilla is also produced on the island of Nosy Be and the neighboring mainland coast of northwest Madagascar near Ambanja and Ambilobe.

Vanilla growers and their families live in small hamlets of fewer than two hundred people. Village life is simple yet demanding. Roads are little more than rough tracks that have not had major improvements made for decades. When cyclones hit the island, the roads are often completely washed out, and only minimally repaired. People travel to the cities either by walking or traveling on trucks or small buses. There is neither electricity nor running water outside the bigger cities, and there are no schools or hospitals. In the cities and larger towns, children have access to education, but the majority of the people who live in the countryside are illiterate. Even in the cities, many families can't afford the fees to send their children to school. This critical lack of essential tools for navigating in the modern world has helped to keep traditional

Malagasy culture intact, something that many people in transitional cultures have lost. At the same time, it has jeopardized their ability to represent themselves effectively or to negotiate a more equitable lifestyle for themselves and their families.

The cycle of vanilla growing in SAVA begins with the spring planting of vines in September and October (Southern Hemisphere). Most plantations are semi-wild, with the older plantations having a variety of wild tutors. New plantations use glyricidia or pigeon peas (lentils) as tutors as both are members of the nitrogen-rich legume family and help to feed the soil. Composted plant material is built up around the tutors and vanilla vines to help hold in moisture and to give the vines additional nutrients.

Pollination coincides with the dry season when the fruit is most likely to "set." Pollination is usually done by the women, though in small families or larger plantations, men and children may also pollinate the flowers. In Madagascar, as in the rest of the vanilla-growing world, this process is known as *la fécundation* or *le mariage de la vanille*, or the "marriage of the vanilla." A more common local expression is "We are going to do flowers," often called out as a greeting as workers walk to their fields. It is also common for families to offer sacrifices of chickens, oxen and cattle, honey, chalk, and beeswax when asking ancestors for favors. Requesting an abundant crop falls into the realm of favors the ancestors can bestow.

Harvest times vary along the coast. Andapa, roughly 62 miles (100 km) northwest of Antalaha, was the area where the majority of vanilla was grown in the 1950s and is harvested between August and October. Vohemar harvests its vanilla between May and July; Antalaha, Maroantsetra, and Mananara-Nord harvest between June and September; and Sambava harvests between May and September. In Madagascar, vanilla is harvested by ripeness to ensure.

*A Malagasy man dumping "cooked"
beans into the "sweating" box*

that the quality of the vanilla will be consistent. This is one of the
reasons why theft is an ongoing problem along the coast, and it requires vigilance on the part of the families to make certain their
vanilla remains on the vines until it's ripe. It's also more labor-
intensive as each bean is checked daily for ripeness.

Until the period between the late 1980s and the mid-1990s,
farmers were paid at the time of harvest when they sold their green
beans to the collectors who then began the labor-intensive processing of the beans. The collectors are the buyers or agents for
the curing houses. The Chinese were the traditional collectors

who traveled in cars and small vans throughout the SAVA region, purchasing the green beans from the farmers and bringing them to the curing houses. To keep the green vanilla from spoiling, the collectors usually began the curing process, then delivered the partially cured vanilla, known as *vrac*, to the export houses where the drying, conditioning, and processing were completed.

Nowadays, most producers know the basics for curing beans. This shift occurred as the farmers realized they could get better prices for their vanilla while at the same time achieving greater involvement in the industry. The entire family harvests the beans and assists in the initial curing, which may be as simple as sun drying or as complex as using the Indian Ocean method of "killing" or "cooking" the beans in hot water, then beginning the sun-drying process. Farmers may sell their *vrac* directly to exporters but most often sell to the collectors. The collectors then classify the beans, continue the drying process, and bring the vanilla to the exporters either by truck or by air shipment to Antalaha.

Originally, Indian Ocean vanilla traveled to Europe and the United States on ships from the deep harbor port in Toamasina (Tamatave). As Antalaha has an airport, most vanilla is sent overseas by air. Not only has air transport shortened the process from harvest to delivery by several weeks, it has also helped to eliminate the problem of the beans' getting moldy from less than optimal conditions en route.

In the vanilla-growing region, homes are built out of bamboo and wood with palm thatch roofs, though with the recent influx of money as vanilla has become more valuable, tin roofs have begun to replace thatch. Rice is still the foundation of the diet, which is supplemented with chicken, beef, pork, tropical fruits, and some vegetables. Along the coasts, fish and seafood are also eaten, but rice is the mainstay, with even a rice-water tea prepared from the

TRADITIONAL INDIAN OCEAN CURING AND DRYING PROCESS

Tons of green vanilla or *vrac* come into the curing houses at harvest time, as 5 to 6 tons of green beans will eventually be reduced to 1 ton of cured, dried, and conditioned vanilla. Since Madagascar produces hundreds of tons of vanilla on average, the curing houses are *very* busy during the harvest season, employing thousands of Malagasy workers.

The beans are first sorted according to maturity and size with *vrac* and split and cut beans placed in separate categories. Batches of green beans weighing 25 to 30 kilos are loaded into open-work cylindrical baskets which are then plunged into containers full of hot water heated to 63°C to 65°C (145°F to 149°F). These are then placed over a wood fire or propane heat. Higher-quality beans are immersed for two to three minutes, while smaller beans and splits are treated for less than two minutes. The warm beans are rapidly drained, wrapped in dark cotton cloth, and placed in a cloth-lined "sweating" box. After twenty-four hours, the beans are removed and inspected to separate any that have not been properly "killed."

The beans will next be carried outside to a plot of dry, easily drained ground, away from dust contamination, where they begin sun drying. The beans are spread out on dark cloths resting on raised, slatted platforms, constructed from bamboo or tables built specifically for drying the beans. After the beans rest in the sun for approximately an hour, the edges of the cloth are placed over them, and the beans are then left for an additional two hours in the sun before they are rolled up in blankets and taken indoors. This is done for six to eight days until the beans become quite supple. During rainy periods the beans will either be kept inside with wood-burning fires to warm them or hot air blown on them to continue the drying process.

The third stage in preparing the beans involves slow drying in the shade for a period of two to three months. The beans are spread on racks, mounted on supports and spaced 12 centimeters (nearly 5 inches) apart in a well-ventilated room. During this slow drying, the beans are sorted regularly; as the beans become ready, they are removed for conditioning.

Conditioning takes about three months. Beans ready for conditioning are again sorted, and each bean is straightened by drawing it through the fingers. This technique spreads the volatile oils that give the beans their characteristic luster. The beans are next tied into bundles of about fifty with black string or raffia.

Vrac will be processed according to its level of readiness, which usually means they will need to go through the shade-drying period, but sometimes they are ready for conditioning. These beans will be sorted according to readiness.

The bundled beans are next placed in tin boxes (cardboard has replaced tin in some export houses) that are lined with waxed or parchment paper. The tin boxes are weighed for uniformity, then loaded into larger boxes for shipment. The entire process of preparing the beans takes six to eight months. Given that it took up to three years for the first vanilla flowers to appear, the beans were on the vines for nine months, and another eight months were spent in the curing and drying process

before shipment, the time from planting to readiness for sale to-
tals nearly five years. That vanilla isn't more expensive, even
during periods of ample harvests, is quite remarkable.

crusty remains in cooking pots. The Malagasy have a long history
of using medicinal herbs for curing illness, and the *ombiasa*, or
healers, are called on when herbs alone are not enough.

Vanilla growers have never incorporated vanilla into their diet
as a flavor nor have they used it in medicine as it has always been
grown as a cash crop. They also have never known how it could be
used. Given that it was grown for the French colonial settlers as a
cash crop for at least thirty-five years before the Malagasy managed cultivation by themselves, there was no precedent for them to
follow for using vanilla. After the French left Madagascar, tourism
has been limited to a few select coastal areas and to the extraordinary wildlife reserves. As a result, vanilla is rarely seen in the
weekly or daily markets (called *ʒoma*), and it has never been included in art or textile design as is true in other parts of the world
where it is grown.

It is only in the larger cities or at the tourist hotels in the protected wildlife reserves that vanilla has been used in cuisine and
beverages. Malagasy who have lived or studied abroad, or who
have assimilated with the French, flavor their rum *(roma)* with
vanilla, honey, sugar, or lemon, which is then served on its own or
in punches. The French, ever innovative and resourceful with local products, have brought vanilla to the level of *haute cuisine*,
commonly using it in savory dishes as well as the more traditional
baked goods and sweets.

Economic Impact of Vanilla in Madagascar

Vanilla has been a major export from Madagascar for so long and is so synonymous with the Indian Ocean islands that most people assume it has always been grown there. It has had a major effect on Madagascar's income from agricultural exports, with everyone *but* the producers benefiting from it. The majority of the money has been made by the business owners of the curing and drying facilities, the exporters, the European and American buyers, and the government. The farmers have consistently assumed the greatest risk yet they have typically received less than 8 percent of the sales from exported vanilla. While the government theoretically was to apply the money earned from export taxes toward improving the country's infrastructure, this didn't happen. In fact, the farmers who live in the vanilla-growing region have been among the poorest in the country despite their living in the area with the greatest natural resources.

Many farmers have traded their vanilla to Chinese and Indian middlemen for food or supplies, and most recently for bicycles, gold jewelry, and other novelties in lieu of cash. Vanilla is known as "green gold" and has even found its way into slang in the same way "bread" has become slang for money in Western cultures. Its intrinsic value is represented on currency and stamps. But until the vanilla shortage of 1999, farmers barely managed to subsist by supplementing their income with other cash crops or by buying on credit against the next season.

For the past four years many farmers have made more money than they ever imagined. Vanilla's soaring value hasn't touched all farmers in Madagascar, but word traveled fast and farmers became

An entrée similar to this is served at a wildlife reserve in eastern Madagascar.

MILK AND VANILLA BEAN POACHED VEAL WITH VANILLA BEAN RICE AND GREEN PAPAYA FRUIT SALAD

Courtesy of chef Nicci Tripp,
Theo's Restaurant, Soquel, California

2 vanilla beans, split lengthwise

4 cups whole milk

1 onion, roughly chopped

1 carrot, roughly chopped

1 tablespoon kosher salt

2 teaspoons black pepper

2 star anise

2 cinnamon sticks

1½–2 lbs veal tenderloin

SCRAPE VANILLA BEAN SEEDS INTO MILK, then combine the balance of ingredients in a bowl, including vanilla pods, and refrigerate overnight.

PREHEAT OVEN TO 350°F. Place veal in roasting pan, add milk and spices, and oven-poach until the veal reaches an internal temperature of at least 170°F, about 25 to 30 minutes.

VANILLA BEAN RICE

1 shallot, minced
1 tablespoon butter
1 vanilla bean, scraped
1 cup jasmine rice
2 cups chicken stock
salt to taste

SAUTÉ THE SHALLOT AND BUTTER until mixture is translucent. Add the vanilla bean and rice.

SAUTÉ UNTIL RICE IS WELL COATED, then add the chicken stock.

COVER AND LET SIMMER on very low heat until liquid is absorbed, about 20 to 25 minutes.

SEASON WITH SALT and keep warm.

VANILLA BEAN JUS

1 teaspoon minced ginger
1 vanilla bean, scraped
1 12-oz can coconut milk
1 tablespoon cornstarch
2 tablespoons water

IN A SAUCEPAN, add ginger, vanilla, and coconut milk and reduce by one-fourth. Add the cornstarch and water to the hot liquid, and mix to thicken.

TO ASSEMBLE
Serve Vanilla Bean Rice at the center of four plates.
Slice the veal and arrange on top of the rice.
Drizzle the Vanilla Bean Jus around the veal and rice.
Top with the Green Papaya Fruit Salad.

SERVES 4

GREEN PAPAYA FRUIT SALAD

1 cup shredded green papaya
1 cup diced pineapple
1 cup diced mango
1 cup diced lychee, canned or fresh
1 tablespoon minced ginger
¼ cup chopped scallion
2 tablespoons olive oil

IN A BOWL, lightly toss the fruits, ginger, and scallion. Add the olive oil and let marinate in refrigerator for 1 hour.

Vanilla-Fragranced Duckling, Madagascar Style

Courtesy of chef Deane Bussiere,
Shadowbrook Restaurant, Capitola, California

1 whole fresh duckling
1 tablespoon kosher salt
1 teaspoon ground white pepper
½ yellow jumbo onion, split into quarters
1 orange, cut into four wedges
2 vanilla beans, split lengthwise
2 cups duck or chicken stock

PREHEAT OVEN to 500°F. Rinse the duckling inside and out, removing the neck, heart, gizzard, and liver. Place the "innards" in the bottom of a roasting pan.

SEASON THE DUCKLING with salt and pepper inside and out. Place onion pieces in the duck cavity. Squeeze juice of the orange over the duckling, then put rinds in duck cavity. With a thin knife, cut a slit on each side of the breast and in each leg/thigh, and insert vanilla-bean halves. Put duckling on top of "innards" in roasting pan.

ROAST DUCKLING for 15 minutes at 500°F, then lower oven to 350°F and roast until a thermometer inserted into the duckling registers 165°F. Remove from oven and allow to cool for 30 minutes.

Remove and discard onion and orange rinds. Using a cleaver, remove the backbone of duck by standing it on its neck end and cutting down each side of the backbone. Remove the rib cage and hip bones by slipping your fingertips around them, then lifting up and twisting the bones off the meat. The wing and leg bones remain.

Set innards aside and defat the roasting pan, then deglaze the pan with the duck or chicken stock. Bring stock to a boil, adding bones and innards, and reduce stock to 1 cup. Remove the two half-beans from the legs of the duckling and add to the cup of reduced stock, then reduce again to ½ cup.

Reheat the two duck halves in oven at 400°F for 12 minutes, until hot and the skin is crisp. Place on two hot serving plates with the breast halves still pierced with the vanilla bean halves. Ladle the hot sauce (with the vanilla bean pieces) over the duck breasts.

Serve with green vegetables and jasmine rice.

Serves 2

more savvy about trading their green gold for cash. Ironically, the influx of money in a culture where money was not traditionally a primary objective, and where the concept of expendable cash has never been an option, has caused problems of its own. Without the concept of saving money for lean times, money is spent quickly and not necessarily on things of enduring value to the well-being of the family.

Now that vanilla has been sold for more than $500 a kilo ($230 per pound) to American and European buyers, everyone is planting vanilla, even in areas where it hasn't been grown since the 1930s. Of course, high-volume production means prices will drop, and prices were poised to drop dramatically when the record 2004 harvest of 1,200 tons of dried vanilla would hit the market at the end of the year. But nature has a strange sense of humor. On March 7, 2004, a category-five cyclone, Gafilo, slammed into the "vanilla triangle" of northeast Madagascar, with winds of up to 160 miles an hour and torrential rainfall. The town of Antalaha was nearly destroyed, and estimates report that more than 100,000 people were left homeless. The cyclone destroyed a large part of the vanilla crop on the northeast side of the island, then passed across to the northwest, destroying everything in its path before moving out into the Mozambique Channel, where it stalled for a day before returning as a category-one cyclone and sweeping across the southern part of the island.

Three of the four Comoro Islands also were hard-hit by the cyclone. In one respect, the farmers were lucky: only part of the crop was destroyed. Windfalls were gathered and sold as low-grade filler. Apparently, the dried beans will amount to 1,000 tons—vanilla that will be extremely valuable to farmers and curing houses alike as they rebuild their homes and lives once again.

THE COMORO ISLANDS

The Comoro Islands were, like the Seychelles, Mauritius, and Réunion, high-volume producers of vanilla during the nineteenth and twentieth centuries. In fact, while the Comoros were at one time second only to Madagascar in production, their crops were usually combined with Madagascar vanilla before shipment to Europe or the United States.

The Comoro Islands are situated at the north end of the Mozambique Channel, 310 miles (500 km) north of Madagascar. The archipelago stretches more than 186 miles (300 km) from north to south and is volcanic in origin, with Mayotte the earliest of the islands and Grand Comore the most recent and the largest. Geographically they are Grand Comore, Andjouan, Moheli, and Mayotte, with the capital city Moroni situated on the west coast of Grand Comore. However, Mayotte elected to remain a French protectorate, at the time of independence; consequently, politically it is not part of the Comoros.

The Comoro Islands were settled roughly at the same time as Madagascar, most probably by Malay-Polynesian travelers. Seafaring Arab traders called it *Djazair al Qamar* (Islands of the Moon), which, over the years, slowly evolved into "Comoro." Arabs who were racially mixed with coastal Africans came later and settled in the islands. The language of the islands is a cross between Arabic and Bantu, not unlike modern Swahili, and is even called Swahili though the two languages are not the same.

The Arabic merchants had a strong influence in the Comoro Islands, introducing Islam, setting up trading centers, and later overseeing the slave trade. The islands have been fought over for centuries, and internal strife has been more common than not. The French had their sights set on the Comoros as they struggled with the British for dominance of the Indian Ocean trade and finally gained full control of the islands in the 1880s. It wasn't until 1975 that the Comoro Islands became independent of France.

The French occupation of the Comoro Islands is similar to that of Madagascar and the Bourbon Islands. The hot, humid climate lent itself well to establishing botanicals for the perfume industry and cash crops for the European market. The French settlers set up vanilla plantations at about the same time as Madagascar did, and used the local Comorians as laborers. Just as in Madagascar, Comorian families eventually took over vanilla cultivation on small family plantations, especially on Grand Comore where there was abundant, fertile land and where 70 percent of the Comoro vanilla was grown. Up until the 1960s, vanilla was cured by Europeans, then taken to Madagascar where it was exported abroad. Unfortunately, just as in Madagascar, the Comoro Islands are all situated in the cyclone belt and every four years or so one or more islands is hit.

Since the Comoro Islands became independent from France, there have been periods of political unrest over leadership of the islands. The Comoros were also caught in the cold-war power struggle that impacted Madagascar. During part of the 1990s, American traders were unable to purchase vanilla from the islands because of political unrest. Shortly thereafter, vanilla prices dropped dramatically. As a result, farmers either let their vanilla go fallow or planted other crops, so there was a period in the late 1990s when vanilla production was minimal. Since the cyclone of 2000 and the escalation of prices, growers, especially on Grand Comore, have again started cultivating vanilla. While the quality of Comoro vanilla is consistently good, its selling price tends to be higher than that of other Indian Ocean countries, putting Comorians at some disadvantage in the world marketplace. Regardless, as long as the Comoro Islands produce vanilla, they will likely have interested buyers.

PUERTO RICO
AND THE CARIBBEAN

There was considerable talk of introducing vanilla cultivation in Puerto Rico and Hawaii after their annexation to the United States in 1898. Before 1909, plants were brought to Puerto Rico from Mexico, at which time more were brought to the U.S. Department of Agriculture in Puerto Rico from the U.S. Plant Introductory Garden in Coconut Grove, Florida. A small tropical agricultural research station developed in Mayaguez. The goal was to make it at least a minor crop for highland farmers, and indeed vanilla became a useful crop for local growers. Then devastating hurricanes in 1828 and 1932 ruined the island's coffee, vanilla, and fruit farms. Restrictions on sugar production and one-crop farming further limited income, so that by 1934 some 75 percent of the entire population of Puerto Rico was directly or indirectly affected by unemployment.

In 1935, the Puerto Rico Reconstruction Administration (PRRA) was established to create new standards of living for Puerto Ricans by correcting the problems of agricultural depression. In the municipalities of Lares and Adjuntas, in the interior of the island, the PRRA purchased 1,645 acres of land where two hundred small farmers began to produce coffee, vanilla, tung oil, perfume plants, and rare fruits and vegetables. Thousands of *Vanilla planifolia* cuttings were planted or distributed to additional farmers, and the island began to produce vanilla again.

During the 1940s and early 1950s, a series of investigations for the improvement of vanilla-curing methods was carried out at the U.S. Department of Agriculture Tropical Agricultural Research Station in Mayaguez. Their research was thorough and remains viable today. While vanilla was ultimately discontinued in Puerto

Rico (fusarium was one of the reasons), the research station continues to boast extraordinary gardens filled with an extensive array of tropical products. And although vanilla was not grown in Puerto Rico for long, the country's legacy as a vanilla producer lives on in recipes such as the Brazo Gitano, a tropical-fruit-and-vanilla-filled jelly roll and Bread Pudding with Coconut Vanilla Sauce.

Several of the Caribbean islands produced vanilla in varying amounts during the time of Spanish rule, but by the late nineteenth century it was still grown in only a few islands. Guadeloupe and Dominica continued to produce vanilla, though Guadeloupe also suffered from the hurricane of 1928, and trade briefly flourished again during World War II after vanilla shipments from the Indian Ocean had been disrupted.

A vanilla grower's association was formed in Dominica in the early 1940s, and it appeared that Dominica would become a small, but consistent, producer of vanilla. Then a disastrous fire burned the warehouse storing the entire season's crop, leaving the islanders without financial resources. Devious practices, such as substituting white cedar pods for vanilla pods in the center of bundled beans, damaged Dominica's reputation, and the shift back to the vanilla of the Indian Ocean island of Madagascar finally killed the industry, though Dominica still produces a small vanilla crop. In Guadeloupe, where *Vanilla pompona Schiede* has been grown for several hundred years, a small quantity is still produced, most of which is used locally, sold to the tourist market, or used in fragrances.

Saint Vincent and Saint Lucia were also vanilla producers. In Saint Lucia, old coffee bushes, originally brought from Liberia, were used as tutors for the vanilla. While the vanilla trade eventually died out, an unusual recipe for hot chocolate has survived to the present.

Because of the early history of vanilla production in the

SAINT LUCIA COCOA TEA

Cocoa tea is a rich, local breakfast drink. When vanilla was grown on the island, it was popular to boil tiny flour dumplings in the cocoa tea, thereby making the drink a complete meal, with the dumplings replacing bread.

2 cups water
½ vanilla bean, slit lengthwise
1 whole cinnamon stick
¼ teaspoon freshly grated nutmeg
1 bay leaf
1 chocolate stick (about 2 oz unsweetened chocolate)
1 cup milk or light cream
sugar to taste
1 tablespoon cornstarch mixed with $\frac{1}{4}$ cup water

BRING WATER TO A BOIL with vanilla bean, cinnamon, nutmeg, and bay leaf. Boil for about 15 minutes. Grate chocolate stick and add to boiling water. Reduce heat and simmer for another 10 minutes. Add milk or cream. Sweeten to taste. Mix the cornstarch with water and slowly add to the hot mixture, stirring constantly. Strain and serve.

SERVES 2

Caribbean, synthetics have been, and continue to be, sold in the local marketplaces. Tourists from cruise ships, visiting the various islands, happily oblige the locals by purchasing what they believe are fantastic buys on vanilla. The synthetic vanillin, sold at about the same price as synthetics in the United States, has often been cut with coumarin or other additives to boost the flavor and fragrance of the otherwise one-dimensional vanillin. Even islands with no traditional history in the vanilla trade ply unsuspecting visitors with their "famous local vanilla." With the area's high unemployment and a ready market of visitors who will remain only a few hours on the islands, it's understandable that the locals offer exotic-sounding tropical elixirs as a way to survive.

WORLD WAR II

With the outbreak of World War II, merchant ships were no longer able to move commodities from the Indian Ocean to Europe, and the Atlantic was closed to all but troop and military ships. After years of diminishing trade in Mexico, the United States relied entirely on Mexico and the Caribbean for vanilla. In 1939, as supplies from Europe dwindled, the Mexican industry increased its plantings, a major boon for the struggling industry. The unofficial estimate of the 1943 crop was between 300 and 350 tons, a 50 percent increase over the previous year.

French Oceania produced approximately 130 tons of vanilla in 1944. However, at this time the United States was buying very limited quantities of Tahitian vanilla for extract manufacturers. Further, with overseas transport from the South Pacific nearly impossible, and a war tax that cut deeply into profits, many Tahitian growers suspended production until the war ended.

Wartime rationing of meat, dairy, butter, eggs, sugar, and other ingredients meant that most homemakers made do without the luxury of pure vanilla; for that matter, they largely made do without baking. The majority of the vanilla that arrived in the United States was destined for the ice-cream industry, but by 1944 ice-cream manufacturers were encountering a drastic shortage of vanilla, vanilla substitutes, and most fruit flavors. Maintaining pre-war quality-control standards was all but impossible.

In a curious moment of ingenuity, manufacturers thought to create vanillin tablets for the baked goods of overseas forces. *The New York Times* ran an article in late 1942 announcing that the army was using vanilla tablets, and then, in March of 1943, the *Times* noted: "To save shipping space and alcohol, the Substance Research Laboratory of the Chicago Quartermaster Department develops vanilla flavoring tablets." While the tablets certainly saved shipping space, the kitchen staff in overseas military encampments likely craved the "real deal," not so much for the flavor as for the welcome kick of 80-proof alcohol. With so much of the world caught in the horrors and upheaval of war, vanilla production in most countries disappeared until the late 1940s.

· 7 ·

THE INDUSTRY
COMES OF AGE

The international impact of World War II was so enormous that countless volumes have been written about the effects it had on our collective lives. With respect to culture and food, the world became smaller and more familiar, as millions of people became aware of, or experienced, cultures other than their own. American servicemen and women returned from around the globe, having sampled foods they never experienced at home. Whether they loved or abhorred these exotic flavors, most agreed that they'd had more than enough Spam and other war rations and were ready for some comforting home cooking and the flavors they associated with security and familiarity.

At first, many basic foods remained in short supply, but, with the exception of continued sugar limitations, rationing was lifted in the United States by November of 1945. Staples were scarce throughout the rest of the world, and in Europe, the black market was the only way people could get many essentials. American families held food drives, collecting canned and dried foods for CARE (Cooperative for American Remittances to Europe). The U.S. government subsidized American farmers to produce extra wheat, soy, and other agricultural products to end the misery of serious food shortages abroad.

With so many men returning to the job market, women, who managed much of the workforce throughout the war, were encouraged to give up their jobs and be homemakers again. Wartime demographics had taken families far from home to be near military bases or to work in the shipyards, so many young women didn't have extended families nearby to rely on to share recipes or to teach them to cook. As domestic help was unaffordable in both the United States and much of Europe, women took to their kitchens in unprecedented numbers, and soon were rewarded with an array of packaged foods designed to make life easier as the postwar baby boom took off. By the mid-1950s, there were frozen TV dinners; quick and simple frozen, canned, and dried entrées; and a greater selection of fresh meats, fruits, and vegetables than had been seen for years. But it was dessert that spoke most clearly of the reward of a new, more prosperous time and the soothing smell of baked comfort foods. Cake and pudding mixes produced by General Mills, Pillsbury, Duncan Hines, Amazo Products, and Jell-O, to mention a few, flooded the market, and there were desserts for all ages and all occasions.

Quick" and "easy" were the key words in advertising in the 1950s. Women were encouraged to prepare great meals for their families, so speed and ease were the main come-ons in advertisements, women's magazines, and cookbooks. Here's an example of a 1950s favorite.

BANANA-VANILLA CREAM PIE

18 vanilla wafers
2 tablespoons sugar
2 tablespoons melted butter
1 tablespoon water
1 package vanilla instant pudding made with light cream
½ teaspoon vanilla extract
3 large bananas, sliced ½-inch thick
½ pint sweetened whipped cream

CRUSH 12 VANILLA WAFERS and mix with sugar, butter, and water. Spread over the bottom of an 8-inch pie plate. Cut remaining 6 vanilla wafers in half and arrange around edge of pie plate.

PREPARE PUDDING according to package directions, using cream and vanilla instead of milk. Add extract and pour pudding into vanilla wafer shell. Chill for at least 2 hours. Stir banana slices in the pudding, reserving a few slices for garnish.

To SERVE, pipe the whipped cream decoratively around the top of the pie and garnish with the remaining banana slices.

SERVES 6

Cookbooks varied from the basics like *Betty Crocker's Picture Cookbook* or the new, revised *Joy of Cooking* to books geared to the more sophisticated palate by culinary greats such as M. F. K. Fisher, James Beard, and Helen Evans Brown. The world-class cooking schools Le Cordon Bleu and L'Ecole des Trois Gourmandes opened in France, the latter designed for Americans and conducted by Bostonian Julia Child along with French cooks Simone Beck and Louisette Bertholle. Even specialty-food stores catering to the "gourmet palate" opened in some big cities around the United States, providing the adventurous with unusual culinary ingredients and delicacies well beyond the scope of the local grocery stores. In the United States, this occasionally included vanilla beans, something that most Americans had never seen. While it wasn't until the late 1980s or early 1990s that vanilla beans became a more familiar household item, Europeans used beans instead of extracts. Sophisticated cooks who had traveled abroad sought out the flavorful beans to provide deeper, fuller-bodied notes to their desserts—usually with no success.

Advances in science and technology, in many cases driven by the government and military during the war, brought significant changes in food distribution. Refrigeration and transportation were vastly improved, making it possible for companies to sell frozen and refrigerated products nationwide. In 1947, the Borden Company introduced Lady Borden Ice Cream, the first premium ice cream to be distributed nationally. Sara Lee Cheesecake was launched in 1950, becoming one of the world's largest bakeries. Dannon Yogurt brought flavored yogurts into the marketplace in the late 1940s, and small ice-cream companies merged and created franchises that expanded during the postwar building boom. Vanilla was a necessary ingredient for the multitude of dairy products and desserts that flooded the market, and the industry sprang back into action.

STANDARD OF IDENTITY

The biggest issue facing the vanilla industry was maintaining quality standards. During the Depression years and throughout the war, imitation vanillas and mixed natural and synthetic extracts largely took the place of pure vanilla for manufacturers, food service, and consumers who were hard-pressed for cash for the expensive—and scarce—vanilla. There were no government standards for flavors and extracts, and the Flavor and Extract Manufacturers Association (FEMA) was not set up to monitor the products their members produced. As label laws weren't enforced, companies could put whatever they wanted on their packaging, even if it didn't remotely match what was actually in the contents. And while the powerful Food and Drug Administration (FDA) could halt the import of synthetics from Mexico and the Caribbean, it was nearly impossible to police internal producers, in part because there wasn't an effective method to identify many of the chemicals found in flavor formulas.

Until the late 1940s, wet chemistry was the primary method of isolating flavors. Using wet chemistry, scientists could crystallize and distill chemical constituents to identify them, but the technology was limited to identifying the major flavors such as vanillin, which comprises less than 30 percent of vanilla's flavor and fragrance profile. Most of the other organoleptic properties of vanilla, (that is to say, those relating to the senses) and other flavors were beyond the reach of available scientific methods.

When gastro and liquid chromatography became possible, scientists could look for and identify components that were in parts per trillion, an amount so minute that as now retired McCormick chemist Dick Hall explains it, one part per trillion is the equivalent of less than one-tenth of an inch of the distance from the earth to the moon—in other words, *small*!

McCormick & Company had a vested interest in the spice and flavor industry. In 1946, McCormick & Company merged with A. Schilling and Company, a San Francisco coffee, spice, and extract house founded in 1881, gaining national distribution and expanding into Latin America. McCormick & Company, by now the largest spice and flavor company in the United States, had the resources to maintain a fully equipped modern laboratory and skilled chemists. Dick Hall came to work for the firm as an organic chemist in 1950. He was hired to find flavor-identical sources (i.e., different plants with similar flavors) or synthetic sources for an array of popular spices and flavors. While this might seem like a contradiction in terms, spices and natural flavors were in short supply during the war, and McCormick & Company was interested in finding alternative options to offer customers when prices of a particular commodity became higher than the market could bear. At this particular time, they were competing with so-called vanillas that didn't contain a single vanilla bean, and their extract couldn't be price-competitive with the adulterated vanillas, they were interested in creating a good-quality synthetic that they could offer consumers who couldn't afford or preferred the flavor of imitation vanilla. So the other part of Dick Hall's job was to help establish a standard of identity for extracts.

In the early 1950s, the FDA had the resources to effectively police foods and flavors. They needed direction, however, if a particular industry wanted to effect change, and with the new technology McCormick & Company knew that there were ways to detect adulterants in extracts. Their first step toward creating the standard of identity was to contact other ethical companies in the vanilla industry who produced quality vanilla. These extract manufacturers were facing the same uphill battle as McCormick & Company, so they supported change, and McCormick & Company filed their proposal with the FDA in 1953.

FEMA members knew about the growing support for a standard of identity, and member alliances were divided nearly fifty-fifty for and against. Those who didn't support the proposal were split into several categories. Companies that produced adulterated extracts wanted to maintain the status quo because they were making lots of money. Others preferred tradition over innovation. They were emotionally tied to the old way of doing business, and as they felt that much of the vanilla beans coming into the market at this time were "junk" anyway, they didn't see the point of pushing for standards that would be difficult to meet. Then there were the companies that felt that since McCormick & Company was the industry giant, it was to the firm's interest to set standards, so they opposed the proposal on principle. They were correct about the vested interest despite the fact that the standard might actually benefit them, too. A huge battle ensued, one that lasted for years.

At the heart of the matter was determining the amount of vanilla bean solids contained per gallon of extract. This wasn't as simple as it might appear. If vanilla beans are carefully handled and don't have a high bacteria count, they won't mold if they are moist and oily. However, moist, oily beans weigh more than drier beans, and as drier beans don't have the same oil content, they tend to be of poorer quality or have a lower level of sanitation. As there were no sanitation standards in the countries where vanilla was grown and processed, it was anyone's guess as to what was the perfect weight for vanilla beans that could travel to the United States without molding but still have enough oil to have good flavor. Once that was established, it was necessary to determine how to get the producers to ship consistently good beans. McCormick had filed for the measurement of 13.35 percent vanilla beans at 20 percent dry weight per gallon of extract.

In 1960, FEMA backed an alternative standard of vanilla based on a wet weight of 13.35 percent of vanilla beans or what would amount to 10 ounces of moisture-free vanilla bean solids. The problem with this measurement was that companies could say they were using the heavier, high-moisture beans when what they were actually doing was using fewer beans. The FDA mulled over the two proposals; finally, in 1962, the official standard of identity was set at 13.35 percent vanilla beans at 25 percent dry weight per gallon.

BUREAU OF ALCOHOL, TOBACCO AND FIREARMS (ATF)

The FDA was not the only government agency overseeing the vanilla industry. Because pure vanilla extract contains alcohol, standards were needed to establish how much alcohol should be required in extracts. All companies that produce products with alcohol (this includes extracts, pharmacological tinctures, and alcoholic beverages) had to register with the ATF (now known, as noted earlier, as the Bureau of Alcohol, Tobacco, Firearms and

Explosives yet still shortened to ATF) and fill out a series of forms, including a "drawback" form. All companies that produce alcoholic products pay a tax to the ATF for the alcohol they use. In the case of extract and flavoring companies, their products are not for consumption in the same way as distilled spirits (at least usually). When they account for their alcohol via the formula for their flavor or extract, they receive a drawback or rebate for the money paid out. As the ATF is in contact with the FDA, they know whether the formulas on the drawback forms match with the FDA laws. If they don't, the ATF won't return the drawback.

Needless to say, while this technical information was important to extract producers, most consumers bought whatever was available at the grocery store or, by now, the modern supermarkets that were springing up around the country. Those who couldn't afford pure extract—or who didn't know the difference—purchased imitation vanilla to flavor birthday cakes, lunch-box cookies, and bake-sale treats to earn money for local fund-raisers.

Chocolate wafer cookies were very popular in the 1950s and 1960s. They were crisp, versatile, and easy to use for lunches or desserts.

CHOCOLATE COOKY ROLL

2 cups heavy cream
2 teaspoons vanilla

1 teaspoon sugar
24 thin chocolate cooky wafers
chocolate or multicolored sprinkles

IN A SMALL BOWL, whip the cream until frothy. Add the vanilla and sugar and beat until thick. Spread one side of each cookie with cream and arrange the cookies standing on edge, on a serving platter to make a long roll. Frost the cooky roll with the rest of the cream. Cover the roll with plastic wrap, and chill for 4 hours.

TO SERVE, sprinkle the roll with chocolate or multicolored sprinkles. Slice the roll at an angle so that each piece has alternating stripes of cream and chocolate cookie.

SERVES 8 HUNGRY CHILDREN

"PLAIN VANILLA"

The headlines of articles about vanilla often begin with "Vanilla is anything but plain," or some variation on that theme. The questions remain, When did vanilla get relegated to the "plain" category, and who is responsible for this somewhat disparaging and certainly puzzling oxymoron?

Tracking the origin of "plain vanilla" has not been easy and is largely based on supposition. Vanilla wasn't readily available and affordable until the early twentieth century. When it became more widespread, it was most often found in vanilla ice cream. Vanilla ice cream by itself is unadorned and therefore could be considered generic, as it doesn't contain nuts, fruits, chocolate, or other flavors. Further, the flavor is soothing (some might call it bland), and the color is a soft, summer white. By making a linguistic leap of faith, it's easy to see how the words "bland," "generic," or "plain" could become synonymous with vanilla.

In the 1940s, there was a surge of engineering projects in the aerospace industry as part of the war effort, and after the war, engineering efforts expanded into electronics. It was probably during this time period that vanilla was first used to describe a simple, unadorned airplane, console, or circuit board. The term was later carried over into the computer world, where it is commonly used by engineers and programmers. As much of this technology began in the now-famous Silicon Valley, it's altogether possible that this was where the term originated.

By the late 1950s or early 1960s, "vanilla" was used in the clothing industry to describe a basic, unadorned wardrobe. It was then propelled into mainstream usage to describe anything generic, sometimes replacing an earlier expression "milk toast" to describe someone who is less than memorable. In current usage, "vanilla" is used in ways that are not only far-fetched but also inappropriate to include here. As anyone who loves vanilla knows, neither the flavor nor the fragrance is generic or plain, but it appears that the term and its usage will be with us for years to come.

The Vanilla Industry Grows with the Baby Boom

The postwar baby boom not only heralded the arrival of more women who were preparing meals and baking desserts for growing families, but it also was a driving force in providing family-style restaurants and franchise chains across the United States. By 1952, there were 351 Howard Johnson's restaurants, a Maine-to-Miami chain located largely at highway turnoffs, and Howard Johnson won a franchise for ten more on the New Jersey highways. He hired chef Pierre Franey to upgrade the quality of his food and then launched frozen meals through supermarkets. Fast-food restaurant chains, often beginning as mom-and-pop diners or stands in the 1920s and 1930s were popping up everywhere as families visited relatives in distant cities or vacationed in station wagons. Diners Club was launched in 1950, followed by American Express in 1958, offering couples and families promotions that were an enticing way to dine out more often. And for those women who were in the workforce or didn't enjoy cooking, the packaged-baked-goods industry was flourishing. While the lower-priced sweets contained synthetic vanillin, niche-market companies offered premium cookies, cakes, and pies containing pure vanilla. Ice-cream producers, soft-drink companies, restaurant chains, bakeries, and food-service companies needed vanilla in greater volume, and the vanilla industry needed to expand to accommodate demand.

Up until the late 1950s, American imports of vanilla beans were steady at about five hundred tons a year. In the 1960s, American imports began to increase. This was in part due to market demand but also to congressional legislation regarding the labeling requirements of frozen desserts, most especially ice cream. The U.S. vanilla extract standards of 1963 and the frozen desserts standards of 1965 were the main measures passed. The result was that once the FDA established statutes regulating the industry, consumption of natural vanilla in the ice-cream industry doubled by the 1970s.

The U.S. Definitions and Standards of Identity for Frozen Desserts were established in order to regulate an industry that had no specific rules or controls either for product quality or the inclusion of ingredients. The law needed to be flexible enough that manufacturers could maintain their formulas and methods of production but stringent enough so that consumers could understand what they were buying.

Ice cream is a case in point, specifically vanilla ice cream. In addition to setting standards for butterfat content, cream, milk, and stabilizers, among others, there needed to be a standard for vanilla itself. Some ice creams contain a mixture of pure vanilla and natural botanicals that provide vanillin which is not from synthetic sources. There are also blends made from vanilla extract as well as synthetically produced vanillin, and some products are made with only artificial or synthetic vanilla flavor. As a result, vanilla extract is the only flavoring with both an FDA standard of identity of its own *and* an FDA ice-cream standard. Frozen-dessert makers pushed back against Category I (as described below) because it required that they use only pure vanilla extract, and eventually Category II (also described below) was included in the law.

CATEGORY I:
VANILLA ICE CREAM

In order to be labeled *pure vanilla ice cream,* or *vanilla ice cream,* the product must be made with 100 percent pure vanilla. It can be made from vanilla extract or beans. Usually pure vanilla ice cream is made with top-quality ingredients as the pure vanilla will not mask any "off" flavor or fragrance notes. "Super-premium" and "premium" ice creams usually have a high butter-fat content, so double-strength pure vanilla extract is most often used.

CATEGORY II:
VANILLA-FLAVORED ICE CREAM

This ice cream may contain up to 1 ounce of synthetic vanillin per unit of vanilla extract used. This is considered a natural and artificial product and must be labeled *vanilla-flavored ice cream.*

CATEGORY III:
ARTIFICIALLY FLAVORED OR
ARTIFICIAL VANILLA ICE CREAM

Artificial vanilla ice cream has less than half of its flavoring derived from pure vanilla. Given the price of pure vanilla, manufacturers usually use no pure vanilla. Typically, these frozen desserts may contain water, ethanol, propylene glycol, vanillin, ethyl vanillin, propenyl guaethol, anisyl aldehyde, and heliotropin. Some of these chemicals are part of the flavor profile of pure vanilla so they impart a vanillalike flavor.

Vanilla-bean ice creams often contain vanilla "seeds." Usually the "seeds" are actually small pieces of ground whole "exhausted" vanilla beans left over from the extract-making process and are used for appearance, not flavor. Real vanilla-bean seeds are only found in high-end ice creams made in small batches, if at all.

Even the ice-cream-making process is highly specific to each producer. Liquid, butterfat, sugar, and flavoring amounts vary, and even the quantity of air whipped into the ice cream varies by company and sometimes even by product lines within a company.

The ice-cream and frozen-dessert industry generates more than $20 billion a year (2002 statistics) in the United States, so it has a lot invested in pleasing ice-cream eaters.

MOVING INTO THE 1960s

The problem, as always, was the dependability of tropical crops. Weather wasn't the only issue—political instability and fluctuating prices made dependence on only a few countries a chancy proposition. If the vanilla industry was to meet the growing demand for vanilla, it would be necessary to establish new resources for vanilla beans. The Indian Ocean countries continued to be the primary producers but their government was involved in vanilla revenues, and high prices brought boycotts from American and European buyers. Tahitian beans were inexpensive until the 1960s and were used by ice-cream and extract manufacturers to provide the distinctive flavor of heliotropin to their products. However,

Vanilla beans undergoing the conditioning or "resting" phase of the curing and drying process. The beans will rest for upward of several months before being boxed for shipment.

when the French became more actively involved in the Tahitian vanilla trade, many of the Tahitian families stopped producing vanilla, and the prices escalated. Interestingly, manufacturers, put off by the high prices, attempted to pull the Tahitian beans from their formulas, but heliotropin is in minute Mexican and Bourbon beans. When the makers discontinued Tahitian vanilla in their formulas, it dramatically changed the flavor note. Eventually, Tahitian vanilla was phased out of most manufacturers' blends, and it wasn't until the 1980s that Tahitian vanilla had a resurgence of popularity in the United States. And the Mexican industry, though revived during World War II, was in decline and unable to meet the growing need of an expanding economy and hundreds of new products requiring vanilla.

Several factors brought change to the vanilla industry in the 1950s and 1960s. One was a new generation of young men who either followed in their fathers' footsteps or came into the industry fresh out of school. Bernard Champon took over the family company, Champon Vanilla, Inc., after his father's death and went overseas to purchase vanilla beans rather than rely solely on telegrams and correspondence. Howard Smith Sr. joined the Virginia Dare Extract Company in 1955. In addition to providing food and beverage formulation experience, Smith contributed his expertise in pharmaceuticals to help strengthen the company's product line. Chat Nielsen Sr. bought out the remaining stock from Richard Massey's widow in the 1950s and was joined in the business in the late 1950s by his son, Chat Nielsen Jr., who then helped to expand the company's wholesale market.

In 1964, Kurt Schussler and his son-in-law, Warren (Nick) Gaffney, bought the assets of Dammann Company, continuing the business under its original name. In 1963, the Todd family business, which had been founded by A. M. Todd in 1869 and was the foundation of the American peppermint and spearmint industries, was joined by Richard Davis Webb. Webb's father had worked for the venerable English firm W. J. Bush (precursor to Bush Boake Allen Ltd., which recently became a division of International Flavors & Fragrances Inc.), and he had been involved with the Champon family in a joint venture after growing up with Bernard Champon. The Todds, looking for new opportunities in flavorings, purchased Jack Zink's share of Zink & Triest in 1964, and the balance of the company was purchased from Bill Triest in 1967.

They retained the name Zink & Triest, and the company became the vanilla component of the A. M. Todd family business.

The Beck family bought out business partner Doyle, changing the company to Beck Vanilla, with ownership of the family business going to Howard and Norman Beck in the 1950s. The vanilla beans for producing their signature vanilla extracts came exclusively from Mexico, but by the late 1960s the Becks were buying from Zink & Triest and the Dammann Company, though they continued to purchase some Mexican beans as well.

Ray Lochhead worked with his family vanilla and flavoring business in Saint Louis until 1964. The family then decided to expand by dividing the family business into territories. Ray came west to California, settling in Paso Robles. Ray's brothers, Jimmy and Johnny, continued the R. R. Lochhead Manufacturing Company in St. Louis. Ray's move instantly gave the family a national base for selling high-quality flavors.

This new generation was interested in bringing more uniformity and consistency to vanilla beans and better quality in extracts. Berend Hachmann, of Aust und Hachmann Ltd. in Germany, a longtime family vanilla business, describes this shift:

"In the early days vanilla beans were judged on appearance, oils, flexibility, and aroma. Anyone working in the industry needed to have a 'nose' to determine if the vanilla met industry standards. In the 1960s, equipment was developed that could measure vanillin content, humidity, and other characteristics heretofore unavailable. A new generation of buyers wanted comparative statistics, depending more on vanillin and moisture content than physical appearance and aroma alone. This brought about a shift in the way buyers and sellers thought about vanilla."

With this technology, it was possible to establish new markets in tropical countries where vanilla had not been previously grown as well as to standardize the beans from countries already producing vanilla. Howard Wolf was McCormick's first global buyer. During World War II he had met Henri Fraise, one of the largest French families in the Madagascar vanilla trade. While McCormick had been buying exclusively from Mexico until then, the company's requirements were too great for Mexico's dwindling industry, so it began purchasing Indian Ocean beans. In the 1960s, Howard set up McCormick's "global sourcing" operation, and negotiated a joint venture with Mitchell Cotts, who headed up a British coffee and tea plantation in Uganda, the Uganda Company. Mitchell was to oversee the vanilla plantations in Uganda, and Wolf helped to set up a mechanical system developed by McCormick scientists that was capable of doing "quick curing." In just a few days, vanilla beans could be cured and dried, a huge difference compared to the usual four months' period using the Indian Ocean or Mexican techniques. While the resulting beans were not quite as flavorful as beans cured and dried in more traditional ways, this process was useful for countries where workers didn't have the experience of curing and drying beans, or for isolated areas where green vanilla beans could be processed on-site instead of risking spoilage by shipping them to distant plants.

In 1970, Benjamin ("Hank") Kaestner came to work for McCormick & Company, training under Howard Wolf before assuming his position in 1972 when Howard retired. He continued Howard's work of expanding vanilla markets during his thirty-three years' working for McCormick.

In 1963, Julia Child began a series of cooking demonstrations on Boston's educational television station, attracting an enthusiastic group of Americans. This marked the beginning of the trend for a more varied and sophisticated cooking style in the United States, a trend that would flourish in the late 1970s and continue to evolve to the present. However, in the 1960s, the idea of gourmet food for the majority of Americans more often included steak and lobster ("surf and turf") or thick slabs of roast beef; a baked potato with sour cream, bacon, and chives; and a dessert that appeared complicated and exotic but could easily be made at home for dinner parties. Baked Alaska fit the bill and was popular in the 1950s and 1960s.

BAKED ALASKA

1 8-inch cake layer (whatever flavor you prefer)
4 egg whites
½ cup sugar
1 teaspoon vanilla extract
1 quart firm vanilla ice cream

PREPARE CAKE as per directions on package. (Freeze the second layer for another use.)

PREHEAT OVEN to 500°F. In a small bowl, beat egg whites until foamy, add sugar and vanilla, and beat until stiff but not dry.

Place cake on a heavy, ovenproof platter. Spoon ice cream onto the cake, leaving a 1-inch border all around.

COVER THE ICE CREAM and cake completely with the egg-white meringue. Brown the meringue lightly in the oven for 2 minutes. Serve immediately.

SERVES 6

THE 1970S

By the late 1960s, the first baby boomers (the post–World War II generation) in the United States and Europe were growing into adulthood. While many followed in their parents' footsteps, there was also a small but influential lifestyle shift occurring, with young people opting to travel the world, join the Peace Corps, or move "back to the land." There was growing concern about the environmental impact of the expanding economy and population growth, and its effect on the planet. Preceded by a small but vocal group of "health food nuts" and "free thinkers" who eschewed the fast pace and stress of modern life, instead opting for a simpler way of living, these young people were the pioneers of the new organic and natural foods market, a movement that would eventually grow powerful enough to influence the food industry markedly. It wasn't that this concept was new; it had simply been lost in the rapidly growing postwar expansion of large corporate farms, fertilizers, pesticides, chemicals, and bioengineered foods created to feed an increasingly hungry planet. Herbal teas, whole grains, and organically produced fruits and vegetables slowly grew in popularity, dropped off for a while, and then took off again in the 1990s with supermarkets that specialized in organic and wholesome food alternatives. Soy substitutes for meats, milk, and frozen desserts became more available, and the market for yogurt and other cultured dairy products grew stronger.

In college towns across the country, but particularly in California, Massachusetts, and New York, cafés and restaurants opened, featuring healthy alternatives to the booming fast-food chains. Moosewood Restaurant opened in 1972 in Ithaca, New York, and became nationally famous with Mollie Katzen's *Moosewood Cookbook*; Ruth Reichl launched the Swallow in 1973 in Berkeley, California, a café that preceded her career as a food critic and author; and the Whole Earth restaurant chain in California were just a few of the profusion of healthy eateries that sprang up in the late 1960s and early 1970s. Chez Panisse, an early model of the shift in chic cuisine, opened in 1971, reflecting the philosophy of owner Alice Waters to use only the freshest, finest-quality ingredients (organic when possible) and to prepare her dishes simply without fancy sauces.

Granola was often synonymous with "hippies" or "the counterculture," young Americans, and Europeans who chose a less structured and stratified lifestyle than the mainstream culture. Ironically, Europeans and Americans had been eating whole-grain cereals for generations, but as the culture "modernized" in the 1950s and 1960s, processed and heavily sugared cereals flooded the markets. Granola was essentially just a throwback to an earlier time.

HOMEMADE VANILLA GRANOLA

2 cups rolled oats
1 cup toasted wheat germ
½ cup chopped toasted nuts
½ cup sunflower seeds
½ cup chopped dried fruits
¼ cup canola, safflower, or sunflower oil
½ cup warmed honey
1 tablespoon pure vanilla extract

Preheat oven to 300°F. Toast the oats in the oven in a large baking pan. Stir them often until they are fragrant and barely beginning to turn golden.

Lower the temperature to 200°F. Add the remaining ingredients, mix well, and return to the oven for another 15 minutes or so, stirring often. When the granola becomes drier and toasty, turn off the oven and allow the granola to dry completely in the oven before storing it in an airtight container.

MAKES ABOUT 4½ to 5 CUPS

At the same time, gourmet cookies became big business, filling the niche left by women who no longer baked. Debbi Fields launched Mrs. Fields Cookies in 1974, a business that in seventeen years would have eight hundred stores worldwide. Famous Amos Chocolate Chip Cookies, begun by Wally Amos, debuted in department and specialty-food stores, and scores of smaller businesses sold their cookies and other baked fare to local stores as well as at music events and craft and street fairs. And, in response to the interest in haute cuisine fostered by food writers, cooking schools, and television food shows, upscale bistros and restaurants opened throughout the United States, in Europe, and in international hotels catering to wealthy tourists. Indonesia became competitive with the Indian Ocean islands as the vanilla industry responded to the continually growing demand for vanilla by the industrial and food service markets, and small producers on tropical islands began to grow more vanilla.

THE VANILLAMARK

In an attempt to identify products containing pure vanilla rather than natural synthetic blends or synthetics, the "Vanillamark" was created and sponsored by the Vanilla Alliance (Unavanille International) of Madagascar, began in Europe in 1968, then came to the United States in 1971. Univanille International owned and controlled the use of the Vanillamark in all the countries where it was registered. By 1976, more than seven hundred products were licensed to display the Vanillamark, which assured that the consumer was receiving a product solely flavored with natural vanilla. The intention was to inform and educate the consumer about pure vanilla and the products that contained it.

The American vanilla industry had mixed feelings about the Vanillamark. Companies that produced premium-quality vanilla felt that it would be a good marketing tool to encourage the public to purchase products containing pure vanilla. It was also a way for the public to identify the manufacturers who produced premium vanilla. There was only one problem: the Vanillamark promoted *only* Madagascar vanilla. In fact, extract manufacturers often used blends of beans from several origins in the formulas they produced for industrial and food service customers. Further, products made with Mexican or Tahitian vanilla didn't qualify for the Vanillamark. And some felt that it was a heavy-handed way to get companies to fund and promote Madagascar vanilla or risk nonacknowledgment of their organizations as quality producers. The biggest vanilla producer, McCormick, chose not to participate. While it supported the concept of a quality brand, it felt that its own name stood for quality and that it didn't need additional branding.

Along with the Vanillamark, Unavanille International hired New York food public relations specialists Lewis and Neale to launch a campaign promoting Madagascar vanilla and to create the Vanilla Information Board. The Vanillamark and vanilla promotion were paid for, in part, by a tax that was instated on all Madagascar vanilla, and paid by exporters. This cost was factored into the selling price to the buyers importing the vanilla into their countries. The campaign was quite successful for a while, making Madagascar a familiar name and synonymous with vanilla. Although Madagascar discontinued the program in the late 1980s, the majority of the American public still believes that Madagascar is *the best vanilla* and assumes that the Indian Ocean is the origin of vanilla worldwide.

AFTER YEARS OF INDUSTRY GROWTH, in 1979 Madagascar was hit with a major cyclone and produced only three hundred tons of dried vanilla. Prices soared to more than $100 a kilo ($45 a pound), at the time unprecedented in the modern history of vanilla. The shortage of vanilla and subsequent high prices put the industry into a tailspin. There were many small manufacturers in Europe in the 1960s and 1970s who were producing extracts, and there were small businesses in the United States who depended on vanilla extracts and beans for their products. When prices soared, they either went out of business or switched to the far less expensive synthetic vanillin or blends. Unfortunately, even when prices returned to normal, many of these clients never returned to using pure vanilla. It would take several years for the industry to regain momentum.

THE 1980s

Until the 1980s, Nielsen-Massey Vanillas produced customized wholesale blends for the industrial and food-service markets, but they had never considered selling their vanilla to the retail market. McCormick controlled the majority of the retail vanilla market, and by the early 1980s there were just a few other companies that offered retail vanilla. The Nielsens supplied a local caterer and cooking-school teacher in Chicago with extract, and the teacher's students constantly asked where he got his vanilla and if they could buy it, too. He approached owners Chat Jr. and Camilla Nielsen about buying smaller bottles, and they agreed to do so as a favor. He came in twice a year and purchased twenty-four bottles that Camilla hand-filled and labeled while her young children napped.

As a result, the two were caught off guard when Chuck Williams of Williams-Sonoma fame called and said he was interested in carrying their retail line in his mail-order catalog. The Nielsens were unfamiliar with Chuck Williams and his growing line of specialty foods and kitchenwares, which had begun in the late 1940s in a hardware store in Sonoma and now sold in mail-order catalogs. They also didn't understand how Chuck assumed they were in the retail business. It turns out that while Chuck was visiting Chicago, he had met the local caterer and seen the small bottles of extract he had been supplied. He asked Chat if they could fill an order for seventy thousand 4-ounce bottles of extract. The Nielsens assumed it would be a onetime deal and agreed to do it.

Chat found a secondhand bottling machine and set it up in their warehouse. They then posted a notice on the local university bulletin board looking for helpers, and in a couple of weeks they had the order together. Once the extracts went into the catalog, Chuck Williams's phone rang off the hook, and the next thing the Nielsens knew, all the gourmet stores wanted to carry their extract.

At a National Association for the Specialty Food Trade (NASFT) show in 1981, the Nielsens were persuaded to have a booth at the San Francisco show in January of 1982. Chat went to the show with some bottles of extract and vanilla bean samples, a charismatic personality, and a lot of information about vanilla. The only thing that saved him over the next few days was the company in the booth next to his, which kept him well-fed on its food samples, as he was so popular he couldn't leave his booth. Even while Chat was packing up at the end of the show, people pitched in to help so they could learn more about vanilla. The enthusiasm expressed by so many people who knew nothing about the flavor they used led Chat to write "The Story of Vanilla," a booklet that the Nielsens continue to use as a promotional handout today.

In the meantime, Hank Kaestner was actively involved in developing new sources of spices and herbs as well as vanilla beans for McCormick & Company. Kaestner says, "I spent my career expanding on Howard Wolf's idea to develop alternate sources of vanilla. I worked in Tonga, Uganda (where our curing plant equipment is still functioning after thirty-five years), Papua New Guinea, and India, as well as countries where vanilla was already established.

"In each country I was able to select an outstanding local partner who assured success of these projects. Although I was given credit for the success, without Mike Kneubuhl in Tonga, Aga Sekalala in Uganda, the A. V. Thomas Company in India, Sam Filiaci in Indonesia, and John Nightingale in Papua New Guinea, I wouldn't have had such good luck in establishing the new vanilla programs. It also helped that I was able to implement 'quick curing' systems with equipment based on the original McCormick patent, which had long since expired, to help my partners cure the beans. This saved time as no one needed to be trained in the traditional methods of curing and drying beans."

THE VANILLA KING

As director of spice procurement, and McCormick's in-house spice expert and vanilla specialist for thirty-three years, Hank Kaestner has well earned his title. He has traveled to remote and nearly inaccessible lands; trekked along overgrown jungle trails and up rain-swept mountains; endured killer bees, fire ants, and scorpions; negotiated for crops with kings and village chiefs; and talked his way out of being killed by a trigger-happy gunman during a revolution in Africa.

During his school years, Hank had discovered he had an ear for languages, a fascination with geography, and a burning desire to visit the intriguing countries and islands that caught his fancy. Good people skills and an innate curiosity rounded out his portfolio of attributes, and after college he was fortunate enough to land a position in the purchasing department of McCormick & Company, located in his hometown of Baltimore.

To say that his job as a purchasing agent was ideal is an understatement. In his years at McCormick, he visited more countries than many people know exist. He used his current language skills as well as learned new languages, he developed friendships on every continent, and he had the opportunity to observe more than 6,500 birds (another of his passions) in their native habitats. "I loved my job, and it gave me the opportunity to pursue my hobby of bird-watching," says Hank. "I had the best of all possible worlds!"

Hank and I met first by phone after I read an article from *The Wall Street Journal* about how Hank had negotiated with the king of Tonga over the right time to harvest the island kingdom's vanilla. Although I was a great fan of vanilla, at that time I only knew that it was an orchid that produced a seedpod that smelled wonderful and added flavor to my sugar when I placed both in a jar. We talked for more than an hour and, based on our conversation, I began the research for *The Vanilla Cookbook* which was later published by Celestial Arts. A couple of months later, I met Hank in person in San Francisco, and so began a long-term friendship as well as my career as a vanilla specialist.

Hank took copies of my book to the vanilla farmers of Mexico in 1987. As a result, when I finally traveled to the vanilla region there several years later, I was already a local celebrity. My slide-show presentations are peppered with his wonderful photographs from around the world, and he has kept me up-to-date on important industry information over the years.

Although he was a buyer for the world's largest spice company, Hank has always been concerned about the welfare of the farmers. Through McCormick & Company, he developed markets for farmers, buying their vanilla at fair market prices and helping thousands of farmers better their lives as vanilla suppliers. There was even a special ceremony in Uganda in honor of Hank's work helping them to rebuild and restart their vanilla production after the difficult years when Idi Amin was in power. He has also partnered with Conservation International in Chiapas, Mexico, to work with the Mexican Lacandon tribe, joined a project with the Nature Conservancy in Sulawesi, Indonesia, and worked with the Peregrine Fund on the Masoala Peninsula in Madagascar.

Asked if he had insights to share from his years of experience and interaction with so many people around the world, Hank replied, "I've learned that people everywhere are caring and considerate. I've been where people had very little and yet they insisted on sharing half of their food and that I stay with them in their modest homes. It's quite humbling to experience such kindness from people, especially as I was a stranger from a different culture and came from a country on the other side of the world."

Knowing Hank, I find it's no surprise that he has experienced such hospitality, as he himself is a caring, compassionate, and considerate man. Though Hank is most certainly the vanilla king, he's also a global ambassador, and he's changed the lives of untold numbers of farmers around the world for the better, assisting them to remain in their home countries, cultivating herbs, spices, and flavors for people whom they will never meet.

During my research, I met Juan San Mames, a Spaniard who lived in Central America and Mexico before immigrating to the United States. His primary business was focused on saffron, but he developed a vanilla business as well. I spent a wonderful afternoon with Juan, learning about vanilla. This meeting was very helpful as there was very little available on vanilla in libraries at the time. It was gratifying to do shows with Juan over the years since our first meeting, and we remain friends today.

This was one of the first savory recipes that I created, using vanilla as a primary flavor. It has remained one of my favorites. Bottled or dried cherries that have been rehydrated in cherry cider can be substituted for fresh cherries.

CORNISH GAME HENS WITH CHERRY-VANILLA SAUCE

4 Cornish game hens
coarse sea salt and coarsely ground pepper, to taste
2–4 tablespoons unsalted butter
2 tablespoons cherry vinegar (or other fruit vinegar)
4 inches of a vanilla bean, split lengthwise
4 teaspoons sugar, or 1 tablespoon honey
1 tablespoon finely chopped fresh tarragon
1 cup ruby port
4 cups Bing cherries, stemmed and pitted

PREHEAT OVEN to 375°F. Rub game hens with salt and pepper and dot with butter. Place in oven and roast, basting several times, until hens are tender, about 1 hour or a little longer, depending on size. Place on platter and keep warm.

PLACE PAN WITH JUICES over high heat, and deglaze pan with cherry vinegar. Add vanilla bean, sugar or honey, tarragon, and port, and mix well. Add cherries and cook until cherries are tender and ruby port has reduced by half. If cherries are tender but sauce hasn't reduced enough, spoon cherries into a small bowl and continue reducing liquor.

> Add salt and pepper to taste, place cherries back in pan of reduced liquor to heat if necessary, then pour over game hens and serve.
>
> Serves 4 to 6

As often happens with new ideas and inventions, at the same time that *The Vanilla Cookbook* debuted, American and European chefs were stretching the parameters of flavors by experimenting with unusual ways to use herbs, spices, extracts, chocolate, and vanilla. World-famous chef Wolfgang Puck, drawing on his European background, served lobster with a vanilla sauce at his trendy Beverly Hills restaurant, Spago, and created quite a stir. Vanilla began to show up on the menus of expensive and innovative restaurants—mainly in the sauces of savory entrées—and increasingly, there were desserts that featured vanilla as the star rather than the backup flavor.

Tahitian vanilla is a case in point. Although it had been used as part of the flavor profile in extract blends, the majority of Tahitian vanilla was shipped to France and then to other areas of Europe where Tahitian vanilla was well received. Until the 1980s, most Americans had no idea it existed. This changed when two young entrepreneurs, Marc Jones and Peter Stone, brought Tahitian vanilla to the attention of American chefs.

Marc Jones's mother, a French woman, moved to Tahiti in the late 1970s and sent some local vanilla to her son who worked as a chef in Los Angeles. While Tahitian vanilla didn't immediately spark his interest, his mother's persistence led him to join forces with Peter Stone and they tested the American market. Chefs were immediately interested in its fruity-floral flavor. Eventually, Tahitian vanilla acquired a niche in the American culinary world, where it is especially popular in fruit and cream-based dishes.

THE 1990s

The general prosperity of the 1980s had helped to fuel the popularity of small, upscale bistros and trendy restaurants that featured such delicacies as tropical produce, exotic ethnic foods, wild game, and fusion cuisine, all bursting with a wide array of flavors. Television was a great outlet for celebrity chefs to introduce cooking fans to less commonly used ingredients, and then to apply them in fresh new ways. "Big flavors" were the buzzword, and we wanted to know more about how to use them. Cookbooks soared in popularity, and people read them as if they were novels.

In the meanwhile, Americans were gaining weight. Life was increasingly fast-paced, and it was common for working people to eat on the go, often skipping breakfast or lunch, and then overeating at night. The market for low-fat foods boomed, and both salty and sweet low-fat or lowered-fat snacks could be found in convenience stores, supermarkets, and specialty-food shops everywhere. To make low-fat foods palatable, intense flavors are needed to boost taste interest. The addition of vanilla enhanced and complemented everything from lowered-fat yogurt and diet protein drinks to cookies, muffins, and cheesecake.

AROMATHERAPY

At the same time, Americans were overstressed and often pushing burnout. Self-help books and spas promoted the concept of slowing down and relaxing by using aromas known to help soothe jangled nerves and exhausted bodies. For decades Europeans had been using herbal blends and the essential oils of flowers and other plants as a healthy, less expensive alternative to medications for relaxation, and Americans took notice. Yoga, meditation, and biofeedback went mainstream and were combined with aromatherapy as people sought relief.

In 1991, Memorial Sloan-Kettering Cancer Center in New York announced in a news release that the fragrance of heliotropin—a sweet, vanillalike scent—was the most relaxing and pleasant of five fragrances tested for the reduction of anxiety and distress during a difficult medical procedure. With a grant from the Olfactory Research Fund Ltd., William Redd, Ph.D., and Sharon Manne, Ph.D., of Sloan-Kettering's Psychiatry Service tested eighty-five patients who were undergoing magnetic resonance imaging (MRI) as part of their initial workup. During an MRI scan, patients lie motionless for up to an hour in the narrow cylindrical core of the scanner. Anxiety associated with this medical procedure causes up to 10 percent of patients to terminate their scans before completion. Results of their initial tests showed that patients exposed to the aroma of heliotropin in the room while undergoing their MRI experienced 63 percent less overall anxiety than a control group of patients who were not given the fragrance during the scan.

An Antidote to Stress

The results of the pioneering aromatherapy tests at Sloan-Kettering prompted a series of additional tests to further determine which aromas produced the best results and how test subjects rated the various fragrances. Heliotropin was consistently rated the most pleasant and most relaxing. Fifty-seven percent of participants said they would still like this scent after an hour of exposure, whereas only 25 to 30 percent of participants stated they would still like the other five scents after an hour of exposure. In a later comparison of twenty-two scents examined in the fragrance tests, heliotropin consistently rated most favorably in terms of having pleasant, relaxing, and moderately intense properties. The researchers concluded that "vanilla, a homey scent which may remind people of food, may be a preferred scent. Its recent rise in commercial popularity is well-deserved."

Mood Enhancement with Vanilla

There appears to be ample evidence that aroma also affects mood. The fact that vanilla is associated with home, food, security, and pleasure helps to evoke a sense of well-being. Realtors often use a vanilla room freshener or put vanilla extract in water in a warm oven before showing a home that's for sale. Vanilla may also have a pheromonelike quality to it as vanilla essences attract attention. People who wear vanilla fragrances have said that people's comments range from "I always feel so calm (or happy) around you" to "What are you wearing? It smells s-o-o-o-o good!"

Veterinarians have found that animals are also attracted to the scent of vanilla, and they sometimes use vanilla to create stimulus and response among very sick animals. The scent also assists in inducing appetite in dogs after surgery. In other veterinary research, it has been found that the vanilla aroma and flavor are important for encouraging calm and stimulating appetite among nursing sows and growing piglets.

The fragrance of vanilla has also been proved to be very calming. A study at Tübingen University in Germany indicated that the fragrance of vanilla reduced the startle reflex among both humans and animals. Further, the animal results showed that the calming effects of vanilla may be attributed more to some essential property of the fragrance than to the "positive childhood associations" commonly used to explain its universal popularity among humans.

Slimming Down with Vanilla

Vanilla's aroma calms and soothes, but it may also have the capacity to help cut down food cravings. A study at St. George's Hospital in London indicates that vanilla can curb the appetite. Under the guidance of Catherine Collins, chief dietician at St. George's, overweight people who were given vanilla-scented skin patches found that their sweet food intake was significantly reduced, leading to greater weight loss than those given dietary advice alone. Collins concluded that an intensely sweet vanilla-scented candle or essence may have a similar effect, though it hasn't been proved in a test environment. Dieticians in the United States working with overweight people are also often testing clients with an array of aromas as a way to reduce food cravings. While vanilla may not work for everyone, it appears to be useful for most. Breathing the aroma of a vanilla bean in a glass tube or wearing vanilla body products may be helpful.

After the Sloan-Kettering success, vanilla became the signature scent in a large variety of products, including carpet fresheners, candles, potpourri, and a number of perfumes. Annette Green, former president of the Fragrance Foundation in New York City, an educational institution, says, "It's all part of the olfactory 'security blanket.'" Green has attributed the increased use of vanilla to the above-mentioned scientific studies.

SEX, LOVE, AND THE VANILLA BEAN

Spring, summer, fall, and winter, we're in love with the idea of love. The perfume industry thrives on our desire to lure and captivate the object of our affection, and vanilla performs an important role in this drama. While a romantic sunset at the seashore and that "special song" may make us swoon, the *big* players in the game of love are taste and smell. There's something about the scent of vanilla that's at once sexy and erotic, sweet and innocent. Throughout the ages, vanilla has been considered an aphrodisiac both as a tincture to enhance passion and as an ingredient in sultry, exotic, and mysterious oriental fragrances, romantic floral bouquets, sophisticated and confident modern perfumes, and even in sensual, relaxing, and calming scents. Judging by its popularity as a fragrance in everything from body care to candles and air fresheners, we must conclude that vanilla has that secret something that draws us in. This brings us to some tests done by neurologist Alan R. Hirsch, M.D., of the Smell and Taste Treatment and Research Foundation, Ltd., in Chicago.

In controlled studies designed to better understand the connection between smell and sexual arousal, Dr. Hirsch had volunteers wear masks scented with an array of odors. Several fragrance combinations were found to be very effective in increasing penile blood flow. These included lavender and pumpkin pie, doughnut and black licorice, and pumpkin pie and doughnut. However, *older* men were most aroused by just one simple smell—*vanilla!* Modern science has proved what native people figured out centuries ago, and what many of us discovered on our own—whether you prefer to eat, drink, or smell it, vanilla is definitely a potent character in the arena of love!

Capitalizing on the various studies testing vanilla's appeal, by the mid-1990s there was an ample selection of perfumes, colognes, toilette waters, and skin-care products that featured vanilla as the primary note, bottom note, top note, or "just plain vanilla" essence, in and of itself. There was something for everyone, including vanilla in men's aftershave and colognes, a fragrance that, until then, had not been used much in men's toiletries. While the inexpensive fragrances were made with synthetics, better-quality perfumes contained pure vanilla esters and oleoresins.

In June of 1994, an article in the "Business Day" section of *The New York Times* announced "Everything's Coming Up Vanilla." The story mentioned that the cosmetic company Coty Inc. had introduced Vanilla Fields cologne nine months earlier and rung up $25 million in sales within four months! This trend was not limited to fragrances. Mark Mitchell, a product manager for McCormick & Company, said that vanilla-extract sales were running ahead of overall food-industry growth because of the use of vanilla in reduced-fat foods. "We're using vanilla to mask 'off notes' in food when you pull fat out. That is a big area of work for us, creating customized vanilla flavors and extracts for reduced-fat food products."

Vanilla became a popular addition to coffee as flavored coffees hit the market. Even cake mixes by companies such as Pillsbury created a stir. French Vanilla, Golden Vanilla, and Vanilla with Fudge mixes shot to the top third of the cake-mix market, according to Matthew Smith, marketing manager of Pillsbury.

The 1990s also brought in a new generation of vanilla traders. Henry Todd Jr. joined his father at Zink & Triest, later to take over the vanilla business. Douglas Daugherty followed his father's footsteps by working with Zink & Triest before becoming co-owner of Vanilla Corporation of America. Michael Champon, Guy Gaffney, George Lochhead, Josephine Lochhead, Bruce Murphy, Craig and Matt Nielsen, and Howard Smith Jr., among others, all came into their respective family businesses, bringing new energy and innovation to the industry.

European trader Berend Hachmann expanded his business to Canada in 1993, joining in partnership with David van der Walde, in Montreal, Quebec. Aust und Hachmann, Madagascar, was founded in 1996. In collaboration with his brother-in-law, Klaus Droege, Berend launched "Planifolia" in Guatemala in 2001, and Aust und Hachmann, Papua New Guinea, began in 2003. Other European companies also expanded the reach of their purchasing to new regions.

In Mexico, Olga Edda Gaya moved back to Gutiérrez Zamora to partner with brothers Orlando and Italo in the family business, which included the production of extract and a vanilla liqueur called Xanath. In Papantla, Pedro Heriberto Larios Rivera's daughter, Margarita Teresa, joined her father during the busy season, and daughter Olympia worked with the newly formed vanilla association. Victor Vallejo and his wife, Gloria, are now being joined by daughters Norma and Alma as the second generation of the family business.

At the same time, new companies were formed. François Bernard and Patrick Barthélémy launched Tripper, Inc., focused largely in Indonesia, Thomas Fricke set up ForesTrade Inc., a Fair Trade business, and Roger Rakotomalala began producing extract from beans from his home country of Madagascar, in conjunction with his tourism business. These are only some of the new companies that have joined the vanilla trade in the last fifteen years.

NEW COUNTRIES START GROWING VANILLA

Naturally, as the demand for vanilla grew, producers who had either grown vanilla in the past, or who had never grown vanilla before, got on the bandwagon. Their interest was also fueled by the drop in prices—first, of cacao, and later, coffee. Despite the low prices for vanilla in the mid-1990s, farmers saw an opportunity and acted on it.

MADE IN THE U.S.A.

When Hawaii was ceded to the United States in the late 1800s, cultivating tropical crops was part of the plan. Ultimately, Puerto Rico, which was outfitted with a research station and large botanical garden, did extensive studies on vanilla and oversaw its planting on home ground. A few growers took up vanilla farming in the Hawaiian islands, but over time the vanilla plantations here slowly faded away.

This changed when second-generation Hawaiian Tom Kadooka became fascinated with plant hybridizing while working at a dairy in the 1940s. He could only find one book on the subject, but he was diligent and determined and went on to become one of the pioneers in the Big Island flower industry, growing orchids, anthuriums, and mums.

Tom was intrigued by an interesting vine climbing on tree ferns, guava trees, and lantana on his sister's land in Ke'ei, Kona. He later learned that it was a vanilla vine. Apparently, there had been a still in the area, and the vanilla was used along with ti plant roots to make a potent bootleg liquor. When he found an article on vanilla genetics, he became even more interested and finally drove 110 miles to Hilo to learn more. Then, like so many others before and since, he fell under the spell of orchids and, specifically, vanilla and in the late 1940s joined the American Orchid Society (AOS).

He opened his nursery in Kainaliu, Kona, and continued to hybridize orchids, selecting rare, beautiful mutations and registering new clones. He put Kona on the orchid-collector's map with orchid cultivars such as *Brassolaeliocattleya* Ports of Paradise "Kainaliu," *Brassolaeliocattleya* Orange Nugget "Kadooka," and a unique *Vanda*, the pride of Kona. He marketed the blossoms of *Vanda* "Miss Joaquim" and selected a special cultivar (a winter variety that produced flowers when flowers were scarce). This nonedible, deep purple clone soon decorated the dinner plates of thousands of guests to Hawaii.

Despite his success with his nursery and orchid work, Tom found his interest in the vanilla culture burned so strongly that he decided to grow the plant. In the 1980s, he started the first orchid club in Kona and has remained the adviser for the Kona Daifukuji Orchid Club since 1983. He introduced vanilla to the members, won them over, and together they embarked on a community-wide vanilla venture. They created a large display at the Annual Honolulu Orchid Society Show in 1994 in Honolulu, where the trustees of the American Orchid Society held their semiannual meeting. It was through the AOS that they met other vanilla enthusiasts such as Robert Itoman of the Kaimuki Orchid Society, who has been teaching vanilla culture since the 1970s at the Lyon Arboretum in Honolulu, and Glen Fukumoto, extension agent in the livestock program of the University of Hawaii College of Tropical Agriculture and Human Resources in Kona. Kadooka's daughter, Janice Uchida, Ph.D., a plant pathologist, and his son, Chris Kadooka, assistant researcher for the University of Hawaii at Manoa, assisted their father's research project, which, by now, was a large hillside greenhouse filled with vanilla plants in pots that were producing thousands of beans.

In 1997, entrepreneurs Jim and Tracy Reddekopp bought a 4,000-square-foot vanilla field in South Kona and began the Hawaiian Vanilla Company, with *sensei* (master) Tom Kadooka as their mentor. Jim expanded his operation on the Hamakua coast on the Big Island of Hawaii. His first major client was Meadow Gold Dairies, a division of Suza Foods, Southwest Region, Dallas, Texas, which established a licensing agreement to market Hawaiian vanilla-bean ice cream. Portions of the proceeds from the sales of this product are donated to the Tom Kadooka scholarship fund, designed to interest young people in the agricultural future of Hawaii. Tom Kadooka's picture graces the company's ice-cream carton, and Meadow Gold's campaign to promote, support, and encourage tropical agriculture for Hawaii's youth is well under way.

Kadooka, now more than eighty years old, continues to do his research on vanilla, striving to create a vanilla plant that will be more resistant to diseases and pests. His dream is that vanilla from Hawaii will gain worldwide recognition to equal that of the famous gourmet Kona coffee.

Jim Reddekopp may be the person to help him realize this

dream. Reddekopp, age thirty-seven at the time of publication, grew up on Oahu, attending Lahainaluna High School as a boarder before going to work in his family's travel business. After moving with his wife, Tracy, and five children to six acres in rural Paauilo in the Big Island's Hamakua district, Reddekopp received a $110,000 federal grant to help him expand the family vanilla business, which specializes in value-added products.

"Value-added products are the only way to go," Reddekopp says. "We grow the only commercial vanilla beans in the United States, but the only way we can compete with the Third World is to take our vanilla and turn it into something interesting to locals and tourists alike."

Whereas Kadooka did the technical research, Jim brought his marketing skills to the enterprise. Using his grant money, Jim and his wife purchased the Kona-side field of a former vanilla grower and began what Jim calls "the Hawaiian vanilla expansion project." He is now contracting growers around the state to produce vanilla.

Kadooka has felt for a long time that vanilla culture could be the future of Hawaii. His feeling is that anyone with a backyard, some black shade netting, a few pots, and some patience could make a nice side business of growing vanilla beans. For the coffee growers it could be an ideal goal, as the pollination season for vanilla beans is the opposite of the busy time in the coffee groves. Agriculture keeps Hawaii beautiful and families employed, a good reason to encourage vanilla as a niche crop.

Carol Zakahi—a close friend of both the Kadookas and the Reddekopps, as well as an orchid enthusiast and, with her husband, a coffee grower in Kona—says that many young people on the Big Island don't want the hard work of growing coffee and macadamia nuts, but they want to find a way to stay on the island and keep the family land. Vanilla could be a part of that.

While the cost of growing vanilla in Hawaii is significantly higher than in most of the vanilla-growing countries worldwide, it is a special niche that can appeal to tourists and mainlanders alike. After all, it's "made in the U.S.A.!"

PAPUA NEW GUINEA

Papua New Guinea is located in Oceania, next to Indonesia and just north of Australia. The main island is divided into two countries: in the west is Irian Jaya, a part of Indonesia. The eastern part is mainland Papua New Guinea. There are also a number of small islands that are coastal provinces of Papua New Guinea.

Papua New Guinea is a mountainous, tropical country, covered with thick forests and divided by four major rivers. Until the end of World War II, it was almost entirely a traditional society. Because of the intensely rugged terrain (the central area is just now being carefully explored and mapped), bands and tribes of people were isolated from one another. As a result, there are far more than seven hundred languages and numerous dialects, and many distinct cultures. English and pidgin are the common languages for communication.

Vanilla was initially produced in Papua New Guinea during the European colonization of the Pacific in the nineteenth century but wasn't grown commercially. *Vanilla planifolia* was next introduced into Kerevat in East New Britain Province from Madagascar in May of 1963. Subsequent plantings included two varieties of *Vanilla tahitensis* in 1968 and *Vanilla pompona* in 1973. However, there wasn't much interest in commercial cultivation until the 1980s, and even then there was fairly small production. It wasn't until after the prices for coffee dropped in the 1990s that vanilla became a major cash crop. East Sepik Province is one of the largest producers of vanilla, and it is estimated that there are at least two million plants grown throughout the country.

To date, vanilla is strictly a cash crop, but because of the high prices in the last few years, it has been very lucrative for the growers, many of whom have sold directly to traders. Because there are less than one thousand miles of paved roads throughout the country, villages and towns are still quite isolated. One innovative way that Papua New Guinea has coped as a transitional society is by making certain that some of the children in their villages attend boarding schools and universities. In turn, those people who have received an education and are fluent in English act as representatives for their villages. Some have returned home to work as farmers, and they are the ones who travel hours over rough track roads to the city where they will visit Internet cafés to locate buyers for their vanilla or other crops. Others have taken jobs in the cities and watch after their families and villagers by returning home frequently and acting as liaisons with the West.

Sun curing and drying are the predominant methods used, and these work well with the Tahitian vanilla they grow. The curing and drying of the *Vanilla planifolia* have not been as successful, as it's dried for the same length of time as the *Vanilla tahitensis* and often gets moldy during export. Because *Vanilla tahitensis* grows so well in New Guinea, in the past few years it has provided a less expensive alternative to beans grown in Tahiti, and some American manufacturers have again incorporated it into blends for the signature heliotropin flavor note.

Interestingly enough, despite vanilla's being a new crop, it has now given rise to a number of standard words in pidgin: *maritim* is the marriage of vanilla or pollinating the flowers; *kisim* refers to the harvesting; and *driem* is the drying process. There's even an expression that's used when someone has a new outfit, something new for their home, or anything new that is special—*pipia blong vanilla*, meaning "It's just rubbish vanilla." However, vanilla has not been incorporated into foods or beverages, and most families don't know how it's used.

The sudden influx of money has been problematic for many villagers. Local banks place arbitrary limits on withdrawals, so few villagers use the banks. Traditionally, a particular shell was used as currency and was buried on family lands until it was needed. Money was not a primary factor, so creating a "budget" is a foreign concept. As a result, a lot of money has been spent on impulse items. The men and women who have received an education or have lived in the cities have advised the villagers to invest their money in better dwellings or education for their children. This has had mixed results. When the prices went sky-high in 2000, people planted vanilla all over the island, creating an oversupply of vanilla. The government, which encouraged the planting of vanilla, is currently researching ways to assist farmers unable to sell their crops.

INDIA

The history of vanilla in India began more than two hundred years ago when the plant was introduced by the British for growing at Kurtallam in the spice garden owned by the East India Company. But it was not exploited as a commercial crop. Vanilla was then introduced to the West Bengal, Bihar, Tamil Nadu, Pondicherry, Karnataka, Kerala, and Assam states in the late 1800s, but whatever projects were planned never materialized. It wasn't until 1945 that vanilla was consistently cultivated at the Kallar Fruit Research Station in the Nilgiris district of Tamil Nadu state in southern India. It was here that research into growing conditions for vanilla was conducted, and a handout on vanilla cultivation was published in 1958.

In the early 1990s, the Spices Board launched an extensive program for growing vanilla in Kerala state, also in southern India. The project was later expanded to include the Karnataka and Tamil Nadu states, and plants started by tissue cultivation were used. The Spices Board created a planting program, nursery and processing projects, and a fund for assisting producers to promote exports of organically grown vanilla and other spices.

The southern states, in peninsular India, contain an interesting mix of highly educated people, many of whom are trained in engineering, computer technology, or electronics; very poor, uneducated people; and tribal farmers. The Vindhya Mountains run east to west, dividing the north from the south and separating the northern fertile river valley of the Ganges (Ganga) from the Deccan Plateau, which extends through much of the Indian peninsula. South India's coastal plains are backed up by the Eastern and Western Ghats where tea, coffee, and spices are grown. The regional forests contain exotic hardwoods such as sandal, which is used for furniture and carvings, and its perfumed oil is found in fragrances and incense. The coastal regions—both east and west—are subject to torrential monsoons, and the area is hot and humid ten months of the year. The tropical heat is ideal for vanilla growing, though some places get too much rain, making it difficult to cure and dry the vanilla.

The efforts of the government-funded Spices Board to propagate and popularize vanilla cultivation in India have resulted in large numbers of farmers' taking up vanilla cultivation—particularly in the Karnataka and Kerala states. Again, there has been an interesting blend of growers. They include young engineers planting vanilla (especially since the prices went up so dramatically in the late 1990s), gentlemen farmers who either have retired from professional careers or are taking advantage of family lands to have a second business, and poorer farmers struggling to support their families. There are even specially funded projects for teaching the poor sustainable farming.

Overseeing one such program is Jai Chaitanya, who runs and manages the Hare Krishna Nature Farm in Karnataka state. Educated and in his thirties, he has dedicated his life to teaching sustainable, organic farming to poor farmers and tribal people. His farm is set up as a working model where people can come from all over India (and the world) to observe and learn the most efficient methods for cultivating and producing a variety of crops. Jai travels to conferences and summits on organic and sustainable farming, and visits other countries in search of the latest techniques that he can apply to his program. Vanilla has been one of the crops that he has cultivated.

Due to the research and development activities of the Spices Board, ten years after the southern states launched their project, they were producing more than 70 tons of green vanilla, and the plantations have continued to grow and expand. In the regions where there isn't adequate natural rainfall, drip irrigation has been introduced as well as shade-cloth production. In areas where there is too much rainfall, harvested vanilla beans have been taken over to the Western Ghats to dry.

India is now facing the problem of overproduction. The Indians, with a long history of entrepreneurship, have already begun to address this by setting up extraction plants. As India is a major tourist attraction, it won't take long for vanilla to find its way into the tourist hotels and shops and for it to be made into value-added products.

Traders who have been in the business for a long time have assumed that India will be knocked out of the vanilla market when the prices drop again. This may be true for those who grow vanilla as a side business, but for the very poor it may prove to be a worthwhile long-term investment.

UGANDA

Uganda, located in Equatorial East Africa, has hot, tropical weather all year, fertile soil, and two dry seasons, which give vanilla growers the unique advantage of having two harvests a year. Given that their cost point is $30 a kilo ($13.60 per pound) for cured, dried beans, vanilla is an ideal crop for a group of people who have experienced more than their share of political violence and poverty.

Vanilla planifolia was first introduced into Uganda during the colonial period around 1918 when Uganda was still a British protectorate. White, Asian, and Indian growers leased vast tracts of land from the government for use in commercial farming. Coffee, cotton, rubber, and cacao were the primary crops, and vanilla was grown as a secondary crop, using the coffee and cacao bushes for supports. Migrant workers came from other regions of Uganda as well as Rwanda, Burundi, and southern Sudan to work on the large plantations.

The Ugandans living in the districts where vanilla was grown were Bantu tribes who lived a traditional lifestyle as cattle herders and cultivators of food crops. They did not grow vanilla, and most didn't work on the plantations in the early years. Later, they began growing cotton, coffee, and cacao as well as working on the European plantations.

As mentioned earlier, McCormick & Company went into a joint venture in the early 1960s to do estate production of vanilla. This project came to a standstill in the early 1970s when Idi Amin came into power and all whites and Asians were expelled from the country. During the nightmarish years of rule by Idi Amin and Milton Obote, the economy collapsed, and what was once known as the "breadbasket of Africa" went fallow. Families who lived near the big plantations took cuttings from the vanilla vines and grew them on a small scale, but they had no market for vanilla until the late 1980s when Aga Sekalala encouraged farmers in the Mukono district to grow it for sale to McCormick & Company.

Vanilla is now grown in ten different districts, primarily on the shores of Lake Victoria and on the banks of the Nile River. The Mukono district, not far from the capital city of Kampala, is the primary vanilla-growing region, followed by the Bundibugyo district on the western side of Uganda. The two regions have rich soil, ample rain, and forests that provide shade for the vanilla. Coffee and bananas are grown alongside the vanilla and provide shade and additional humidity.

The growers are from several tribes, each with its own languages, but Luganda is the commonly used language for communication between different groups. Growers who also cure and dry their vanilla speak English as well, but in the villages English is rarely used. Plantations are family enterprises on small plots of land, with as few as one hundred vines to as many as forty thousand. There are also some larger estates of 10 to 40 acres. The success of these farmers, especially in the Mukono district, encouraged farmers from other parts of the country to set up associations for growing vanilla. The United States Agency for International Development (USAID) set up a project in 1996 to assist farmers with cultivation techniques to produce higher yields and establish standards of quality and other technical assistance, including teaching the Indian Ocean style of curing and drying the beans. Not all areas have electricity, but some growers who do, or who have warehouses in or close to Kampala, also use high pressure 5,000-watt sodium lights. These mimic sunlight for about two hours each day to speed up the drying process, especially during periods of rain.

Growers who don't cure and dry their own beans are paid at the end of the harvest. The money goes for school fees for their children, the purchase of farm animals for household use and extra income, and long-term investments such as buying trucks and doing home improvement.

Unlike growers in most countries where vanilla is a new crop, the Ugandans use vanilla to flavor their food, alcoholic beverages, and tea. They also refer to harvest payment and shopping with earnings as "vanilla."

The quality of Ugandan vanilla is excellent. Help from McCormick & Company and USAID has ensured a standard of quality that matches Indian Ocean and Mexican vanilla. The majority of exports are to the United States. Uganda will be able to weather the drop in vanilla prices and, if the country remains stable, will benefit from vanilla growing in the coming years.

MEXICO REVISITED

In the latter 1950s, Mexico's vanilla production decreased dramatically as Totonac growers took work on cattle ranches and citrus plantations instead. The booming petroleum industry along the gulf was also a major draw for young men as family plots on the *ejidos* were too small to support multiple generations. The established families, who cured and dried the vanilla, stayed in business, buying whatever vanilla was available, processing it, and shipping it to the United States. It remained popular for its quality, and

VANILLA MEMORIES FROM A MEXICAN CHILDHOOD

Yolanda Arzani

I am a descendant of an Italian family who immigrated to Mexico in the late 1800s. They were originally from Piovera, in the Alessandria province in the region of Piedmont in northwest Italy. They were farmers and traders. They started in the vanilla business around 1893. My grandfather, José Francisco Arzani Giovannini, had three brothers, Domingo, José Luís, and Felio. José Luís and Felio went to live to Mexico City, and only my grandpa and Uncle Domingo stayed in Gutiérrez Zamora to work in the vanilla business.

My father told me that my uncle Domingo was very well-known and respected in the United States. The vanilla traders looked for his signature on the vanilla packages as proof of high quality. Someone in New York even brought my uncle north one time to save a shipment of vanilla that got moldy. Although Uncle Domingo also sold some vanilla to the States, he preferred working with the vanilla than acting as a trader, so he sold to one Señor Collado, an exporter who then sold the vanilla to a broker.

In 1969 my dad decided that if Señor Collado could sell our vanilla, he could do it, too, so against my grandpa's wishes, Dad started to look for customers. The first shipment he sold was *picadura* (cuts and splits) as the customer wanted the vanilla for shampoos, soaps, and perfumes, and off the vanilla went to Philadelphia. Dad continued to trade vanilla to the United States, Chile, Argentina, and Japan until 1979 when my grandpa passed away and my uncle took control of the business.

My grandfather's brother, Uncle José Luís, who lived in Mexico City, knew the Coca-Cola distributor in Mexico City and put him in touch with my dad. Even though my father spoke no English, he negotiated a contract with Coca-Cola and started selling our vanilla to them around 1970.

One of my favorite childhood memories is the vanilla itself. I grew up saturated with that beautiful aroma at my grandparents' home where everything smelled like vanilla. Their home was divided into three parts. The smallest area was the house itself. Next was *la bodega* (warehouse and offices), which had an old desk, two rocking chairs, and a big scale and safe. And then there was the patio. Their patio was like no other I can remember; it was huge! There were two *quemadores* (curing ovens), and later they added another two in addition to a large area of cement where the vanilla would dry.

My grandpa spent a lot of time sitting in his rocking chair, waiting for the Totonacas who passed by, selling their green vanilla. At the end of the buying season, we had green mountains of vanilla all over *la bodega*. It was now time to start with the processing. For that, we needed *los trabajadores*, the workers. In those days there was a very strong vanilla union that set the men's salaries. There were three levels of workers: *el maestro*, *oficial primero*, and *oficial segundo*. The men were always happy, or at least I always saw them smiling and talking to each other. They treated us with a lot of respect no matter that we were just kids. One time I wanted to share that happiness and decided to join them on their job. I brought my little chair close to my grandma and asked her to show me how to do it. She started to show me how to *despezonar la vainilla*—process the vanilla. My grandpa saw that and called my grandma and talked to her. When Grandma returned, she told me that I couldn't work with them. I was very sad when she explained that the liquid that came out of the vanilla would burn my hands. I didn't understand why it would burn my hands but not burn the hands of the men. I figured that my grandpa didn't want me to do it, but I stayed there on my chair, enjoying the company of all of them.

Later, I found out why my grandpa did not want me to work with them. I was always curious about my grandpa's thumbnail; it was long and yellow. The other thumbnail wasn't as long but it, and most of his fingernails, were also yellow. He told me that he needed the strong, long thumbnail to cut the *pezón* (tip) of the vanilla beans, and the liquid coming out from the vanilla beans burned his fingers and caused the nails to discolor and deteriorate. At that moment I realized why he didn't want me to work in the vanilla, and I loved him more for taking care of me and thought that his hands were the most beautiful hands I ever touched.

At noon all the activities stopped for lunch. *Los trabajadores* had lunch right there at *la bodega* and Grandpa and Grandma dined in their home. I remember my grandpa always ate with his sterling silverware; they were very heavy and his fork was *chueco* (crooked), like it was molded to his teeth. My grandmother gave their silver set to me as a memento after my grandpa died.

My most vivid memory of the vanilla is the big vanilla carpet on the patio. The *trabajadores* laid out *petates* (mats) and then brought the vanilla out to spread on them. They used a cotton cloth that was about 1 meter long by 20 to 30 centimeters (roughly 40 inches by 8 to 11 inches) to roll up the vanilla, and then they carried it in their arms out to the mats. I wished to roll in the vanilla so many times, and I regret never having done it at least once! I think my grandpa felt the same way about the vanilla as he often slept in *la bodega* surrounded by *espigeros* (shelves) and big wooden boxes full of vanilla.

My grandpa was very good at curing vanilla and an expert at classifying it. His eyes were not good, but his fingers were very sensitive. He was quite accurate in classification; by just touching the skin of the vanilla, he knew its quality. To export the vanilla, they packed it in a special way. The vanilla was in *mazos* (about fifty beans wrapped in cord), then packed in large tin boxes lined with wax paper. My grandpa separated the best *picadura* for the family. And he made each person feel very special when he presented the beans to them. He used to tell my sister that he picked that *picadura* just for her, so she could make her very own extract. My sister treasured that *picadura* for years after my grandpa died. Eventually, she had to give it to my mother as she was moving out of Mexico and had no way to keep it.

I know that no matter how far away I am from that time, the vanilla will be with me forever. No matter if I haven't a single bean with me, I can close my eyes and be transported to those days and smell its aroma and feel its texture. I feel so lucky to have had such a flavorful childhood!

those who knew vanilla well still considered it the finest in the world. Yolanda Arzani, born in Gutiérrez Zamora, describes what it was like to be a part of the Mexican vanilla industry in the early 1970s.

In the late 1970s and early 1980s, a new generation of Mexicans came into the industry. Some, like Pedro Heriberto Larios Rivera, had family members who had worked in vanilla in the past, and others were interested in being a part of a tradition that was deeply ingrained in Totonacapan. Most were educated as engineers and had a more technical approach to cultivating, curing, and drying the vanilla.

Theirs was not an easy undertaking as the rain forest was gone, destroyed by the petroleum industry and cattle grazing. Rainfall, which had always been inconsistent, was even more erratic due to the loss of the forest cover. Because of this, it was hotter and less humid. Most of the vanilla-producing countries had a lower price point for their vanilla, so competition was fierce. But by the late 1980s the citrus industry, which had done quite well in the area until Brazil undercut them price-wise, was slowing down. Ever resourceful, some Mexican growers converted orange groves into vanilla fields, using the orange trees as support and shade for the vanilla. They banked on Mexico's earlier reputation for producing the finest beans in the world and went to work.

By the turn of the millennium, intercropping vanilla with citrus was increasingly popular, especially along the southern growing area of San Rafael, not far from the once famous Misantla Valley. Growers are also experimenting with shade cloth and greenhouse production and other more modern techniques for expanding production. And as tourism in the region is growing, there is also a market for Mexican beans and vanilla crafts in Papantla and at the increasingly popular ruins of El Tajín. The state government even took a nominal interest in the vanilla growers and in late 2001 set up the *Consejo Veracruzano de la Vainilla* (Veracruz Vanilla Council), funded by the government, and headed locally by Victor Vallejo. Vallejo was born in Michoacán and raised in Mexico City before moving to Papantla to raise cattle, set up a cheese business, and grow vanilla. He has been a good liaison for the Mexican industry as he is bilingual and bicultural, adept in negotiating with both the government and industry and not swayed by the rivalries

DON FERNANDO PATIÑO: VANILLA ORNAMENT ARTIST

Fernando Patiño, master ornament maker and national treasure of Mexico, was born in Papantla, Veracruz, and lived there the majority of his life. His grandparents came from Spain at the time of major European immigration to tropical Veracruz, during the mid-1800s. The family settled in Papantla and coastal Tuxpan, working in agriculture and livestock ranch-

Vanilla ornaments are made of the highest-quality vanilla beans as
they need to be flexible and maintain their shape once woven or bent
into place. Ornaments can be very simple or as elaborate as
full, beautiful crowns given to royalty around the world.
Note: the Vanilla Queen has several crowns and even a scepter!

ing. This was a period of expansion and excitement throughout
the region, and the vanilla industry was flourishing. By the time
Fernando was born in 1908, Papantla was a wealthy community and tourist destination for Mexicans with the means to
travel.

Fernando's father, Sotero Patiño Pardo, worked at the Casa
Subieta as a "gang" or crew foreman, overseeing the sorting,
bundling, and packaging of the vanilla beans. This was his

bread and butter. His avocation was wood carving, and he had a flair for turning sections of wood into pieces of art.

Fernando remembered trips on horseback with his father through the rolling hills from Papantla down to the steaming tropical coastal town of Tuxpan to visit family. One of several children, he was the observant child, the one who would later recall the history of his famous town with uncanny clarity. During the years when vanilla was queen in Mexico, when there were twenty-one large family businesses where the vanilla was cured and dried, Fernando's beautiful younger sister, Eloisa, charmed her way into the homes of high society, thereby opening the door for her big brother to join her at the fabulous balls and midnight buffets of the wealthy. Fernando experienced the days when the plaza was a sea of white as the Totonacs came in from the ranchos for the festival of Corpus Christi, riding the finest horses, the women adorned with exquisite gold filigree jewelry. This was the *bella epoca*, when life was good.

By the mid-1920s, however, his father, Sotero, knew that the industry was in grave danger. He decided to parlay his avocation into a life as artisan, creating magnificent figures and decorations of vanilla. During his lifetime he crafted exquisite ornaments for European royalty, museums, and world expositions, all constructed from the finest Mexican beans.

Fernando was young and restless; becoming an apprentice artisan in his twenties held little fascination for a man with an inquisitive mind and a yen for travel. He worked with family in the livestock industry, traveled yearly to Southern California and Arizona, and lived a life of adventure. Then his mother suffered a stroke, and his father was unable to support the family alone. Fernando returned home and assumed responsibility for the care of his family. In 1950 he went into the family business and discovered that he had the hands and imagination for creating fine art. At the time of his father's death, he was a master craftsman, supporting not only his bedridden mother but also his beloved sister and her daughter. Throughout his life he unflinchingly remained devoted to family, never marrying, instead assisting his sister in raising his niece, Rocio, who learned to create vanilla art seated next to her famous uncle.

Fernando was a small, unassuming man with a passion for his work. In most respects quiet and retiring, he would come alive as a magnificent storyteller at his workbench as his nimble fingers twisted, bent, shaped, and tied supple vanilla beans into works of art. Over his lifetime Don Fernando received considerable recognition for his art. In the 1990s he was the subject of several documentaries in Mexico and Japan. His decorative work is in museums and possessed by royalty—he even made artifacts for the pope. His family was probably more taken by his celebrity status than he was. He really preferred to visit with friends and guests while he replicated the Pyramid of Niches or the flying *Voladores* from fragrant beans. Until his mid-eighties, he never wore glasses, his needle pulling deftly through the beans and his still flexible fingers creating the delicate and intricate weaving of baskets and bowls.

By his early nineties, Fernando was no longer able to work, whiling away his time sitting in the family room, observing the activities of a family that had a constant stream of visitors passing in and out throughout the day. His favorite pastime was to tell his stories to visitors who came from many countries to meet the man who, with his father, created a new industry for Papantla, a community business born of resourcefulness and creativity.

and jealousies of vanilla producers and *beneficiadores* who have been in the industry for generations.

THE TURN OF THE MILLENNIUM

The flood in Mexico in late 1999 and Cyclone Hudah in Madagascar in early 2000 destroyed much of the two countries' vanilla crops, and prices skyrocketed. In 1998, cured, dried vanilla was selling for less $20 a kilo ($9 per pound); in 2000, it was selling for nearly $100 a kilo (a little over $45 per pound). The year 2001 saw prices climb higher, and by 2002 vanilla was selling for more than $200 a kilo ($91 per pound). Needless to say, this was incentive for anyone who lived in an area that could produce vanilla to plant vines or bring dormant plantations back to life. Fiji, Tonga (especially on Nuku'alofa), Tahiti, the Comoros, Guatemala, Costa Rica, Caribbean countries, and even tiny islands in the South Seas all hoped to cash in on the vanilla boom as prices soared ever higher. By early 2004 the highest-quality vanilla from the Indian Ocean and Mexico was selling for $500 a kilo ($227 per pound) or more!

At the same time, vanilla continued to make headlines. Vanilla was declared the new flavor of the year in *Food Distribution Magazine*. Lynn Dornblaser, editorial director of *New Product News* in Chicago, said in 1999 that "vanilla isn't so vanilla anymore. No longer synonymous with 'boring,' vanilla-flavored products are popping up in every aisle. . . . We've always seen vanilla, but now it is sought after as the flavor of choice, not the bland carrier for other flavors." After the terrorist attack in the United States on September 11, 2001, comfort foods were increasingly sought out, and vanilla ice cream and other vanilla-flavored products were high on the list of foods that soothed.

ROBBERY

As prices for vanilla skyrocketed, so, too, did the problem of theft, and no vanilla-producing region has been exempt from frustration and violence. In Madagascar, beginning after the hurricane of 2000, workers in the curing houses were subject to pat-down searches. As the prices went higher and robbery became a daily problem, the rules got stricter. Because theft is very difficult to control, and because the vanilla market was beginning to resemble the illicit drug market in value, locks and security guards were simply not enough of a deterrent. Now, workers were required to change their clothing on entering the area and on leaving at the end of the workday. The vanilla beans were put into shipping containers and welded shut at night. The containers were opened with a welding torch the next morning.

Farmers, unaccustomed to having anything so valuable, kept their processed vanilla in their homes, but it was now necessary to have family members guarding their homes all the time. Some acquired guns and slept with their vanilla. But as the prices went up, the situation grew dire. In the autumn of 2003, a Malagasy couple who were buyers for one of the big vanilla exporters were ambushed and murdered as they drove from a plantation outside

Sambava. *La Gazette de la Grande Île* reported that on November 28, 2003, eight robbers armed with assault rifles broke into a family's home in the town of Andrampengy, murdered a couple, and seriously wounded their child, then stole two hundred million Malagasy francs from the sale of the family's processed vanilla. Two days later, there was another armed robbery in Andrampengy, where the thieves stole 100 kilos (220 pounds) of top-grade vanilla ready to be exported. Violence is unusual in the Malagasy culture, but with vanilla worth so much, the problems continued until the government brought in military reservists as well as police to patrol the roads in the SAVA region.

Papua New Guinea has had a major problem with crime in the bigger cities but not in the bush until 2001. In the words of one local, Maisen Windu:

"There is a lot of robbery along the Sepik Highway in East Sepik Province. Initially, vanilla was introduced to Maprik province, and the people of Maprik kept it a secret from the western part of Maprik. Due to intermarriage, travel throughout the region, and so forth, the people in western Maprik found out, and then two or three years ago the people in the Sepik area found out. The Maprik growers travel with their vanilla about 120 to 150 kilometers [up to 100 miles] to the city of Wewak. It is along this route that people are robbed by thieves and hooligans.

"My brother in-law is a public motor vehicle driver who transports people from Maprik to Wewak to sell their vanilla. He was one of the victims of robbery. The truck was held up, and those who had vanilla for sale were robbed and he was punched and kicked. Now the vanilla has spread around the country and everyone in the region is involved in the cultivating of vanilla. Thieves go directly to the vanilla gardens and steal from the farmers."

With their new money, growers have purchased assault rifles to protect themselves and their crops. Gangs of thugs known as "the Rascals" are armed with automatic weapons and assault rifles and terrorize people passing through the vanilla regions.

In Indonesia, farmers have harvested their vanilla very early to avoid robbery. Java local Effendi Sutadisastra said that in late 2003 the problem of robbery was so great in his region that his vanilla was picked at four months to avoid total loss. A few months later, the price of green vanilla had risen to $47 a kilo (about $21 per pound). Unfortunately, no one had any vanilla to sell.

Farmers build small huts in their fields and sleep in the huts, armed with machetes, from the time beans appear until harvest. There are neighborhood watches with observation lookouts up in the trees. Growers work as a team to protect their crops, including all of them harvesting the same day.

Guns of any type are illegal in Indonesia. At the same time, there is no tolerance for deviant behavior, and villagers often take the law into their own hands as the police and the system are corrupt. At the very least, robbers are beaten when caught. In 2003 several men caught stealing vanilla in Lampung were tied to trees, doused with kerosene, and burned to death.

When told about how Indonesians deal with vanilla robbers, a frustrated man in India said, "Here we would like to do the same to the thieves as they do in Indonesia, but in reality, we handle it the traditional way. We report the robbers to the police and have them arrested. We pay money to the cops so that they are thrashed and incapable of thieving for about a month, and then they will be back in business once again.

"One safeguard taken by buyers of green beans in Kerala state is to register the location and address of all sellers of green beans when they come in with their vanilla. The addresses are cross-checked with known growers of the area, which discourages the thieves to steal green beans. This is a concerted effort between the genuine growers and the buying industry. How long this will last I don't know, but at least it is a positive step."

Mexico has had a long history of robbery and violence surrounding the vanilla industry. The most recent serious incident was in 1986. Several men from Oaxaca hired out to work on a rancho for the vanilla season. When the owner of the rancho had been paid, they first murdered his wife, two other workers, and seriously wounded a third, then ransacked the house, looking for the money but without success. They then ambushed the owner on the road and killed him. Ironically, he had been paid by check and hadn't yet cashed it. The bank stopped payment of funds, then confiscated the money to pay back a loan the owner had taken to cover his costs for the season. The sole survivor, Cesar Arellano, who now manages Rancho Beatriz, could have identified the men had they been caught, but they crossed the mountains into Oaxaca and disappeared.

This year, Mexico was proactive, bringing in two helicopters and military personnel who had roadblocks in place before harvesting began. However, their diligence backfired in an amusing incident involving Victor Vallejo, the former head of the Veracruz Vanilla Council, a trade group, and his wife, Gloria. Victor went out to the family ranch to pick up cheese for delivery in a neighboring city. Seeing vanilla beans that had fallen off the vines, he collected them and put them in a bag in the back of the car. He then drove home and gave Gloria the car to deliver the cheese. Gloria was stopped at the checkpoint, and the officers asked if they could examine her car. Unaware that the vanilla beans were in the back of the car, she readily agreed. They found the beans and started questioning her. She explained that her husband was the head of the Vanilla Council for Veracruz and that he must have gathered the beans from their ranch that day. They asked to see her driver's license. In Mexico women keep their maiden name, so the license said "Caserín" instead of "Vallejo." They apologized profusely . . . and took her into the station.

The police then called Victor and asked him his wife's name. When he told them, they said, "Okay, we'll release her, but you have to come to the station to pick up your vanilla." Victor, ever ready with a quick response, said, "Actually, the beans are worth more than my wife. Why don't you keep her and just give me back the beans."

The scarcity of vanilla has diminished its popularity as vanilla products have become less available and retail prices have climbed steeply. It will be interesting to see if it will again soar in popularity as the prices fall.

· 8 ·

THE POLITICS OF OUR PASSION

As we have seen throughout this book, the vanilla industry has been controlled by the volatile issues of weather, political instability, war, the whims of governments, plant disease, and industry and consumer interest. That vanilla only thrives in a narrow, politically vulnerable equatorial band, that it is so labor-intensive, and that it is most affordably produced in countries with a large and hungry labor force puts it at a distinct risk in terms of availability. As most of the vanilla-growing regions are susceptible to cyclones, typhoons, or hurricanes, as well as to drought and, now, the increasingly common El Niño fluctuations, it is difficult to predict with any certainty the outcome of a particular crop at the time of pollination. Added to the mix of political coups, wars, and theft, there is no guarantee that even the most abundant and promising crop will reach its destination intact and on time . . . or even at all.

MARKET CONTROL
IN MADAGASCAR

For years governments and producers have volleyed for market control. While the Mexican Totonacs once controlled the world vanilla industry through planting, pollinating, and selling—or withholding—the crop, once the Indian Ocean plantations were developed, it didn't much matter what Mexico produced. This is with the notable exception of the period during World War II when vanilla from the Indian Ocean islands was unobtainable. So it came as no surprise that when Madagascar gained its independence from the French in 1964, the government would want to manage the industry.

Madagascar became a state-controlled market. Importing vanilla from Madagascar to Europe and the United States was like having a special broker's license. Buyers came to Paris to purchase vanilla, and the government set the selling price and yearly quotas. There were fewer than a dozen major buyers in attendance, with an attorney who acted as arbitrator over discussions and didn't permit individual companies to monopolize sales or band together. In fact, the buyers jealously purchased their beans in private meetings with sellers—never on the floor—and with hopes that they alone might be given deferential treatment.

Under industry regulation, the price had little to do with supply and demand, and it certainly wasn't free market, but it was predictable, increasing at the rate of about 2 to 3 percent per year. Everyone knew and accepted the terms and conditions. As there was no need for intensive speculation, quality was controlled, vanilla stayed on the vines the necessary eight to nine months to

Malagasy woman carrying a basket of vanilla beans

produce premium quality, and everyone benefited except, perhaps, the growers themselves.

The obvious advantage to this arrangement was price stability. Other vanilla-producing countries set their prices based on Madagascar's standard. Countries new to the vanilla trade typically sold at a little under Madagascar's current price. Mexico, however, banked on its longtime reputation for quality when setting its price. Additionally, the cost of living in Mexico was considerably higher than in Madagascar but, as there has continued to be a relatively small but consistent demand for Mexican vanilla, the growers survived.

There were, of course, disadvantages to the Madagascar system. It created an inefficient price structure with no reference to supply and demand. It also led to rampant corruption. The government-levied taxes never improved the lives of the Malagasy or the infrastructure. And the middlemen and traders made the lion's share of the profit, with the farmers receiving only a small piece of the pie.

Deregulation

In 1994, everything changed. A new political regime brought about industry deregulation. The International Monetary Fund–imposed conditions were not well accepted. As the quota system ended in Madagascar, buyers and sellers alike were confused about quantities of available product as well as the taxes that had historically affected vanilla sales. If the sellers paid the government tax, then they didn't earn as much money as those who didn't. If they didn't pay the tax, they were disregarding the law. Where there had been only a few major exporters before, there were suddenly dozens of exporters, most of them new to the market. As vanilla has been a primary economic driver in Madagascar, everyone wanted in on the action.

Then prices collapsed. Farmers stopped caring for their plants as they couldn't make an adequate return on their investment. Vanilla supplies that had been in storage to ensure against a shortage were burned, ostensibly because of a market glut and painfully low prices, but also, in part, because of the mold on poorly stored beans. Vanilla prices went into a free-fall, with vanilla selling for as low as $12 a kilo ($5.50 per pound) or less, down from a high of $74 a kilo ($33.50 per pound) a few years before. The price drop impacted all vanilla-growing regions. Only producers with a niche market demand (Tahiti, Mexico, and parts of Indonesia) and the very poor had incentives to grow vanilla. With prices at a low not seen for years, demand for natural vanilla increased, especially in the United States. Vanilla grown or purchased before the price collapse traveled from port to port. Known as "vanilla touriste," it circulated for a few years but was eventually sold.

Then, in September of 1999, a company in Europe needed 20 tons of vanilla and couldn't find it. With prices so low, farmers had planted minimal vanilla. Word went out to brokers, and suddenly the demand grew to 100 tons. In September of 1999, prices were at $25 a kilo ($11.35 per pound); six months later the prices shot up precipitously.

In October of 1999, Mexico was hit by a tropical depression, triggering the kind of flood that occurs only every thousand years. Hundreds of people and thousands of animals were killed, vast areas were inundated, and a large percentage of the vanilla crop was destroyed. In March of 2000, Cyclone Hudah flattened a swath of northern Madagascar, causing extensive damage to vanilla in storage as well as to the current vanilla crop and plant stock. Demand far outpaced supply, and prices soared.

The past four years have brought continued troubles to the industry. Damaged plants needed time to recover. Mexico was faced with drought following the pollinating seasons of 2002 and 2003, limiting supplies to fewer than 10 tons countrywide each year. At the same time, heavy rainfall caused by El Niño during pollination in Madagascar caused the flowers to fall from the vines. The 2003 crop brought roughly 400 tons of dried vanilla, far less than the normal annual volume of 1,000 tons or more.

The troubles experienced by Madagascar and Mexico certainly assisted newer industry players such as Uganda, Papua New

A woman with her child in a vanilla grove in Madagascar

Guinea, and India, but even they couldn't meet the unexpected increased demand for vanilla created by the soft drink and alcoholic beverage markets' launch of new vanilla-flavored products. By the end of 2003, prices were more than $500 a kilo ($227 per pound) in Madagascar.

After the Madagascar cyclone in 1979 pushed prices to $150 a kilo ($68 per pound), manufacturers turned to synthetics during this time, and never resumed using pure vanilla when the prices dropped. Others say that the market did come back but that it took almost ten years to recover.

Overall demand for vanilla has dropped from 2,200 tons of dried vanilla to about half this amount in the past four years, this despite the increased use of vanilla in the beverage and gourmet ice-cream industries. Farmers, eager to take advantage of the extraordinary prices, have overpollinated their plants in an attempt to maximize their potential earnings. While this will work in the short term, it means that plants will quickly become exhausted and not produce well the following year.

Assuming that weather and politics cooperate, the 2004 harvest in Madagascar should bring 1,000 tons of vanilla beans onto the market late in the year. If this happens, there will be more than enough vanilla to go around.

Unfortunately, because of the current value of the vanilla, the issue of theft is real and immediate; most farmers will harvest before their vanilla is fully mature, which means the quality will be less than ideal. And, because everyone who is currently growing vanilla is pushing production to the point of exhaustion while the prices are high, the plants will produce less in 2005. Regardless, so many farmers have been struck with vanilla fever that there is a glut on the market, and prices are already dropping.

Predictions were that the prices wouldn't fall as precipitously as they rose over the past two years but, rather, would decline in steps, but in reality this isn't happening. Most farmers know that the current boon has been a serendipitous moment of fortune and that it won't last. However, in India, top prices were paid to the producers of green beans, and the middlemen have been overly optimistic about what they can earn for their processed beans. A hard lesson that producers and buyers have experienced over the years is that it's like musical chairs—you don't want to be left standing without a chair and your arms full of vanilla when the market collapses. A drop over a year's time from $500 a kilo ($227 a pound) to $100 ($45 a pound) or less could ensure a major loss for anyone sitting on several tons of vanilla beans.

Given the multitude of challenges and obstacles involved in producing vanilla, and given the majority of vanilla users that reside in an entirely different environment far from where it's produced, there have been ongoing attempts to manipulate and control the production of vanilla ever since the Europeans first learned of it nearly 500 years ago. As growing vanilla commercially in temperate climates wasn't a viable option, and as the synthetics couldn't emulate the flavor profile, until recently there has been a reluctant acceptance of this reality, coupled with an eye trained to watch for other possibilities.

A lot has changed in the last fifteen years. Scientists, largely funded by flavor corporations, have diligently worked to unlock the secrets of vanilla. The intention is to modify and strengthen plant stock so that it can grow in a wider range of climates and be more disease resistant, as well as to isolate the organic compounds that make up the complex flavor and fragrance of vanilla, with the end goal of creating flavor-identical alternatives.

First International Congress on the Future of the Vanilla Business

In November 2003, Daphna Havkin-Frankel, Ph.D., a specialist in vanilla and vanillin production at the Biotechnology Center for Agriculture and the Environment at Rutgers University in New Brunswick, New Jersey, organized and chaired the first international congress to address the future of the vanilla business. Speakers included scientists and academics from around the world who specialize in a variety of areas of vanilla research and study. Also speaking were members of the vanilla industry with expertise in particular vanilla-producing regions, a patent attorney, a representative of the American-based Flavor and Extract Manufacturers Association, and one vanilla producer.

The objective of the congress was, in the words of Dr. Frankel, "to create a perspective on the overall context as well as specific issues of the vanilla business. One burning issue is the economics and trading of cured vanilla beans. I hope that this meeting will help to sort out the root cause of the problem and offer some solutions. We are also looking forward to gain knowledge and understanding on the various aspects of the business. New scientific developments may also unravel long-standing questions on the biology and technology of vanilla and vanillin."

The two-day congress addressed phytochemical genomics (approaches for gene discovery) for the flavor and pharmaceutical industries; the market and future for natural vanilla; analytical approaches to vanilla quality and authentication and composition of vanilla beans from different geographical regions; flavor-extraction techniques; the biology, biotechnology, chemistry, and physics of vanilla and vanillin; and specific applications of vanilla in foods, perfumery, pharmaceuticals, and aromatherapy.

NATURAL FLAVOR-IDENTICAL ALTERNATIVES

Perhaps the most controversial topic of discussion concerned the use of "flavor-identical alternatives." This subject has become increasingly interesting to American flavor manufacturers in the past several years because of the escalating prices of natural vanilla beans (and, therefore, extract) and consistent instability in tropical growing regions. However, whereas in Europe flavor-identical vanillas have been used and accepted for some time, flavor-identical vanilla alternatives have not met the FDA criteria for listing as Category I vanilla, which requires that the entire flavorant be produced from pure, natural vanilla from vanilla-bean extractives.

The law, with regard to flavor-identical alternatives (also called WONF, or "with other natural flavors") states that in order for a vanilla flavor to be presented as a natural substance, a vanillin not coming from vanilla beans must be obtained through one of the following: enzymatic or microbiologic process; or physical process; or created from a natural raw material. In other words, a vanillin-based product is considered natural if it's derived from plant synthesis, though not necessarily from vanilla beans. The FDA ruling says the natural flavor must come from vanilla beans.

As can easily be imagined, this is a loaded topic. Scientists have focused on the biotechnology of producing better and stronger vanilla plants and alternatives to traditional vanilla-bean extractives. Flavor companies are interested in flavor salads or bouquets that are marketable, high-quality, and less expensive alternatives to the more expensive traditional vanilla beans. Vanilla-bean traders are concerned about their livelihood as providers of natural vanilla to the industrial, food-service, and consumer markets. Extraction manufacturers are anxious about remaining within the law, despite the sharp rise in costs of the vanilla. And farmers want to maintain their livelihoods.

The unanswered question is where the middle ground exists where we can provide an affordable, high-quality product that

THE ETHICS OF PLANT MANIPULATION

In 1987, plant scientist Walter Goldstein joined ESCAgenetics Corporation in San Carlos, California. ESCAgenetics evolved from the bankruptcy of the International Plant Research Institute (IPRI), and was launched in 1978 with considerable corporate funding to "do excellent and unusual things in plant-cell culture research to improve nutrition for mankind." Walter, who has a biotechnology background in clinical chemistry, came in as research director of a staff of fifty people; all of the projects they were involved with were food and plant related.

Their primary project was to produce a facsimile vanilla flavor through plant-tissue culture in order to provide new opportunities for "flavor salads." They believed this would open a lot of doors of opportunity for people everywhere, not only for those in the flavor industry but also for farmers for whom they could create disease-resistant plant stock.

Using cell manipulation of root tissue, Walter and his team created compounds that they could first grow in petri dishes and slowly work up to large fermentation vessels. The resulting material was now a substance, not a plant.

Ethical questions were raised within the flavor industry, not as to whether the concept of their work mattered but as to whether the end product was natural or not. Walter maintained that phyto-vanilla was natural. You could "grow" the cells, which then would be purified and made into an extract that would have the flavor of natural vanilla. The researchers were focused on identifying the hundreds of chemicals in vanilla to create a synergistic flavor, and they had created a pretty good profile in their facsimile.

Despite the potential of controversy, several of the big food and flavor houses were interested in their project, and ESCA-genetics were being courted to develop their program at an international level. Things looked good. Then somewhere between 1992 and 1994, an article came out in the *San Francisco Chronicle* with a sensational headline and accusatory text, suggesting that the results of scientists' work would essentially "rape the Third World."

Suddenly, the project no longer seemed reasonable. The initial business plan stipulated that there was a place in between the natural and the synthetic that would create new opportunities for flavor systems that would be beneficial in the same way that potatoes that were disease-resistant or foods that could be grown in salt water could benefit humanity.

Walter said that initially he was quite hurt by the critical tone of the article because he had thought his work would ultimately help people, a goal that was important to him. "At first my position was that business and commerce around the globe would benefit from our accomplishments. After all, it was cheaper than natural vanilla and they'd want to buy from us. I had hoped to boost and diversify agriculture.

"After reading the article in the *Chronicle*, it made me reflect on what would happen to the livelihood of the farmers. I was looking at the project as a scientist. I learned that you can't do things solely for money. You have to look at a lot of different ideas and then figure out where a difference can be made. I would still like to do something with vanilla, but I now want to think of ways that our work would benefit, not hurt, the growers."

doesn't undermine the thousands of people whose lives depend on the production of vanilla beans and other tropical foods and flavors that we use daily in the developing world.

GENETIC ENGINEERING AND BIOTECHNOLOGY OPPORTUNITIES

So what about biotechnology? We've been modifying plant stock for hundreds, if not thousands, of years in ways both subtle and extreme. Is it a piece of the evolutionary process, or is it a death sentence for the traditional farmer? The answer perhaps lies in the end goal and use of the vanilla.

In order to provide a ready supply of vanilla at a stable price, scientists have created new methods for growing vanilla that contradict the traditional techniques that served well in a natural forest environment. For instance, early attempts to grow vanilla in dense plantings were initially successful and simplified the labor-intensive hand pollination and harvest considerably, so that a lot of vanilla could be produced efficiently in a concentrated area. The problem was that when disease breaks out—and historically, it always has—because the plants are so close together, *all* the plants sicken and die very quickly, the soil becomes contaminated, and the producer is back to the starting point, usually without recovering his initial financial investment.

Plant biologists have identified the varieties of fungus that bring on disease and death, and have modified plants to breed stronger, healthier, disease-resistant stock. Through scientific studies of how vanilla creates and synthesizes vanillin and the many other organic compounds that make it unique, it will be easier to identify how to produce and process vanilla beans with greater concentrations of the flavor profile sought by extract manufacturers, making the vanilla more valuable for both the growers and the users.

In shade-cloth production of vanilla, tutor trees can be eliminated through the use of bark composite posts wrapped in chicken wire or wooden or cement supports to hold the vanilla, and the use of shade cloth to provide consistent, even, filtered light. Plants reproduce earlier in this environment, can produce a larger volume of beans with less stress, and save labor costs for pollinating and harvesting, providing producers with a faster and better return on their investment. (This method of growing vanilla is not without drawbacks; if fusarium infects one plant, all the plants will die in short order, especially when they are planted close together.)

Most farmers won't argue against these types of genetic modification as they make it possible for them to grow larger crops of healthier plants more quickly and efficiently, ostensibly for a better return on the growers' investment.

On the other hand, the dark side of this same useful technology means fewer jobs for laborers, and the opportunity for a few producers to have a larger control of the overall crop. While these advances benefit those few farmers and provide buyers with a higher-quality product and less hassle for procurement, we'll see greater unemployment in areas traditionally in need of more jobs.

Also, if shade-house growing is efficient in the tropics, who's to say that, with a few more modifications, it can't be applied in industrialized countries more efficiently than in developing countries? Does this mean that traditional growers will migrate to newly producing industrialized countries in search of whatever work they can find? And, ultimately, is it cost effective to continue to grow vanilla at all, given that it's so labor-intensive, when vanillin from other plants can cheaply and efficiently be synthesized from other plant sources? In other words, why not phase out vanilla as we know it in return for something more practical and affordable?

ETHICAL SOLUTIONS

These and other questions have yet to be effectively addressed, and it will require serious consideration on the part of social scientists as well as scientists involved in plant technology to find the midground that addresses all the issues involved in feeding and supporting our increasingly small and hungry planet. In the meantime, these are short-term solutions that can assist in creating a more equitable environment for the tropical producers of the foods we crave.

CERTIFIED ORGANIC
NICHE MARKET

Before the price of vanilla rose so dramatically at the turn of the millennium, there was a growing demand for niche-market vanilla. Food-service industries (restaurants and small, gourmet producers and bakeries) increasingly sought high-quality beans, often certified organic, for consistency with the other ingredients they used for discerning customers. When the prices topped $150 a kilo ($68 a pound) at source, most of the farmers who relied on the extra money that certification provided—money that counterbalanced the overall low prices for vanilla beans—discontinued certification as they could make the same amount of money without the extra financial investment.

Fortunately, the market for certified organic vanilla is not going to go away anytime in the foreseeable future. In fact, it is gearing up for dramatic growth. Further, there will continue to be a demand for natural flavors from vanilla-bean extractives. Markets that were poised to grow just before the price increases put their product launches on hold until the market prices drop. Soy products—soy milks, yogurts, iced desserts, etc.—depend on flavorants to make their products more palatable, and natural vanilla plays a considerable role in soy- and rice-milk products for people seeking lactose-free alternatives. The consumers of these products are largely socially conscious, health-conscious individuals who consistently choose the pure and natural over heavily genetically engineered products.

FAIR TRADE

The coffee industry is emerging as a leader in the establishment of Fair Trade, an international program where small farmers with less than 10 to 15 hectares (25 to 37½ acres) of land can be certified as producing organic, sustainable, high-quality crops. Those farmers meeting these criteria are then accorded Fair Trade status, and they receive a living wage for the sale of their coffee. This became a critical issue when overplanting of lower-grade robusta coffee plants created a huge oversupply of coffee in the world marketplace, causing a steep drop in coffee prices and forcing thousands of small farmers who produce fine-quality arabica coffee out of business. To date, there is a relatively small market for Fair Trade coffee, but through the work of TransFair, Oxfam, Global Exchange, ForesTrade, and other organizations, as well as socially conscious coffee roasters who only purchase Fair Trade for resale, coffee consumers in industrialized countries are slowly becoming aware of the value of supporting Fair Trade practices, not only because it's the ethical thing to do but also because it provides consumers with better-quality coffee. While Fair Trade coffee costs more, the extra money makes it possible for the growers' children to remain in school longer, and for their families to have nutritious food and access to medical and dental care. Lest we question the standard of living of coffee farmers, it's interesting to note that most of them don't drink the product they produce—they are in dire need of selling every coffee bean in order to survive.

The Fair Trade program has gained popularity among manufacturers of other products as well. Cloves, cinnamon, and other spices are now being grown under Fair Trade policies, and the cacao (chocolate) industry is starting to adapt Fair Trade and sustainable farming practices in some countries. To date, vanilla has not formally become part of the growing trend of sustainable projects, largely because of its current high prices. However, farmers are well aware that this boon won't last, and as they become more aware of alternative opportunities through word of mouth and the Internet, they have become increasingly interested in participating in programs that will improve their overall condition.

In and of itself, Fair Trade won't be enough to protect tropical farmers who are caught in a rapidly changing physical environment that has not yet evolved socially into a more equitable system. We can hope that education will help to bring change, and we certainly need to consider social systems that will create a more evenly balanced standard of living.

Change of this nature doesn't come quickly or easily. However, those of us who are fortunate to live in industrialized countries have the collective power to encourage (and, when necessary, pressure) corporations to purchase sustainably produced food products, where farmers receive a fair price for their labor. Yes, it may cost us a little more, but the small increase in price is more than compensated for by the higher standard of living it provides to those who live in the tropics.

The lives of all of us existing on our small planet depend on the plants that purify and create oxygen, and the ever diminishing supply of water and other resources that keep us alive and healthy. While it may be simplistic to infer that your choice of pure vanilla will make the world a better place, remember that the products we use daily and usually take for granted—coffee, chocolate, vanilla,

Women in Madagascar working with vanilla beans

sugar, corn, wheat, potatoes, meat, and so much more—are all produced by families whose lives depend on our choices. There is a place for synthetics, and natural flavor-identical alternatives, within the scheme of things. After all, 97 percent of all vanilla value-added products are produced with flavor alternatives. But what if we used even 2 percent more natural vanilla in the world—think of the difference this would make for the producers! This wouldn't necessarily require that we increase our per capita consumption of ice cream by several gallons a year. Instead, consider putting a few drops of vanilla extract into foods you prepare daily—coffee, hot cereals, fruit salads, fresh vegetables, and entrées. There are myriad ways we can use pure vanilla by thinking "outside the box," as you will find in the next chapter. Simple choices made by those of us in industrialized nations can mean the difference between abject poverty and survival in developing countries. Let's take advantage of all available opportunities to make a difference every day.

· 9 ·

OUT OF THE CUPBOARD
AND ONTO THE TABLE

Now that we have followed vanilla's journey around the world as a cash crop and commodity, and have explored the importance of using pure, natural vanilla in more ways than just enhancing cookies and ice cream, it's time to help you take a leap of faith in your daily food preparation and bring vanilla out of the cupboard and onto your tables for daily use.

During the last nineteen years, I've done a *lot* of experimentation with vanilla with sometimes surprising, but always delicious, results. I encourage you to experiment as well, especially after reading—and hopefully, trying—the recipes included here. My only caveat regards all spices, herbs, and other flavorings: go lightly at first when you add vanilla to savory sauces, salad dressings, vegetables, fruit salads, and many other foods. You can always add more, but sometimes less *is* more, as vanilla is sometimes better as a flavor enhancer in recipes rather than the shining star.

Let's start with some basic information that will help to clarify terms, techniques, and uses of vanilla.

ALL ABOUT VANILLA EXTRACTS AND FLAVORS

Originally, everyone used vanilla beans as a flavoring agent because vanilla extract has only been commercially available for a little more than a hundred years. The first extracts were made at apothecary shops (the first pharmacies and drugstores) and were more like a tincture or syrup. They were strong and very sweet and were often used to calm upset stomachs and "hysteria" (a term used also for uncontrolled laughter, which needs *no* antidote in my opinion). Along with extracts, there are additional products to choose from: natural vanilla flavor, cookie vanilla, imitation vanilla, vanilla blend, double-fold vanilla, vanilla paste, vanilla powder, and more.

Pure vanilla gives us one of the most complex flavors in the world, having well over 250 (and quite possibly up to 500) organic components creating its unique flavor and aroma. I'm often asked if one type of vanilla is better than another. In fact, they're just different so it's a matter of your own personal taste. Even the same species of vanilla beans grown in different parts of the world will vary in flavor and aroma due to climate and soil differences. While some beans are higher in natural vanillin content than others, this isn't the only indicator of flavor or quality.

How do you decide which product to buy? Your preference may be influenced by what your family traditionally used for vanilla flavoring—the taste to which you are accustomed. The following pages explain more about the products on the shelf. You may want to experiment with some to decide which most appeals to you.

PURE VANILLA EXTRACT

There are about 150 varieties of vanilla, though only two are used commercially in extracts—*Vanilla planifolia* and *Vanilla tahitensis.* Vanilla extract is made by percolating or macerating chopped vanilla beans with ethyl alcohol and water. The process is usually kept as cool as possible to minimize flavor loss, though some manufacturers feel that there must be heat to create the best extraction. Most companies use a consistent blend of beans, sometimes from several regions, to create their signature flavor. The extraction process takes about forty-eight hours, after which time the extracts mellow in the tanks with the beans anywhere from days to weeks—depending on the processor being used—before being filtered into a holding tank where the amber-colored liquid extract remains until it is bottled.

While the FDA has specific regulations in the United States regarding commercial extract manufacturing, there are variables that create significant differences in flavor and quality. For instance, the FDA requires a minimum of 13.35 ounces of vanilla beans to a gallon containing a minimum of 35 percent alcohol to 65 percent water mixture.

There are minimal regulations regarding the quality of the beans, so these can range from premium quality to the driest cuts and splits containing only small amounts of natural vanillin. Although 35 percent is the standard alcohol requirement, premium vanilla extracts often contain a higher percentage of alcohol in order to extract more flavor from the beans. More alcohol is okay with the FDA; less than 35 percent is not.

The extract may also contain sugar, corn syrup, caramel, colors, or stabilizers. As vanilla is naturally sweet, it isn't necessary to use additional sweeteners, though some companies use 25 percent or more sugar in their extracts, and some use 3 to 5 percent sugar as a stabilizer. Adding 20 percent or more sugar to a newly made extract is like fortifying any alcoholic product. Some manufacturers use corn syrup instead of sugar. The sweeteners take the edge off the harshness of the un-aged product, which is, at least partially, why some companies continue to use a significant amount of sugar or corn syrup in their flavorings. Extracts made with premium beans and little to no sugar offer a fresh, true flavor to dishes. Though these extracts may be expensive, the flavor is cleaner and carries well to the finished product. Vanilla ages during the time that it goes through the channels from factory to your shelf. Some companies hold the extracts in their manufacturing area for months to make certain the extract is well aged before they ship it out.

Vanilla extracts continue to develop body and depth for about two years, at which time they stabilize. They will keep indefinitely as long as they're stored in a cool dark place such as a pantry or cupboard that's away from the stove or bright sun. Refrigeration is not recommended.

Comparing extract quality is a lot like comparing whiskeys. There's a significant difference between low-end and call- or name-brand bourbon and scotch. Part of the difference has to do with allowing a whiskey to age properly, without the use of chemical additives. The same is true for vanillas. Premium extracts may be more expensive, but the flavor will be significantly better because they've been made from the finest ingredients; contain few, if any, additives; and are naturally aged. This means that your fabulous secret family recipe for cookies will be even better if you use quality vanilla extract.

VARIETIES OF PURE VANILLA EXTRACTS

MEXICAN VANILLA is made from *Vanilla planifolia* (often called *Vanilla fragrans*) plant stock that is indigenous to Mexico. It is a very smooth, creamy, spicy vanilla. It's especially good in desserts made without heat or with a short cooking time. Dark chocolate, cream desserts, alcoholic and nonalcoholic beverages, ethnic foods, wild game, poultry or meat, and foods spiced with chili peppers all benefit from Mexican vanilla.

Bourbon vanilla is a generic term for *Vanilla planifolia* that comes from the Indian Ocean islands. This is the vanilla most of us are familiar with as it's the most commonly used variety in extracts. In the 1800s, the French developed large plantations on Réunion, known then as the Île de Bourbon, which is how the name "bourbon" came into being. Although vanilla extract is high in alcohol content, it is not made from bourbon whiskey. Bourbon vanilla extract may or may not be made from beans from Madagascar. Bottles labeled "Madagascar Vanilla Extract" probably contain Madagascar beans.

Bourbon and Mexican vanillas have the familiar natural vanillin flavor that we associate with vanilla ice cream and other vanilla-flavored desserts and beverages. Bourbon vanilla is best used in baked goods, ice cream, and anything where a traditional vanilla flavor is desired. Mexican and Bourbon vanillas are interchangeable with regard to their similar flavor profile.

INDONESIAN VANILLA can be much like Bourbon vanilla, or it can have distinctive differences. Some growers harvest their beans too early and use a short-term curing process that gives the vanilla a woodier, phenolic flavor. As the early harvest keeps the beans from fully developing their flavor profile, it can be harsher and not as flavorful. It's important to note that not all Indonesian vanilla is harvested too early; premium-grade Indonesian vanilla is excellent.

Frequently Indonesian vanilla is blended with Bourbon vanilla to create a hardy extract. Indonesian vanilla tends to hold up well in high heat, so anything slow-baked or exposed to high heat (e.g., cookies) benefits from its hardiness. Indonesian vanilla is also quite good with chocolate as its flavor overrides the sweetness of chocolate and gives it a beneficial flavor boost. Chocolate's popularity is due, in part, from the sparkle it receives from other flavors as it tends to be somewhat dull on its own.

TAHITIAN VANILLA *(Vanilla tahitensis)* comes from *planifolia* stock that was crossbred with *Vanilla pompona* in the Philippines in the early 1800s. It went to Tahiti where it was further crossbred and is now classified as a separate species, as it's considerably different in appearance and flavor from Bourbon vanilla. It carries many of the characteristics of *Vanilla pompona*, a variety of vanilla rarely used commercially except in perfume.

Tahitian vanilla is sweeter and fruitier and has less natural vanillin than Bourbon and Mexican vanillas. Instead, it contains heliotropin (anis aldehyde), which is unique to its species. This gives it a more cherrylike, licorice, or raisin-y taste. It has a very floral fragrance, the bean is fatter and more moist than Bourbon vanilla, and it contains many fewer seeds inside the pod. Tahitian is especially nice in fruit compotes and desserts, as well as in sauces for poultry, seafood, and wild game. My recommendation is to try both to see if you have a personal preference. If you still can't decide, combine the two flavors to create your own blend.

Note: Hawaiian vanilla extract has come onto the market recently though it's not readily available except in the Islands. The flavor is very similar to Mexican or Madagascar (Bourbon) vanilla as it's also made from *Vanilla planifolia.*

Natural Vanilla Flavor

People who prefer not to use an alcohol-based extract can substitute natural vanilla flavor found in regular and specialty-food stores and some supermarkets. It usually is made with a glycerin or a propylene glycol base. Although the flavor comes from vanilla beans, it doesn't fit the FDA profile for extracts, so it must legally be called "natural vanilla flavor."

Note: The texture of natural vanilla—especially in a glycerin base—is viscous and a little darker than vanilla extract. It also smells somewhat different. In uncooked foods and beverages it tastes fairly similar but with a slight aftertaste; in cooked or baked foods, it's more similar to extract.

Vanilla–Vanillin Flavoring

Vanilla flavor is a mixture of pure vanilla extract and synthetic substances—most commonly, synthetic vanillin. (*Note:* This product cannot legally have "natural" on the label.) There are a couple of common brands that contain a blend of natural and synthetic vanillas. If you grew up with a natural/synthetic blend, this may taste more familiar to you than a pure extract.

IMITATION VANILLA

Imitation vanilla is a mixture made from synthetic substances, which imitate part of natural vanilla's smell and flavor. Imitation vanilla in the United States comes from synthetic vanillin, which mimics the flavor of natural vanillin, *one* of the components that gives vanilla its extraordinary bouquet.

The two most common sources for synthetic vanillin have been lignin vanillin, a by-product of the paper industry, which has been chemically treated to resemble the taste of pure vanilla extract, and ethyl vanillin, which is a coal-tar derivative and frequently far stronger than either lignin vanillin or pure vanilla.

In the 1930s, the Ontario Paper Company was struggling with sulfite liquor, a by-product of papermaking, which was polluting local streams near its plant. Company chemists realized it could be turned into synthetic vanillin, a viable but curious ecological solution to a big problem. If you grew up on synthetics, imitation vanilla will be a familiar flavor to you. Given the fact that vanilla isn't *that expensive*, you might consider learning to enjoy the real deal.

NATURAL VANILLIN

Natural vanillin is one of the more than 250 organic components that make up the flavor and aroma of vanilla, and it's the one we most associate with vanilla. Vanilla beans sometimes have pure vanillin crystals that develop on the bean's surface. The crystals give off an iridescent sparkle in sunlight and are quite edible.

COUMARIN

Coumarin is a derivative of the tonka bean, which comes from *Dipteryx odorata,* a tree native to Brazil. Some of the organic constituents that make up its flavor are similar to, or the same as, those in pure vanilla. Coumarin is frequently found in synthetic vanillas from Mexico, Central America, and the Caribbean as it's cheap and makes synthetic vanilla taste more like the natural kind. Unfortunately, coumarin is considered toxic, especially to the liver, is potentially carcinogenic, and has been banned from the United States since the 1950s.

COOKIE VANILLA

Cookie Vanilla is a brand name for a blend of vanillas created by one of the American vanilla manufacturers. It's a blend of Tahitian and Bourbon vanillas, which makes it sweet and floral. If you enjoy the flavor of Tahitian vanilla but feel pure Tahitian vanilla is too expensive for your budget, then use Cookie Vanilla or make your own blend of Tahitian and Bourbon vanilla extracts.

VANILLA POWDER

There are several types of vanilla powders commercially available. Some are made from sucrose that has been ribbon-sprayed with vanilla extract, and some are a dextrose-vanilla extract mix. They are good for adding to beverages if you want a slightly sweet product that dissolves easily. You can also mix them into powdered or granulated sugar for a vanilla-flavored sugar and sprinkle the powders on finished foods such as cinnamon/vanilla toast or on top of a cake when it's warm from the oven. Some companies use a mixture of pure vanilla and synthetic vanillin in their powder as the synthetic holds up well in the heat of convection ovens. Also, be aware that many of the vanilla powders from Europe are actually completely synthetic. Check the ingredients to see if it's natural or not.

GROUND VANILLA BEANS

Vanilla beans ground to a fine powder are sometimes confused with vanilla powder. Ground vanilla beans are occasionally used in commercial and industrial products. Ground vanilla is absolutely exquisite in food. Because it isn't based in an alcohol carrier, you won't lose flavor when you cook or bake with it. As a result, you can use about half the amount of beans as extract.

EXHAUSTED VANILLA BEANS

Exhausted vanilla beans are the ground residue of the extraction process. They may still hold some flavor and are added to commercial vanilla ice creams (often called "vanilla-bean" ice cream) and other products. They are used in the industrial production of commercial products but not in home cooking.

Single Fold, Double Fold, Etc.

The word "fold" connotes concentration in liquid vanilla extracts and synthetics. Single fold (written 1x) is the standard concentrate of pure vanilla extract. Double fold (2x) is twice as strong, and so forth. Concentrations can go up to twenty-fold or higher, but the extract isn't very stable above fourfold. In candy making, where liquids can change the chemistry of the finished product, a multi-fold extract concentrate is useful.

Vanilla Paste

Vanilla paste is a sweet concentrated vanilla extract with ground, exhausted vanilla beans in a corn syrup base. It's often used as a time-saving shortcut instead of whole vanilla beans.

Vanilla Oleoresin

Vanilla oleoresin is a semisolid concentrate obtained by removing the solvent from the vanilla extract. A solution of isopropanol is frequently used instead of ethanol for its preparation. Some flavor and aroma are lost during removal of the solvent, but it does contain essential oils. Vanilla oleoresin is used in nonfood products. Unfortunately, it isn't always stable in candle and soap making, which is too bad, as it's considerably less expensive than vanilla absolute.

VANILLA ABSOLUTE

Vanilla absolute is the most concentrated form of vanilla. It is often used in perfumes and other aroma-based products. Because it's so expensive, most candles, soaps, and other scented specialty merchandise are made from synthetic vanillin, though vanilla absolute would be the most effective natural vanilla for candles and soaps. Vanilla absolute is used in very high-end products in small quantities, often as part of a blend with other fragrances.

NATURAL FLAVOR-IDENTICAL ALTERNATIVES OR WONFS

Natural flavor-identical alternatives are synthesized vanillin from plants other than vanilla. WONFs are "with other natural flavors," indicating that the vanilla product also contains vanillin from other sources.

HOW TO CHOOSE AND USE VANILLA BEANS

Choosing Beans

Terms used for vanilla beans are similar to those referring to extracts. Beans grown in Mexico are called Mexican beans. Beans from the same plant stock are called Bourbon beans if they grow in Madagascar, the Comoros, or other Indian Ocean locations. While

Vanilla planifolia beans that you can purchase in grocery stores are almost always from the Indian Ocean, in the future you may have more options to choose from. This is especially true in upscale markets and online, as vanilla beans may be marketed like chocolate based on the subtle differences in flavors found in various growing regions.

Vanilla beans do vary in flavor and fragrance, depending on their place of origin. Soil and climate differences as well as methods of curing the beans imbue unique qualities. Vanilla grown only 20 miles apart can have subtle but distinct differences in flavor and appearance.

Tahitian vanilla is a different species and has an entirely different fragrance and flavor profile. Tahitian beans are becoming more available in the marketplace and can also be found online.

Tips for Choosing Quality Beans

PREMIUM BEANS, regardless of where they come from, should have a rich, full aroma, be oily to the touch, and sleek in appearance. Tahitian beans are not as shiny as Bourbon or Mexican beans. This is a normal characteristic of the species. *Beans to avoid* are those with very little scent, or those that are smoky, brittle or dry, or mildewed.

BOURBON BEANS are long and slender, with a very rich taste and smell. They have thick, oily skin, contain an abundance of tiny seeds, and carry a strong vanilla aroma. Bourbon beans from Madagascar and the Comoros are described as creamy, haylike, and sweet, with vanillin overtones. *Planifolia* beans from other regions will be similar if they are picked at peak ripeness and properly cured.

Mexican beans are very similar to Bourbon beans, though they have a more mellow, smooth quality and a spicy, woody fragrance.

Tahitian beans are plumper and more moist than Bourbon beans. Their skin is thinner, they contain fewer seeds, and the aroma is fruity and floral. They are often described as smelling like licorice, cherry, prunes, raisins, or wine.

All three types of vanilla are equally good to use, though their flavors are quite different. I suggest that you experiment to determine which flavor you like most. Or you may find, as I have, that you will choose beans that best pair with the food or beverage you are preparing.

Using Vanilla Beans

Frequently, I come across recipes that call for scraping the seeds from the vanilla bean and discarding the rest. What a waste! The entire bean is filled with flavor, and, in fact, the pod has more flavor than the seeds. You can cut the bean and use a portion at a time or you can use the whole bean, depending on the amount of flavor you wish.

To cut open a bean, lay it flat on a cutting surface. Holding one end of the bean on the surface, carefully slice the bean open lengthwise. When you separate the bean, thousands of tiny seeds are exposed. This step shows why it is classified as a seedpod rather than a bean. By cutting the bean open before placing it in liquid, more of the surface is exposed, and therefore a greater intensity of flavor is released. You can scrape the seeds from the pod before removing the bean if you choose.

Vanilla beans can generally be used several times, depending on how strenuously you've handled them. For instance, if you've placed a vanilla bean in a pitcher of lemonade or a container of mulled cider or wine, the bean will still contain a lot of flavor after the beverage has been consumed. However, if you soak a vanilla bean in a hot cream mixture, then scrape out the seeds and pith, you will probably still have some flavor left in the pod but it won't be very strong.

Rinse and dry the bean pieces after using them. If there is only the pod left, or if you've used the bean several times for flavoring beverages, let the pieces dry, and retire them to the sugar or coffee jar as they will exude a delicate flavor and fragrance for some time to come. Beans that have been used once or twice can also be ground up and serve to add additional flavor to ice creams, cookies, and many other foods.

Keeping Beans

Don't throw out dry or withered beans. They will probably rehydrate in warm liquid and will still contain flavor. I don't recommend attempting to cut open very dry beans until they are rehydrated, as it's easy to have the knife slip. If you prefer, grind them in a coffee grinder or blender and use them in a recipe that calls for ground beans.

Vanilla beans will keep indefinitely in a cool, dark place in an airtight container. Don't refrigerate or freeze beans as this can cause them to harden and crystallize. In the humid tropics where beans are grown, they are wrapped in oiled or waxed paper and stored in tin boxes. As I live in a cooler, dryer climate, I keep my beans wrapped in plastic in an airtight plastic tub or glass jar. If you live in a hot, humid climate, this isn't a good idea as beans can mildew easily, especially if additional moisture collects inside the container.

Bourbon beans may develop a frosting of natural vanillin crystals if you keep them for a while. This usually occurs over time and not when the beans are first cured and dried. Called *givre* in French (which means "light frost"), these crystals indicate that the beans are high in natural vanillin and are of very good quality. The crystals are quite edible and very flavorful. If you are uncertain whether the beans are covered with crystals or mildew, take them into the sunlight. The crystals are similar to mineral crystals and will reflect the sun's rays, creating the colors of the rainbow. Mildew, on the other hand, will be dull and flat in the light, and may also smell bad. If the bean is mildewed, throw it away as the mildew will spread to uninfected beans.

MEXICAN AND CARIBBEAN VANILLA EXTRACTS

A common misconception exists about Mexican and Caribbean vanilla. People rave about the fabulous deal they got on a giant bottle of vanilla extract in Mexico, Haiti, or Guadeloupe, among other places. Further, they'll say it has such a unique flavor and it's stronger than any vanilla they've ever used. Well, sorry, folks, it isn't pure vanilla extract. In fact, chances are the product in the big bottle is synthetic.

Because vanilla originally came from Mexico, Central America, and the Caribbean, and because at one time Mexico produced the world's finest vanilla, it seems it would follow that the same holds true today. In actuality, *nearly all* of the so-called vanilla extract coming from these countries is synthetic.

Mexico, Central America, and the Caribbean have sold cheap synthetic vanillas for decades with the hope of cashing in on the association between Mexico and vanilla. The ruse has worked. By adding coumarin to synthetic vanillin, the flavor is a little more like pure vanilla. But coumarin, from the tonka tree, can be toxic and cause liver damage if used in quantity. We've outlawed its use in the United States since the 1950s. Due to media coverage about coumarin, the synthetics from Mexico now rarely have coumarin in them but some countries still use it.

Although there are label laws in Mexico, they are never enforced; in some of the other countries, there are no restrictions. So, don't count on the label for an accurate account of the ingredients. Needless to say, synthetic vanillas are a big industry as most tourists have no idea they are being duped and the products are easy to sell.

How do you know if you're buying pure vanilla? Here are a few questions to ask yourself:

- Is the product amber colored, dark and murky, or clear? Clear is a sign of pure, synthetic vanillin. It's often called "crystal vanilla." Dark and murky indicates synthetic vanillin, most likely ethyl vanillin derived from coal tar. The vanilla may also be dark because it contains red dye, which has been banned in the United States, or a lot of caramel coloring. If it's truly amber colored, it may be natural vanilla.

- What is the alcohol content? Usually the synthetics range from containing no alcohol to about 2 percent alcohol (which acts as a stabilizer). There are some vanilla-vanillin blends and some cheap-quality vanillas that have 25 percent alcohol, but they aren't worth buying, either.

- How much did you pay for it? This is the biggest tip-off. If the product is in a big bottle and you paid less than $20, it's absolutely not pure vanilla extract. Pure vanilla extract often costs more in Mexico because only one company makes quality extract, and this in only small quantities.

The only brand of pure vanilla extract in Mexico that I recommend is made by Vai-Mex (the Gaya family) in Gutiérrez Zamora, Veracruz. It usually can be found only in the Veracruz region. If you want safe, good-quality, pure Mexican vanilla extract, buy it in the United States. And if you want synthetics, buy them here, too. They're the same price as you'd pay in Mexico, but American synthetics aren't adulterated with dangerous additives.

RECIPES

My feeling about recipes is that they should be considered an inspiration or guideline but are not necessarily "set in stone." Unless you are an experienced baker, you don't want to get too creative with pastries or breads, as with baked goods, measurements really matter. With most other foods, you can have a bit more leeway. If you want to make the recipe for Candied Winter Squash (see page 357), it's fine to use whatever squash you have on hand. You can use all brown sugar or all maple syrup or substitute honey instead. You can make it a little sweeter or a little less sweet, and you can change the amount of the spices to taste. The only consideration would be if you are using summer squash, in which case you would want to make it less sweet, and the cooking time would be shorter—you get the idea.

What I hope will happen is that you will include vanilla in foods and beverages that you would have never considered before. A friend recently told me that he added vanilla extract to the gravy of a leg of lamb and everyone raved about the flavor. So, give it a try and you'll probably be happily surprised.

An ad for Kellogg's extracts from the turn of the twentieth century.
Kellogg carried a full line of products, not just cereal, at the time.

HOMEMADE VANILLA EXTRACT

Homemade extract is easy and fun to make. It usually isn't as strong as commercially made extracts but it may have a fuller flavor. The pleasure of creating your own product and the sensual experience of working with the fragrant beans make this project quite satisfying.

It doesn't matter which alcohol you choose for making the extract—it's more a question of what you prefer. Vodka has the least flavor to interfere with the taste of the vanilla. Because rum is sweet, it's the best for making cordials, and vanilla brandy imparts a delicious flavor when poured over freshly baked cakes or added to winter fruit compotes.

You can also add other spices to the alcohol to make a spiced rum, vodka, or brandy. In Réunion, Madagascar, Uganda, and the Caribbean countries, many families have their own spiced rum blends that they serve for sipping. Sometimes medicinal herbs are added to the alcohol and used for coughs, stomach ailments, or other health concerns.

For gift making, decant the extract into special bottles, add one vanilla bean to each, attach a label, and voilà—you have a very attractive gift. I sometimes tie a couple of extra beans to the bottle with raffia and include directions for making more extract. You can also turn your homemade extract into a vanilla cordial for a truly unique and elegant gift.

5 vanilla beans
1 pint high-quality vodka, rum, or brandy

SPLIT THE VANILLA BEANS lengthwise down the center to expose the seeds, keeping the ends of the beans intact. Place beans in a bottle with the vodka, rum, or brandy. Store in a cool, dark place such as a cupboard or closet for at least 4 weeks. Shake the bottle several times a week.

TO USE, either remove 4 of the beans for another purpose (you can add them to a fresh bean to make more extract, or you can use them for cooking), or let all the beans remain in the bottle, and periodically add more alcohol to keep the bottle replenished. Eventually, the beans will lose their strength but they should contain flavor for many months.

MAKES ABOUT 1 PINT

Fragrant and Flavorful Vanilla Sugar

Vanilla extract is a relative newcomer to Europe, whereas vanilla beans have been used for flavoring beverages, foods, and more since the 1600s. Many families keep a vanilla bean in a large jar of sugar, then use the vanilla sugar to flavor their cookies, cakes, and custards.

Most recipes for making vanilla sugar usually suggest placing a vanilla pod in the sugar jar. While this gives some flavor and fragrance, the sugar won't be strong enough to adequately flavor baked goods unless it remains undisturbed for months. As most of us don't want to wait that long, here is a recipe that will give you a beautiful vanilla sugar with a full bouquet of flavor and fragrance right away.

Place 5 vanilla beans—either fresh or only used once—in a very low oven (150°F, or less). Allow the beans to dry (about 15 minutes), then cool on a wire rack. Break the beans (and pods) into small pieces and place in a clean coffee grinder, blender, or food processor, and process until pulverized. Run the pulverized pieces through a strainer and regrind the larger ones.

One tablespoon of ground vanilla beans is sufficient for 1 to 2 pounds of granulated or confectioners' sugar. This will be strong enough to use right away, but if you place the vanilla sugar in an airtight jar and store for a week, you will be amazed at the bouquet when you open the jar.

If you find the residue of the ground vanilla is more than you want for whatever you are preparing, then sieve the sugar as you add it to your recipe.

FLAVORED OILS, VINEGARS, HONEY, AND SYRUPS

Making your own vanilla oil, vinegar, honey, or syrup is extremely simple. You have endless possibilities as to the medium; you simply need to decide the flavor you'd like to create.

For instance, olive oil can have a strong flavor that could overpower the flavor of vanilla, but if you use a light olive oil or grape seed, safflower, or sunflower oil, the flavor of vanilla will come through nicely.

With vinegars you might consider a very mild white wine, a cider, or a fruit vinegar for using in salads or to enliven vegetable dishes.

The other consideration is the flavor of the vanilla itself. Tahitian vanilla imparts a wonderful fruitiness to salads and a floral bouquet when sautéing seafood. Bourbon and Mexican vanillas have more natural vanillin and also have "dusty," creamy notes, so they are a good choice to use with meats, tofu, portobello mushrooms, and sauces.

For 1 pint of oil or vinegar, 1 vanilla bean is sufficient unless you want immediate flavor (as in the next few days), in which case you can use two beans. Slit the bean lengthwise so that the vanilla flavor infuses more easily. There's no need to heat either the oil or vinegar to activate the process. Within a week, the oil will have some flavor. You can establish one bottle of vanilla oil or vinegar, then refill it as needed. The vanilla bean will continue to impart flavor for over a year.

To make vanilla honey, choose a very light-flavored honey such as star thistle, clover, or orange. For every pint jar of honey, you will want one plump bean. Split the bean lengthwise, scrape out the seeds, and blend into the honey. Then cut the bean in half and put the two pieces into the honey. The vanilla bean will need to infuse the honey for at least a week for the flavor to be noticeable.

Maple syrup and vanilla are an amazing duo—so good, in fact, that at least one maple sugar company is selling bottles of syrup with a vanilla bean included. Again, simply add 1 or 2 beans to your syrup and let it infuse at least one week to notice the flavor. The flavor will grow more intense over time.

You can create multiflavored syrups by making a simple syrup, then infusing it with berry or cherry juice and a vanilla bean, or with spices such as cloves, cinnamon, cardamom, or allspice and vanilla.

VANILLA SIMPLE SYRUP

1 cup sugar
1 cup water
1 vanilla bean, split lengthwise

PUT SUGAR, WATER, AND VANILLA BEAN in a heavy saucepan and cook on medium-high heat, stirring until sugar dissolves. Bring to a boil, and keep at a low boil for 2 minutes. Remove syrup from heat, allow to cool, and flavor as desired. Keep the vanilla bean in the syrup until you are ready to use it. You can use the bean again.

A FASTER WAY TO MAKE VANILLA SYRUP is by adding 2 vanilla beans to a bottle of light corn syrup (such as Karo Syrup) and allowing the vanilla to infuse for a week. The fastest way is by adding a tablespoon of extract to a bottle of corn syrup and you're ready to go. You can also add a vanilla bean to give more depth of flavor to the syrup over time.

MAKES ABOUT 1½ CUPS

THE PERFECT VANILLA CREAM SODA

1 cup sugar
1 cup water
1 vanilla bean, split lengthwise
2 tablespoons pure vanilla extract, or to taste
soda water

IN A MEDIUM SAUCEPAN, place sugar, water, and vanilla bean, and cook on medium-high heat until sugar is dissolved. Bring to a boil, and allow to boil for about 3 minutes or until syrup thickens slightly. Remove from heat and allow to cool. Remove vanilla bean and save for another use. Add vanilla extract. You'll want a strong vanilla flavor.

TO MAKE THE SODA, put 4 tablespoons of the Vanilla Simple Syrup in a tall glass. Add ice and fill with soda water. Taste and adjust flavor accordingly.

Note: You can make cream sodas from just the extract. Add another tablespoon of the extract to the simple syrup once it cools.

VANILLA COFFEE LIQUEUR

Homemade coffee liqueur that is quite similar to Kahlua is a popular holiday gift that can be made several months in advance. While it's best to make the liqueur by the month of October, it's perfectly okay to make it later in the season—just add a note indicating that it should age a bit more to "bring up the exotic notes of the coffee and vanilla."

4 cups sugar
1 cup instant coffee powder
1 cup boiling water
2 vanilla beans, split lengthwise
3 cups brandy, vodka, or bourbon

MIX TOGETHER the sugar and coffee powder. Pour the boiling water over the mixture and stir until all ingredients are well dissolved and blended. Place the vanilla beans in a bottle, pour in coffee mixture, and add brandy, vodka, or bourbon. Age at least 30 days in a cool, dark place, turning and shaking the bottle gently every few days.

MAKES ABOUT 5 CUPS

STRAWBERRY BANANA SMOOTHIE

Smoothies are a perfect breakfast food, or great with a book and hammock or any other relaxing activity. Use whole or 1 percent milk if you prefer, soy milk, or fruit juice, and choose your favorite fruits. The second-best thing to there being a healthy fast food is the fact that smoothies are very adaptable. Here's one version. Make up your own—just be sure to perk it up with vanilla!

    1 cup skim milk, soy milk, or rice milk
    ½ cup vanilla nonfat yogurt
    1 teaspoon pure vanilla extract
    1 small to medium banana
    2–3 tablespoons honey (more or less to taste)
    1–2 tablespoons protein powder (optional)
    2 cups frozen whole strawberries,* no sugar added
        (blueberries, raspberries, peaches, nectarines, man-
        goes, or pineapple can be substituted)

COMBINE ALL INGREDIENTS except frozen fruit in a blender; gradually add fruit and process until smooth and thick.

SERVES 4

*Fresh strawberries may be used, but freeze in a single layer before using.

McCormick's Bee Brand Vanilla
Extract from the early 1920s

GRILLED OR PAN-FRIED PORK CHOPS WITH FRESH APPLES

You can use this basic recipe with a loin of pork or lamb chops.

  4 loin or rib pork chops
  2 tablespoons butter
  2 tablespoons brown sugar
  ¼ cup apple juice or cider
  3 large, firm, sweet apples, cored, peeled, and cut into 12
     slices (summer apples, such as Gravenstein, will work
     in this recipe; you may need to add a little extra sugar)
  ½–1 teaspoon pure vanilla extract, or to taste
  salt and pepper to taste

GRILL OR PAN-COOK pork chops until just done (don't over-cook). Place on a platter in a warm oven.

ADD BUTTER and brown sugar to pan used to cook pork chops and set over medium heat. Stir butter and sugar to blend well, allow to caramelize slightly, and loosen small pieces of the pork chops.

ADD APPLE JUICE or cider and apple slices. Cook apples just until done, then remove with a slotted spoon and set aside.

REDUCE THE PAN JUICES to 2 to 3 tablespoons. Remove from heat and add vanilla, salt, and pepper. Add apples slices and return to heat until apples are hot. Pour over the pork chops. Serve with rice or potatoes.

Note: This recipe can also be made with peaches or nectarines. You will need less sugar and less juice as stone fruits have lots of natural juices.

SERVES 4

SHRIMP WITH
COCONUT-VANILLA SAUCE

This is a very rich recipe. You can use light coconut milk or substitute evaporated milk for the cream if you wish to lighten the recipe up a bit.

  2 lbs of medium-large shrimp
  2 tablespoons olive oil
  ½ cup dark rum
  1 Tahitian vanilla bean, split lengthwise
  1 cup heavy cream
  ¾ cup coconut milk
  salt and freshly ground pepper to taste
  lemon wedges and parsley for garnish

Peel and clean shrimp, keeping tails on. Heat the olive oil in a frying pan or wok. Sauté the shrimp for 2 to 3 minutes or until they have turned pink. Discard them from the pan and set aside. Discard the remaining olive oil in pan.

Add the rum and vanilla bean to the frying pan and reduce rum until it's nearly evaporated (down to about 2 tablespoons). Add the cream and coconut milk, and reduce the mixture by half. Scrape seeds out of the vanilla pod and discard pod. Add salt and pepper to taste. Shrimp can either be mixed into the sauce and served or mounded on a rice pilaf with the sauce poured on top. Garnish with lemon wedges and parsley.

Serves 6 to 8

FRESH CREAMED CORN

This is especially good made with fresh white corn.

4 cups fresh or frozen corn (white or yellow)
¼ cup (4 tablespoons) unsalted butter
1 5-oz can whole or low-fat evaporated milk, or 5 oz
    light cream
5 oz chicken or vegetable stock
1 heaping tablespoon cornstarch
1 heaping teaspoon sugar
1 teaspoon pure vanilla extract
salt and pepper to taste
parsley, chopped chives, fresh herbs, or tomato chunks
    for garnish

If using fresh corn, cut kernels from ears, removing all corn silk. Place butter in a large frying pan or 4-quart pan over medium heat. When butter is melted, add corn and stir to combine. Add evaporated milk or cream, stock, cornstarch, and sugar. Cook, stirring constantly until the mixture thickens, about 5 to 6 minutes. Add vanilla and salt and pepper and serve garnished with parsley, chopped chives, fresh herbs, or tomato chunks.

SERVES 6

MOROCCAN ORANGE SALAD

This makes a refreshing salad or light dessert.

1 tablespoon lemon juice
2 tablespoons fresh orange juice
3 tablespoons confectioners' sugar
½ teaspoon pure vanilla extract
½ teaspoon cinnamon
romaine leaves, washed and dried
3–4 oranges, peeled and sliced
½ cup slivered or chopped blanched almonds
8 dates, sliced lengthwise

IN A SMALL BOWL, combine lemon and orange juices, confectioners' sugar, vanilla extract, and cinnamon.

ARRANGE LETTUCE LEAVES on a serving plate. Layer orange slices decoratively onto plate. Spoon juice/sugar mixture over the oranges and sprinkle almonds and fresh dates on top. Chill until serving.

SERVES 4

CANDIED WINTER SQUASH

Squash is delightful with vanilla. You can try this with almost any variety of squash you like.

2–3 medium butternut, delicata, acorn, or banana
　squash
⅓ cup brown sugar
2 tablespoons maple syrup
2 tablespoons butter, softened
1 teaspoon finely shredded orange peel
½ teaspoon ground cinnamon
¼ teaspoon ground cloves
2 teaspoons pure vanilla extract

SCRUB SQUASH, cut in half, and remove seeds. Place cut side up in a large roasting pan. In a mixing bowl, combine remaining ingredients. Spoon mixture into squash halves.

COVER SQUASH WITH ALUMINUM foil and bake for 30 minutes. Baste sugar mixture over squash, leave uncovered, and bake another 20 minutes, or until squash is tender.

SERVES 4 TO 6

CHIPOTLE-VANILLA SALSA
AND BARBEQUE SAUCE

This sauce is excellent as a marinade or glaze for slow-cooked pork, ribs, beef, or grilled chicken. It will also enliven a pot of beans and give kick to tofu! You can adjust the heat by adding more or less chipotle.

> 4–8 medium chipotle chiles in adobo (¼–½ cup)*
> 5 cloves garlic, peeled and cut into small pieces or mashed
> ¼ cup apple cider vinegar
> 2 tablespoons olive oil
> ¼ cup honey
> ¼–½ cup water or broth (depending on thickness desired in sauce as well as desired heat)
> 2 teaspoons pure vanilla extract
> 1 teaspoon fresh lime juice, or to taste
> salt and pepper to taste

PLACE CHIPOTLE CHILES along with sauce clinging to peppers in a food processor. Add remaining ingredients and puree until smooth. Sieve puree through a mesh sieve to remove seeds and fiber. Season with salt and pepper to taste.

COOK SAUCE FOR 20 MINUTES, bringing it almost to a boil, and then let it simmer. Turn off heat and let rest till cool. Will keep, chilled, up to 1 week.

MAKES APPROXIMATELY 1½ CUPS OF SAUCE

*Found in all Mexican groceries and many supermarkets.

VANILLA MOUSSE

This is *rich*, but if you fantasize about the concept of a true vanilla mousse, *this is it!* A bit of work, but worth the effort.

1½ cups sugar

1 cup water

2 vanilla beans, split lengthwise

8 egg yolks

1 quart heavy cream

pure vanilla extract to taste

crystallized flowers and shaved chocolate for garnish
    (optional)

IN A SMALL SAUCEPAN, boil sugar, water, and vanilla beans rapidly for 5 minutes. Cool. Beat egg yolks on top of a double boiler and whip into the syrup gradually. Cook custard over very hot, but not boiling, water, stirring constantly, until mixture becomes creamy and thick. Remove vanilla beans, and scrape out seeds. Press custard through a sieve and stir over a bowl of ice water until it cools.

IN A BOWL, WHIP HEAVY CREAM until it is stiff enough to hold a shape, add vanilla extract to taste, and fold the cream into the cooled custard to form your mousse.

THIS CAN BE FROZEN and served half-frozen, or it can be spooned into cups and served chilled. Garnish with crystallized flowers and shaved chocolate, if desired. Flavored liqueurs can be added instead of the vanilla extract for a delicate secondary flavor, if desired. SERVES 6 TO 10

OLD-FASHIONED FRENCH
VANILLA ICE CREAM

This is what vanilla is all about. I suggest you experiment when you make ice cream; try Tahitian vanilla one time, and Bourbon (or the similar Mexican) the next. You'll definitely taste the difference between either the one or the other. Then, if you like both flavors, create your own blend.

   6 egg yolks
   2 cups milk
   1 cup sugar
   ¼ teaspoon salt
   1 vanilla bean, split lengthwise
   2 cups heavy cream
   1 tablespoon pure vanilla extract

IN TOP OF A DOUBLE BOILER, beat egg yolks and milk until well blended. Stir in sugar and salt, and add vanilla bean, first scraping the seeds into the mixture. Place in top of double boiler and cook, stirring constantly until thick and the mixture coats a metal spoon.

COOL, THEN COVER and refrigerate until chilled. Remove vanilla bean, stir in heavy cream, and add vanilla extract.

POUR INTO ICE-CREAM MAKER and prepare according to manufacturer's instructions. When frozen, pack down and allow to ripen for about 2 hours before serving (if you can actually wait that long).

MAKES ABOUT 1½ QUARTS

VANILLA WAFERS

I've used a pastry bag to make these cookies as small as coins. They're a wonderful accompaniment to a rich chocolate dessert or a cup of espresso or hot chocolate.

- ¼ cup (2 tablespoons) unsalted butter, room temperature
- ⅓ cup vanilla sugar
- 1 teaspoon pure vanilla extract
- ¼ cup egg whites
- ⅓ cup unbleached all-purpose flour

PREHEAT OVEN TO 400°F. Generously grease two or three heavy, large cookie sheets. In a medium bowl, beat butter and sugar until light and fluffy. Add the vanilla extract and mix. Beat in egg whites. Gradually mix in flour (batter will be soft). Drop batter by level teaspoonfuls, 3 inches apart, onto prepared cookie sheets. Bake until edges are golden brown and centers of cookies are still pale, about 7 minutes. Transfer cookies to wire racks and cool completely. Store in an airtight container.

MAKES ABOUT 30 COOKIES

A Watkins ad, circa the 1950s

FRESH BERRY COFFEE CAKE

I like this recipe very much with fresh raspberries or boysen-berries. You may want to make two at a time as it gets eaten very quickly!

1 cup fresh berries
3 tablespoons brown sugar
1 cup unbleached flour
⅓ cup sugar
½ teaspoon baking powder
¼ teaspoon baking soda
½ cup vanilla yogurt
2 tablespoons melted butter
1 teaspoon vanilla extract
1 large egg
3 tablespoons toasted sliced almonds
¼ cup vanilla confectioners' sugar
1 teaspoon milk
¼ teaspoon pure vanilla extract

PREHEAT OVEN to 350°F. In a bowl, combine berries and brown sugar. Set aside.

IN A LARGE BOWL, combine flour, sugar, baking powder, and baking soda. In a small bowl, combine yogurt, butter, vanilla extract, and egg; mix well.

ADD LIQUID INGREDIENTS to flour mixture, stirring just until moist. Spoon two-thirds of the batter into an 8-inch round cake pan coated with cooking spray or lightly buttered; spread evenly. Top with berry mixture. Spoon remaining batter over berry mixture; top with almonds. Bake for 40 minutes or until a wooden pick inserted in center comes out clean. Let cool 10 minutes on a wire rack.

COMBINE CONFECTIONERS' SUGAR, milk, and vanilla extract; stir well. Drizzle over cake. Serve warm or at room temperature.

SERVES 6

LIGHT VANILLA-CARAMEL FLAN

This is a lightened version of traditional flan, full of flavor but easier on the waistline. You are welcome to use whole milk if you prefer, or soy or rice milk can be substituted. If you like the flavor of Tahitian vanilla, this is a good recipe to use it for.

For the syrup:
   ⅓ cup sugar
   1 tablespoon water

For the filling:
   ½ cup sugar
   2 large eggs

2 large egg whites
1½ cups low-fat milk
1 cup evaporated skim milk
1 vanilla bean, split lengthwise
2 teaspoons pure vanilla extract
mint sprigs and fresh fruits for garnish (optional)

PREHEAT OVEN to 325°F. Spray six 6-oz custard cups or ramekins with cooking spray or butter.

FOR THE SYRUP: In a small, heavy saucepan, combine sugar and water, and cook over medium-high heat, for 5 minutes or until golden, stirring occasionally. Immediately pour the syrup into custard cups, then set aside.

FOR THE FILLING: In a large bowl, combine the sugar, eggs, and egg whites; stir well with a whisk. Add both milk and evaporated milk and blend until smooth. Scrape the seeds from the vanilla bean into the batter and save the bean (or pod) for another occasion. Add vanilla extract. Divide the mixture evenly between the custard cups. Place cups in a 13-by-9-inch baking dish, and add 1 inch of hot water. Bake for 1 hour or until knife inserted in center comes out clean. Remove cups from pan and cool completely on a wire rack. Cover and chill at least 3 hours.

TO SERVE, loosen edges of custards from cups, using a thin, sharp knife. Place a dessert plate upside-down on top of each cup and invert custards onto plates. Drizzle any remaining syrup over custards. Garnish with mint sprigs and fresh fruits, if desired.

SERVES 6

CREAMY, DREAMY CHOCOLATE-VANILLA TRUFFLES

It's true: chocolate is *nothing* without the beautiful flavor of vanilla! And this recipe for chocolate-vanilla truffles is an exceptional way to enjoy our two favorite flavors.

½ cup heavy cream
2 vanilla beans, split lengthwise
2 tablespoons unsalted butter, softened
8 oz finely chopped bittersweet or semisweet chocolate
1 tablespoon dessert sugar (optional)
1 cup unsweetened cocoa powder
cornstarch (if using melon baller)

IN A HEAVY SAUCEPAN, place heavy cream and vanilla beans over medium heat until the cream bubbles around the edge. Remove from heat and allow to steep for several hours or overnight. Reheat again until the cream bubbles around the edge, remove from heat, remove vanilla beans, and pour into a measuring cup.

POUR ⅓ CUP of the cream mixture into a bowl and add butter and chocolate, submerging the chocolate completely with a wooden spoon. Add dessert sugar if desired, then scrape seeds from vanilla beans into the chocolate mixture. Save the vanilla beans for making vanilla sugar. Slowly stir mixture with a rubber spatula until it is completely blended and smooth. Chill, uncovered, for 30 minutes to 1 hour, or until a spoon of the chocolate ganache holds its shape.

USING A PASTRY BAG or a melon baller dipped in cornstarch, make truffle balls and place on a baking sheet. Chill at least 30 minutes or until completely firm.

ROLL EACH CHOCOLATE TRUFFLE between the palms of your hands and then roll in cocoa powder. Place in decorative candy cups and serve, or store in the refrigerator in an airtight container for several weeks.

MAKES ABOUT 30 TRUFFLES

Hopefully these recipes have provided you with an idea of the versatility of pure, natural vanilla. Please consider using vanilla often, in the way that you use other favorite herbs, spices, and flavors. By doing so, you will discover precisely how unique vanilla is and how effectively it brightens and enhances a broad spectrum of foods. And by always using pure, natural vanilla, you will also assist in keeping the cultivation and processing of this extraordinary orchid a viable tropical industry.

· BIBLIOGRAPHY ·

Acuna-Soto, Rodolfo, David W. Stahle, Malcolm K. Cleaveland, and Matthew D. Ther-
rel. *Centers for Disease Control Historical Review* 8, no. 4 (2002)."Megadrought and
Megadeath in 16th Century, Mexico."

Aguilera Madero, Roció. *Recetario Totonaco de la Costa de Veracruz* (newsletter). Consejo
Nacional para la Cultura y las Artes, 2000.

———. *La Voz del Vainillero* (newsletter). Papantla, Mexico: Unión Agricola Regional
de Productores de Vainilla, n.d.

Arbell, Mordechai. *The Jewish Nation of the Caribbean*. Jerusalem: Gefen, 2002.

Bouriquet, Gilbert. *Le Vanillier et la Vanille dans le Monde*. Paris: Paul Lechevalier, 1954.

Brillat-Savarin, Jean Anthelme. *The Physiology of Taste*. Trans. by M. F. K. Fisher. New
York: Harcourt Brace Jovanovich, 1978 (orig. pub. 1949).

Brown, Mervin. *Madagascar Rediscovered: A History from Early Times to Independence*.
London: Damien Tunnacliffe, 1978.

Cameron, Kenneth M. *Phylogenetics and Character Evolution Within Vanilloideae (Orchi-
daceae)*. New York: New York Botanical Garden, n.d.

Castro de DeLaRosa, María Guadalupe. "Voladores and Hua-Huas: From the Pre-
Columbian to the Present, an Ethnography and Ethnohistory" (doctoral disserta-
tion), University of California, Los Angeles, 1992.

Chenaut, Victoria. *Aquellos Que Vuelan: Historia de los Pueblos Indígenas de México, los Totonacos en el Siglo XIX.* Mexico City: Centro de Investigaciones y Estudios Superiores en Antropologia Social, 1995.

———, ed. *Procesos Rurales e Historia Regional (Sierra y Costa Totonacas de Veracruz).* Mexico City: Centro de Investigaciones y Estudios Superiores en Antropologia Social, 1996.

Coe, Michael D. *The True History of Chocolate.* New York: Thames and Hudson, 1996.

Demard, Jean-Christophe. *Jicaltepec: Terre d'Argile, A Chronicle of a French Village in Mexico.* Paris: Les Editions du Porte-Glaive, 1987.

Díaz, Bernal del Castillo. *The Discovery and Conquest of Mexico 1517–1521.* Trans. A. P. Maudslay. New York: Farrar, Straus, 1956.

Drysdale, Helena. *Dancing with the Dead.* London: Hamish Hamilton, 1991.

Farmer, Fannie Merritt. *The Boston Cooking-School Cook Book.* Boston: Little, Brown, 1934.

Fulling, Edmund H. *Economic Botany*, vol. 7. New York: New York Botanical Garden, 1953.

Galbraith, S. J. U.S. Department of Agriculture, Division of Botany (bulletin). Washington, D.C.: U.S. Department of Agriculture, 1898.

Harvey, H. R., and Isabel Kelly. *The Totonac* (Handbook of Middle American Studies). Austin: University of Texas Press, 1969.

Hernandez Cano, José Luís. "Aroma y Sabor de la Vainilla." Thesis, University of Veracruz, 1997.

Hispanic American Historical Review, The, 28 (1948; monograph by Henry Brunman).

Humboldt, Alexander von. *Ensayo Politico Sobre el Reino de la Nueva España.* Mexico City: Porria, 1978.

Imágines de Papantla (compiled from a collection of history, stories, and images of Papantla, Mexico, and the surrounding region from the Conquest to the 1930s). 1992.

Jefferson, Thomas. *Thomas Jefferson's Cookbook.* Charlottesville: University of Virginia Press, 1976.

Kander, Mrs. Simon. *The Settlement Cook Book.* Milwaukee: The Settlement Cook Book Company, 1947.

Kelly, Isabel, and Angel Palerm. *The Tajín Totonac*, Part 1. Washington, D.C.: Smithsonian Institution, 1950.

King, John, M.D. *The American Dispensatory.* Cincinnati: Moore, Wilstach Keys, 1859.

Liebman, Malvina W. *Jewish Cookery from Boston to Baghdad.* Miami: E. A. Seemann, 1975.

Murphy, Dervla. *Muddling Through in Madagascar.* London: John Murray, 1985.

Purseglove, J. W., E. G. Brown, C. L. Green, and S. R. J. Robbins. *Spices.* London and New York: Longman, 1981.

Soyer, Alexis. *The Gastronomic Regenerator.* London: Simpkin, Marshall, 1846.

———. *The Modern Housewife or Menagere.* London: Simpkin, Marshall, 1849.

Trager, James. *The Food Chronology.* New York: Henry Holt, 1995.

Vanilla Curing and Its Chemistry. Mayaguez, Puerto Rico: Federal Experiment Station U.S. Department of Agriculture, 1938.

Zaleta, Leonardo. *Postales de Papantla.* Papantla, Mexico: Amatl Litográfica, 2001.

Additional Resources

Extensive interviews were conducted with individuals from numerous companies involved in the vanilla industry, botanists at the New York Botanical Garden, the Smithsonian Institution, as well as interviews and oral histories from producers in India, Indonesia, Madagascar, Mexico, Papua New Guinea, Tahiti, Tonga, Uganda, and Hawaii. The Internet was used extensively, especially for biographical, geographical, and historical information.

· CREDITS ·

Botanical print of vanilla orchid, courtesy of the LuEster T. Mertz Library of the New York Botanical Garden, Bronx, New York

Photograph of vanilla beans on the vine, courtesy of Tripper, Inc.

Photograph of vanilla orchid close-up, courtesy of Julio Pineda

Photograph of ruins of El Tajin, Veracruz, Mexico, courtesy of Patricia Rain

Photograph of ruins of *Voladores* "flying" from seven-foot-high pole in Mexico, courtesy of Patricia Rain

Print of vanilla vine, courtesy of Tripper, Inc.

Photograph showing close-up of raceme where vanilla flowers will later form, courtesy of Tripper, Inc.

Photograph of vanilla growing wild up a tree trunk, courtesy of Patricia Rain

Papantla coat of arms with vanilla vines, courtesy of Patricia Rain

Promotional fan from McCormick, courtesy of McCormick & Company, Inc.

Veracruz ad for Mexican vanilla beans, courtesy of McCormick & Company, Inc.

Bee Brand ad and recipes, courtesy of McCormick & Company, Inc.

Photograph of Watkins assembly line in the 1930s, courtesy of J. R. Watkins Company

Watkins double-strength imitation vanilla ad, courtesy of J. R. Watkins Company

Watkins vanilla bottles, courtesy of J. R. Watkins Company

Sauer's ad with vanilla bottle, courtesy of Warshaw Collection of Business Americana-Food, Archives Center, National Museum of American History, Behring Center, Smithsonian Institution

Photograph of women working with beans in Madagascar, courtesy of Aust und Hachmann

Photograph of Madagascar man dumping beans in sweating box, courtesy of Aust und Hachmann

Photograph of Tahitian vanilla orchid, courtesy of Patricia Rain

Photograph of women sorting beans in warehouse in Indonesia, courtesy of Tripper, Inc.

Photograph of vanilla beans "cooking" with Balinese offering, courtesy of Tripper, Inc.

Photograph of tattooed vanilla beans, courtesy of Brad S. Wise

Photograph of vanilla beans being conditioned on racks in Mexico, courtesy of Patricia Rain

Photograph of ornaments made from vanilla beans, courtesy of Patricia Rain

Photograph of Madagascar woman with basket of vanilla beans on head, courtesy of Aust und Hachmann

Photograph of woman with child in vanilla grove in Madagascar, courtesy of Benjamin H. Kaestner

Photograph of woman in Madagascar working with beans, courtesy of Aust und Hachmann

Kellogg's Extracts print, courtesy of Warshaw Collection of Business Americanan-Food, Archives Center, National Museum of American History, Behring Center, Smithsonian Institution

McCormick's Bee Brand Vanilla ad, courtesy of McCormick & Company, Inc.

Watkins vanilla ad with cake, courtesy of J. R. Watkins Company